Islamic Finance and Corporate Governance

EMERALD STUDIES IN ISLAMIC ECONOMY AND FINANCE

Islamic Finance and Corporate Governance: Synergies for Sustainable Growth

EDITED BY

MUHAMMAD ALI
Taylor's University, Malaysia

SYED ALI RAZA
Iqra University, Pakistan

NOR SHAIPAH ABDUL WAHAB
Taylor's University, Malaysia

CHIN-HONG PUAH
Universiti Malaysia Sarawak, Malaysia

HANUDIN AMIN
University Malaysia Sabah, Malaysia

AND

ABADULLAH
Faysal Islamic Bank, Pakistan

emerald PUBLISHING

United Kingdom – North America – Japan – India – Malaysia – China

Emerald Publishing Limited
Emerald Publishing, Floor 5, Northspring, 21-23 Wellington Street, Leeds LS1 4DL.

First edition 2025

British Library Cataloguing in Publication Data
A catalogue record for this book is available from the British Library

ISBN: 978-1-83662-347-2 (Print)
ISBN: 978-1-83662-346-5 (Online)
ISBN: 978-1-83662-348-9 (Epub)

Printed and bound by CPI Group (UK) Ltd, Croydon, CR0 4YY

To our dear families, whose steadfast support, endless encouragement, and unwavering belief have been the foundation upon which this work is built. Your love and guidance have been a constant source of inspiration, and it is with deep appreciation that we honour you in these pages. Thank you for being the cornerstone of our journey and for enriching our lives in countless ways.

Contents

List of Contributors

Abadullah	Faysal Islamic Bank, Pakistan
Rosimah Ahmad	Taylor's University Malaysia, Malaysia
Muhammad Ali	Taylor's University Malaysia, Malaysia
Hanudin Amin	Universiti Malaysia Sabah Malaysia, Malaysia
Muhammad Ashfaq	IU International University of Applied Sciences, Germany
Muhammad Asim	Karachi University Business School, University of Karachi, Pakistan
Abdul Kadir Barut	Recep Tayyip Erdoğan University, Turkey
Ng Sok Choo	University Malaya-Wales, Malaysia
Abdul Samad Dahri	Shaheed Benazir Bhutto University, Pakistan
Abdul Razak Abdul Hadi	University Kuala Lumpur Business School, Malaysia
Salman Bashir Memon	Shaheed Benazir Bhutto University, Pakistan
Aisha Naz	Iqra University, Pakistan
Muhammad Asim Rafiq	National University of Modern Languages (NUML), Pakistan
Raja Rehan	International Islamic University Malaysia (IIUM), Malaysia; ILMA University, Pakistan
Auwal Adam Sa'ad	International Islamic University Malaysia (IIUM), Malaysia
Amir Firoz Shamsi	Bahria University, Pakistan
Manisha Singh	VIT Bhopal University, Bhopal
Premagowrie Sivanandan	Taylor's University Malaysia, Malaysia
Sachin Prakash Srivastava	Dr Vishwanath Karad MIT World Peace University, India
Sonali Srivastava	Jaypee Institute of Information Technology, India
Muhammad Faisal Sultan	Khadim Ali Shah Bukhari Institute of Technology (KASBIT), Pakistan
Sumaiya Syed	Shah Abdul Latif University, Pakistan

Jahangir Tanveer	Khadim Ali Shah Bukhari Institute of Technology (KASBIT), Pakistan
Imam Uddin	Institute of Business Management, Pakistan
Nor Shaipah Abdul Wahab	Taylor's University, Malaysia
Lee Chin Yee	Taylor's University, Malaysia
Rosylin Mohd Yusof	Universiti Utara Malaysia (UUM), Malaysia

Foreword

As CEO of Faysal Bank – the largest bank in the world to have successfully transitioned from a conventional institution to a fully-fledged Islamic bank – I am pleased to introduce this book, which offers a detailed look into the evolving synergistic relationship between Islamic finance, corporate governance, and sustainable growth.

The book addresses key topics such as the integration of ESG principles in Islamic investments, the role of strong governance in Islamic banks, and the growing influence of fintech on the industry. These discussions provide practical insights alongside well-founded theories, offering a balanced view of both current practices and future possibilities.

There is also a focus on important areas like Sukuk and Takaful, highlighting their role in maintaining financial stability. Concepts such as Musharakah Mutanaqisah for elderly care and Zakat management are explored, showing how Islamic finance can be applied to address contemporary social challenges.

With the increasing focus on ethical and responsible finance, the themes explored in this book have become highly relevant. The in-depth research presented here will appeal to professionals, policymakers, and academics in the Islamic finance industry by providing clear insights into how responsible governance and finance can contribute to sustainable growth.

Regards,
Yousaf Hussain
Chief Executive Officer
Faysal Bank Ltd

Preface

Muhammad Ali, Syed Ali Raza, Nor Shaipah Abdul Wahab, Chin-Hong Puah, Hanudin Amin, and Abadullah

This book explores the various topics that create the intersection between three key areas of Islamic finance, corporate governance, and sustainable growth. The intersection between these areas develops a useful understanding of how Islamic finance and corporate governance is an essential aspect of sustainable growth. The book sheds light on the role of ethical investment such as environmental, social, and governance (ESG) in promoting sustainable goals. This book includes the debate on how social responsibility can be integrated into the Islamic banking framework for modern practices and ethical foundations. It also explores the governance mechanism in microfinance and Islamic banking institutions. Similarly, this book presents the governance framework, opportunities, and challenges related to Islamic fintech. The inclusion of Sukuk and Takaful governance frameworks in Islamic financial institutions is also included in the book. These areas are essential for the sustainable performance of Islamic finance. Additionally, the book also introduces a new direction within Islamic banking and corporate governance through Musharakah Mutanaqisah for elderly care, integrating financial literacy to ensure sustainable retirement. This topic can be a useful way to expand the boundaries of Islamic banking and corporate governance for sustainable performance. Lastly, it addresses strategic Zakat management to amplify social impact within corporate social responsibility, underscoring the importance of ethical and socially responsible practices in Islamic finance. Overall, this book provides a useful guide and innovative approaches for policymakers and managers to enhance their knowledge on various key topics of Islamic finance and corporate governance.

Acknowledgement

We extend our sincere gratitude to the gifted writers who shaped the story of this book with their commitment, knowledge, and teamwork. They are the real designers of this project, and each chapter has benefited from their contributions, which have given it more depth and richness.

We would also like to thank our families for being our steadfast source of support and for giving us the time and space we needed to learn about the intricacies of contemporary finance.

We express our gratitude to the hardworking staff of the Emerald publishing team. The dedicated staff of Emerald publishing has played an essential role in transforming concepts into the concrete information that is contained on these pages. We received wonderful support from team Emerald throughout the publishing process.

Finally, we would like to thank all of you, the readers. We are inspired by your dedication to overcoming the obstacles of contemporary finance and your quest for knowledge. We all contributed to this book, and we genuinely hope it will be a useful tool for you as you pursue your managerial goals.

Chapter 1

Islamic Corporate Governance and Sustainable Financial Growth

Raja Rehan[a,b]*, Abdul Razak Abdul Hadi*[c] *and Auwal Adam Sa'ad*[a]

[a]*IIUM Institute of Islamic Banking and Finance (IIiBF), International Islamic University Malaysia (IIUM), Kuala Lumpur, Malaysia*
[b]*Department of Business Administration, ILMA University, Karachi, Pakistan*
[c]*University Kuala Lumpur Business School, Kuala Lumpur, Malaysia*

Abstract

The former financial fiascos from Enron to slumps of capital markets during covid-19 pandemic are also measured as a failure of corporate governance systems. However, the circumstances are different for Islamic financial institutes as they competently handle the rising risk and prove beneficial for their nominees during financial disasters. This highlights the Islamic finance offered services and products around the globe which are considered and proven themselves for delivering sustainable financial growth. The Islamic finance regulatory bodies such as the financial services board (IFSB) and the accounting auditing organization for islamic financial institutions (AAOIFI) established several governance standards (GSs) that open the way for Islamic finance institutions to develop vigorous Islamic corporate governance procedures. The AAOIFI and IFSB frameworks for Islamic corporate governance clarify that there must be a central Shariah board, supervisory council, internal compliance, internal audit, and external independent audit to ensure the Shariah obedience of Islamic finance institutions. The AAOIFI and IFSB familiarized GSs support the establishing of Islamic corporate governance procedures that are rooted in Islamic principles, thus, when executed they deliver sustainable financial growth. Besides, Islamic corporate governance guarantees risk sharing, ethical business practices, social responsibility, and

Islamic Finance and Corporate Governance: Synergies for Sustainable Growth, 1–22

doi:10.1108/978-1-83662-346-520251003

environmental goals that are aligned with Shariah philosophies. The integration of Islamic finance governance procedures with corporate, social, responsibilities (CSR), sustainable development goals (SDGs), and environmental, social, and governance (ESG) creates a comprehensive approach that offers sustainable financial growth. Thus, the amalgamation of Islamic finance ideologies with vigorous corporate governance procedures guarantees social and environmental development and offers the utmost sustainable growth.

Keywords: Islamic finance; Islamic corporate governance; AAOIFI; IFSB; sustainability

1. Introduction

Islamic finance refers to all those financial practices, assets, and products that are offered and function by following Islamic laws (Hanif et al., 2024). Typically, some of the key principles on which Islamic finance stresses are forbidding of interest, that is, riba, the avoidance of speculation, that is, maisir, ethical investments, risk sharing, asset-backing, and not investing in several businesses prohibited in Islam like gambling, alcohol, etc. Likewise, the key products of Islamic finance are Sukuk, that is, Islamic bonds; Murabaha, that is, cost-plus financing; Ijara, that is, leasing; Mudarabah, that is, profit-sharing; and Musharakah, that is, joint venture (Siregar & Irmayuliana, 2024). Visibly, Islamic finance boosts sustainability by accentuating social responsibilities, ethical investments, and aligning financial performance with social and environmental goals. Islamic finance emphasizes Islamic principles to boost social justice, financial inclusion, and sustainable financial growth. Remarkably, the after-effects of prior financial crises, that is, from Enron to slumps of capital markets during covid-19 pandemic, forced financial concerns and stakeholders to reevaluate the conventional modes which they approached for the allocation of their investments. This rapidly highlighted Islamic finance and its presented services and products which are measured best to handle all sorts of financial fiascos and dissimilar inflation regimes (Alkassim Farid, 2019). Accordingly, Islamic finance which is also discussed as a shift from a conventional finance encompasses distinctive attributes that spin around risk sharing, participatory measures, and adherence to Islamic rules (Asif, 2022; Saeed, 2016). Evidently, during former financial messes, the circumstances were different for Islamic financial institutes as they competently handled the rising risk and proved beneficial for their nominees (Wahyono, 2022). For instance, during the covid-19 pandemic, when the slipping of inflation resulted in the dwindling of the global conventional financial markets, Islamic finance presented an alternative (see Table 1.1) and utmost sustainable risk-adjusted growth (Dharani et al., 2022).

Table 1.1 demonstrates the financial performance of Islamic and conventional indexes during the first quarter (Q1) of 2020, that is, the beginning period of covid-19 pandemic. Visibly, during the first quarter (Q1) of 2020, the conventional S&P global broad market index (BMI) dropped to −22%, whereas, the

Table 1.1. Comparative Returns (Islamic vs. Conventional Indexes).

S#	Benchmark	Shariah Indexes (%)	Conventional Indexes (%)	Variance
1	S&P BMI (global)	−17.2	−22.3	5.1
2	S&P (Pan-Arab compositive)	−20.6	−23.4	2.8
3	DJIM (world)	−16.6	−22	5.4
4	DJIM (Asia)	−14.3	−19.8	5.5
5	DJIM (Europe)	−16.8	−24.8	8
6	DJIM (emerging markets)	−15.9	−24.4	8.5
7	DJIM (developed markets)	−16.7	−21.6	4.9

Source: Sherif (2020).

Shariah-based S&P BMI dropped only −17%. This drive of Shariah indexes is consistently spotted across numerous regions, as Dow Jones Islamic indexes for Europe and emerging markets outperformed 8% more than their traditional peers (Sherif, 2020). Likewise, in the first quarter of 2021, the Shariah indexes presented higher returns than conventional funds. Hence, the sustainable return and growth of Islamic finance during the periods of financial disasters are the core reasons that lead to a surge in Islamic finance's global worth and acceptance. Currently, due to its ethical principles, resilience, and increasing global demand for Islamic-compliant financial services, Islamic finance experienced significant growth. Resultantly, it has increased its exploration and integration with recent technologies such as blockchain, metaverse, and artificial intelligence to boost its operations and grow in international finance (AL-Hawamleh et al., 2024). In the same vein, Islamic finance lines up with ESG measures for promoting ethics-based investments, environmental stewardship, and social fairness via Sahirah-based rules and principles. Remarkably, core fiascos of the financial world are not only considered a failure of conventional finance, but it has also been measured as letdowns of corporate governance (Haron & Siraj, 2024; Tahir and Sohail, 2012).

The corporate governance is a mechanism that is made by a business such as processes and a set of rules by which it is directed and controlled. The key corporate governance elements are accountability, control, stakeholders' rights, equitable treatment, transparency, and board structure (Drew et al., 2006). Technically, in the absence of corporate governance, the agency problem, that is, conflict between owners and managers arises (Gwala & Mashau, 2023). The corporate governance in Islamic finance formulates business governance principles by considering Islamic laws for transparent, ethical, and responsible management. At first glance, Islamic finance and corporate governance seem to be poles apart. Later, it becomes clear that there is a substantial synergy between them. However, the Islamic finance industry must follow all set of procedures known as Islamic laws and regulations to exercise corporate governance measures. The Islamic finance regulatory bodies such as the IFSB and the AAOIFI proposed several GSs that provide guidelines for the Islamic finance institutions.

The Sharia supervisory councils ensure that executed corporate governance policies comply with Islamic rules and regulations. For that, Shariah councils added several layers of oversight and moral scrutiny and strictly monitor all those corporate sectors that are tagged with Shariah businesses. This is to create a stable, ethical, and socially responsible financial system that operates by following Islamic laws. Thus, the integration of Islamic finance and corporate governance which share several common philosophies and values offers sustainable finance that promotes financial inclusion, environmental stewardship, and social equity (Yusuf et al., 2024). The integration of Islamic finance and corporate governance offers sustainable growth by adding ethical morals, plainness, and accountability to business operations (Dai, 2024). Islamic finance is sturdily associated with the governance conceptions of fairness and justice as it is directed by Islamic rules and regulations that encourage risk-sharing and ethical investments. For instance, the interest is prohibited in Islamic finance and the debt-based transactions are backed by asset tangibility. Hence, the connection between Islamic finance and corporate governance builds up trust among shareholders, boosts long-term investment perceptions, and promotes financial stability. Typically, the developed corporate governance frameworks in the Islamic finance systems are in line with Islamic laws. The Shariah councils and boards ensure that the corporate governance procedures of Islamic-tagged businesses are consistent with Islamic rules. Therefore, this integration of corporate governance and Islamic finance not only attracts ethical investors but also develops a resilient economic system that eventually fosters sustainable financial growth (Setiawan, 2023). Visibly, the implementation of corporate governance procedures by considering Islamic rules and regulations offers sustainable financial growth for the Islamic finance industry in the last decade (see Table 1.2).

Table 1.2. Market Growth of Islamic Finance Assets (USD Billion, 2014–2022).

S#	Country	Islamic Finance Assets *CAGR % (2014–2019)	Islamic Banking Assets Shares % (2020)	Islamic Banks Net Profit % (2021)	Islamic Banks Net Profit % (2022)
1	Malaysia	6.50%	11.10%	40.60%	44.70%
2	Saudi Arabia	8.80%	24.90%	53.80%	72.10%
3	The UAE	7.70%	8.70%	35.10%	42.10%
4	Qatar	10.70%	6.10%	40.10%	32.40%
5	Kuwait	6.30%	6.30%	33.80%	51.50%
6	Indonesia	19.70%	2.00%	24.90%	31.80%
7	Bahrain	5.60%	1.80%	29.90%	36.80%
8	Turkey	3.10%	2.60%	27.40%	48.20%
9	Bangladesh	14.20%	2.10%	36.00%	37.80%

Source: Compiled by authors based on IFSB (2023), Alpen Capital (2021), and Musaffa (2020).

Table 1.2 displays the year over year (YOY) swiftly mounting Islamic finance industry's financial growth. Noticeably, the Islamic finance overall assets have increased its total size in the last decade, specifically, during the financial years 2014–2022 mainly in all key Islamic countries. Remarkably, the Shariah Councils operating in these countries ensure that the implemented corporate governance structures for Islamic-tagged businesses are in line with Islamic rules and regulations to sustain the landscape and obtain utmost sustainable growth (Capital and Advisors, 2021).

2. The Corporate Governance Structure of Islamic Finance Institutions

Islamic corporate governance is a set of directorial measures through which Islamic financial institutions oversight and ensure the board of directors' accountability, responsibility, and management of Shariah-based committees (Abdulrahman et al., 2023). Fundamentally, Shariah-based governance plays a key role to confirm the integrity of the Islamic corporate governance system. Typically, the governance of Islamic financial institutions is different than its counterpart system as Islamic financial system is based on Shariah rules and regulations. Also, with investors and stakeholders, several regulatory bodies and Islamic communities are involved in the Islamic finance governance structure. The framework of Islamic corporate governance is a mechanism that is developed by Shariah regulatory bodies to ensure compliance with Islamic rules and to mitigate several upsurging non-compliance risks (Haqqi, 2014). The global Islamic finance standard-setting bodies such as the IFSB and AAOIFI have proposed several procedures and standards of Islamic governance to operate Islamic financial institutions (see AAOIFI, 2015; Hilmy & Hassan, 2019; IFSB, 2006). Thus, to satisfy the investors and to ensure vigorous practices of Shariah compliance, Islamic financial institutions must follow all the set measures by IFSB and AAOIFI. The IFSB-10 explained the Islamic governance system by considering the background of the Islamic financial institutions:

> It is an institutional and organizational framework by which Islamic financial institutes ensure the existence of an efficient and independent supervision that oversight the adherence of all shariah laws and regulations for the issuance of shariah relevant pronouncements, review of all shariah compliance and for the dissemination of all appropriate shariah linked material (IFSB, 2009).

The above-given clarification for the Islamic governance system by the IFSB-10 is clear that the Islamic governance system contains three dissimilar features and main functions which are governance, control, and compliance to ensure the implementation of Shariah-based governance in the Islamic financial institutes. Notably, these three key functions also distinguish (see Table 1.3) the corporate structure of conventional financial Institutions from the Islamic institutions financial systems.

Table 1.3. Islamic and Conventional Governance Structure Features.

Main Functions	Shariah Governance Structure	Conventional Governance Structure
Governance, control, and compliance	Shariah supervisory board, Shariah review (internal and external), internal Shariah-based compliance unit	Board of directors, auditors (internal and external), financial compliance unit, officers, departments

Source: Authors' own elaboration.

Table 1.3 clarifies the process and structure of the Islamic financial governance structure that contains a Shariah supervisory board, internal and external Shariah review committee, and internal Shariah-based compliance unit. Additionally, it also displays the dissimilarities in the core functions of Islamic and conventional financial systems. Technically, Islamic corporate governance is functioning by following the GSs issued by two dissimilar international Shariah standard-setting bodies that are the IFSB and the AAOIFI. The IFSB and AAOIFI-issued standards (see Table 1.4) suggest how the Islamic corporate governance structure operates in the Islamic financial institutes.

Table 1.4 presents the AAOIFI and IFSB-issued GSs for Islamic financial institutes. The AAOIFI declared 13 dissimilar GSs that explain the Islamic corporate governance framework for Islamic financial institutes.

The AAOIFI developed GS 1 to construct standards and provide guidelines on the reporting, composition, appointment, and description of the Shariah supervisory board. Likewise, GS 2, that is, Shariah review is developed to create guidelines, establish standards, and assist the Shariah supervisory board in ensuring that all regulations, fatwas, that is, clarification and guidelines are consistent with the Shariah principles. The GS 3 is for the internal Shariah assessment in all those financial institutions that are tagged with Shariah. In the same vein, the GS 4 explains the role and responsibilities of the audit governance committee (AGC) and audit firms for Islamic financial organizations. The AAOIFI developed GS5 which is set for the governance principles to develop the Shariah governance practices in the Islamic financial institutions. Notably, the GS5 also assists AAOIFI with standards setting. Afterward, GS7 is introduced that is for the formation and measures of the corporate social responsibilities for Islamic financial institutions. The GS8 is to guide the central Shariah board on its definition, appointment, independence, responsibilities, and other related matters. Subsequently, the GS9, that is, for the Shariah compliance function is set to be in line with and harmonize the Shariah principles for Islamic financial institutions to standardize the procedures and principles as per the worldwide practices. The GS10 is used to set and construct procedures for all rating agencies that apply for Shariah compliance and rating of Islamic financial institutions. Besides, the GS11 is built on former standards to improve the management of internal Shariah audit operations and functions in

Table 1.4. AAOIFI GSs for Islamic Finance Institutions.

S#	AAOIFI GSs	IFSB GSs
GS* No. 1	Shariah supervisory board appointment, composition, and report	Guiding principles for corporate governance of Islamic financial institutions
GS No. 2	Shariah review	Guiding principles on governance of Islamic collective investment schemes
GS No. 3	Internal Shariah review	Guiding principles on governance of Takaful undertakings
GS No. 4	Audit and governance committee for Islamic financial institutions	Guiding principles Shariah governance systems for Islamic financial institutions
GS No. 5	Independence of Shariah board (SSB)	Guidance note on the practice of smoothing the profits payout to investment account holder
GS No. 6	Statement of governance principles for Islamic financial institutions	
GS No. 7	Corporate social responsibility: conduct and disclosure of Islamic financial institutions	
GS No. 8	Central Shariah board	
GS No. 9	Shariah compliance function	
GS No. 10	Shariah compliance and fiduciary ratings	
GS No. 11	Internal Shariah audit	
GS No. 12	Sukuk governance	
GS No. 13	Waqf governance	

Note: GS, governance structure.

Source: Compiled by authors based on AAOIFI (2015) and IFSB-10.

Islamic financial institutions with the consistency of Shariah rules and regulations. GS12 and GS13 are built for the governance of Sukuk, that is, Islamic bond and waqf. The GS12 is built to provide guidelines for dissimilar stages of Sukuk such as its issuance procedure, management, termination, or restricting phases. Moreover, the GS13, that is, for the waqf governance ensures to meet all waqf-related activities objectives.

Additionally, like AAOIFI, the IFSB declared five different governance principles for Islamic finance institutions. The IFSB GS1 is for guiding key principles to Islamic financial institutions. Then, the IFSB GS2 is to provide a guideline on governance such as issuance, restructuring, etc., of Shariah-based investment schemes and GS3 is for Takaful governance and its related activities. The GS4 guide about the principles, rules, and regulations for Islamic financial institutions. The last GS5 of IFSB is to offer guidance notes to make smooth procedures for profit disbursement to investment scheme account holders.

Fig. 1.1 explains the AAOIFI corporate governance framework for Islamic financial institutes. The AAOIFI Islamic governance framework clarifies that there must be a central Shariah board, Shariah supervisory board, internal Shariah compliance, internal Shariah audit, and external independent Shariah audit to ensure the Shariah compliance of Islamic finance institutions (Ginena & Hamid, 2015). Functionally, the internal Shariah review is conducted by Islamic financial institutions. The Shariah review is handled by the Shariah supervisory board that scrutinizes the Shariah compliance for Islamic finance services, products, business-related transactions, and activities. After that, another Shariah review testing is conducted by internal and independent Shariah audit, that is, measured as an internal exercise of audit for the Islamic financial institutions. The second external independent Shariah audit is to analyze the Islamic financial institutes' compliance by following the Shariah guidelines, rules, and instructions that are imposed by the Shariah advisory council and Shariah supervisory board. The AAOIFI explained this procedure as an internal and external Shariah audit, respectively (Hasan, 2011). The developed Islamic Corporate Governance structure by Shariah regulatory bodies such as AAOIFI and IFSB ensures that Islamic-tagged firms are not involved in all those activities that are forbidden in Islam and also offer risk-adjusted sustainable financial growth. Hence, the developed framework and procedures for Islamic corporate governance by AAOIFI and IFSB governance promote sustainable growth by ensuring ethical business practices, risk management, and social responsibility, aligned with Sharia principles.

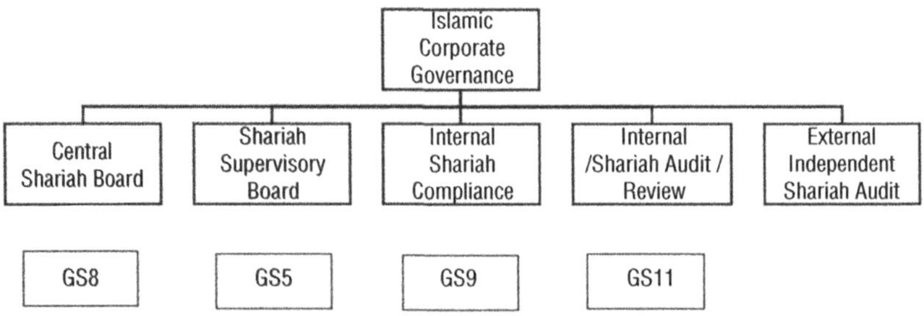

Fig. 1.1. AAOIFI Islamic Corporate Governance Framework. *Source*: Compiled by authors based on Hilmy and Hassan (2019) and AAOIFI (2015).

3. Islamic Corporate Governance and Sustainable Financial Growth

Islamic corporate governance, that is, aligned with Islamic principles focuses on ethical business practices, social responsibilities, and risk management, thus, offering sustainable financial growth. Undeniably, the amalgamation of Islamic finance ideologies with vigorous corporate governance procedures applies to foster sustainable growth in numerous ways that are explained in the next subsections of this section.

3.1. Islamic Corporate Governance Practices Heightened Ethical Values

Ethics deals with principles of wrong and right behavior of a person or society (Ricoeur, 1973). Islam clarifies that anything that endorses the well-being of a person or society is ethically righteous; however, anything that harms others is wrong. Thus, in Islamic finance, ethics mentions the obedience to Islamic principles which stress justice, social responsibility, and transparency to ensure that all financial practices of business are unbiased, fair, and beneficial for society and investors (Agustian et al., 2023). The ethical system enlightened in Islamic finance is perpetually divine and constructed on the foundation of Islamic rules (Omar, 2013). However, daily basis business practices and operations mostly pose challenges when it steadily tries to implement ethical principles. This situation raises a question how Islamic-tagged businesses mix ethical values into their corporate governance policies. On the flip side, the combination of ethical reflections in all aspects of business processes becomes imperative, specifically, for those businesses that are tagged as Islamic businesses. Notably, Islamic finance stresses more on ethics in businesses and explains that they must operate with integrity, morality, and by considering social responsibilities (Sarib et al., 2023). Therefore, the incorporation of corporate governance with Islamic finance creates a vigorous framework that enhances ethical values and sustainable growth. Also, Islamic finance holds the foundation of Islamic laws which prohibit speculation, interest, and investment in all those businesses that are forbidden in Islam, hence, promoting socially and ethically responsible financial practices.

The ethical foundations of Islamic finance guarantee that investments are made in ethical and socially responsible plans that promote overall social well-being (Gardezi, 2023). Thus, when Islamic finance synergizes with corporate governance procedures, which emphasizes accountability, shareholders rights, transparency, etc., offers economic stability and utmost risk-adjusted return (Bhatti & Bhatti, 2010). Moreover, the integration of financial activities, robust corporate governance, and ethical considerations not only fosters investors' trust and decreases inequality but also boosts investments in environmental and social sustainable plans. Hence, this integration drives comprehensive and enduring financial growth that ultimately heightens ethical values. Indeed, the integration of Islamic finance and corporate governances foster ethical values and then ultimately delivers sustainable financial growth. Thus, the practices of Islamic corporate governance not only heightened ethical values but also meaningfully contributed to sustainable financial growth (Jan et al., 2021). Notably, these adopted practices of Islamic corporate governance are rooted in Islamic ideologies that lay emphasis on justice, accountability, social responsibility, and transparency. Remarkably, the foundation stone of Islamic corporate governance is the Shariah supervisory boards and councils which certify all corporate activities that must be in line with Islamic law and foster the trust of investors. Additionally, Islamic corporate governance encourages an investor-oriented tactic by matching the benefits of stakeholders, workers, clients, and in the end the whole community (Ali & Hussain, 2024). This holistic view boosts investments in sustainable socially responsible projects by lining up financial goals with ethical and social essentials. Eventually, via using these heightened ethical values, Islamic corporate governance not only delivers sustainable financial growth but also makes sure that financial growth is equitable and beneficial for the whole society. The ethics-based equation model that is proposed by AAOIFI in its ethics codes includes justice, that is, Adl and benevolence, that is, Ihsan. Principally, the Ahsan and Adl model explains that to attain and preserve justice, the concern must give priority to Ihsan in all dissimilar circumstances. Likewise, experts must pursue Adl, that is, justice in their work functions (AAOIFI, 2019). Clearly, the AAOIFI ethics-based model clarifies that Islamic finance is appropriate for one and all. Also, the risk-sharing concept of Islamic finance is among one of the main concepts of Islamic corporate governance. The risk-sharing mechanism of Islamic finance is measured as a key principle that differentiates Islamic corporate governance from its counterpart, that is, the conventional governance system (Sekreter, 2011).

3.2. Islamic Corporate Governance and Risk-sharing Mechanisms

Islamic corporate governance risk-sharing mechanisms play an important role in nurturing sustainable growth by inserting transparent, socially responsible, and ethical performances into financial structures (Franzoni & Ait Allali, 2024). Mainly, by evading forbidden activities like speculation-based investments and interest-linked transactions, Islamic corporate governance diminishes systemic risks and encourages financial stability. Likewise, the adoption of risk-sharing procedures, that is, sharing of profit and loss, Islamic corporate governance lines up the benefits of investors and stakeholders that foster a collaborative and robust financial environment (Rashid et al., 2024). Hence, the foundation of Islamic corporate governance is constructed on Islamic rules and regulations. This ensures all financial activities of the businesses are in line with Islamic rules and regulations that promote risk-sharing, ethical values, and prevention of exploitation. Evidently, the global banking sector declared the healthy growth of Islamic banking institutions (see Table 1.3) because of their risk management competencies. Islamic banking adopts robust Islamic corporate governance mechanisms for handling the risks. The management of risk in Islamic banking is vital to provide safeguards against probable risks and to preserve stability for financial institutions. The ISFB sets the corporate finance tents for Islamic-tagged banks by approving and issuing principles and standards (Ling et al., 2024). Typically, the IFSB clarifies the procedures for disclosure, identification, and handling of risks that are connected with Islamic finance-offered services and products.

Table 1.5 displays the percentage-wise YOY financial growth in Islamic Banks assets from 2018 to 2020. Visibly, the banking sectors operational in core Islamic nations reported robust YOY growth which confirms their ability to handle existing risks of the market. This is because Islamic corporate governance emphasizes accountability and transparency that force full disclosure, fairness, and honesty that build up the trust of investors and also eliminate risk and corruption. For instance, with adopting corporate governance-connected principles, Islamic finance offers dissimilar risk-sharing products like Mudarabah, that is, sharing of profit, and Musharakah, that is, joint venture which provides a platform and procedures for investors to not only share profit and losses on their investments but also enhance responsibility and mutual cooperations. Similarly, Takaful, that is, Islamic insurance encourages social solidarity by granting members against losses and financial damages on their pooled funds (Alam et al., 2023). Takaful corporate governance structure is very identical to conventional insurance governance procedures; however, it is highly regulated by the AAOIFI (Zuki et al., 2024). Also, Sukuk, that is, Islamic bonds offer interest-free returns which ensure that investors share the risk and reward both on their investments. Technically, the AAOIFI set dissimilar governance principles and standards for Islamic financial institutions. The AGC of AAOIFI for Islamic financial institutions is responsible for the enhancement of the internal controls. The AGC measures contain the monitoring and ensuring that the corporate systems of Islamic financial institutions are in line with Islamic principles. Importantly, the risk-sharing mechanisms of Islamic corporate governance are consistent with CSR measures that promote ethical values, social and environmental growth and lead to sustainable, risk-free utmost financial growth (Hossain et al., 2014).

Table 1.5. Islamic Banking Assets Growth (2018–2020).

S#	Country	Year-wise Growth (%)		
		2018	2019	2020
1	Saudi Arabia	29.00%	44.60%	50.60%
2	Malaysia	22.80%	29.50%	30.10%
3	The UAE	20.30%	18.50%	18.90%
4	Qatar	19.70%	26.60%	26.60%
5	Kuwait	37.90%	40.60%	42.50%
6	Bahrain	12.70%	15.70%	15.20%
7	Oman	12.80%	13.70%	14.30%

Source: Compiled by authors based on Bank Negara Malaysia, Bahrain, UAE, Saudi, and Oman Central Banks Reports.

3.3. Islamic Corporate Governance, CSR, and Sustainable Growth

In the recent era, there has been a long continuing deliberation among intellectuals on adopting those initiatives in businesses that are measured as socially responsible activities (Gillan et al., 2021; Friedman, 1962). Therefore, numerous scholars (see Broadstock et al., 2020; Freeman, 1984) have advised that businesses must fulfill their social responsibilities that are beyond the expansion of nominees' capital and businesses' market value. Hence, for businesses, social responsibility is normally functionated by executing the exercises of CSR. Typically, CSR refers to a business' initiative by that a company fulfills it's on the environment and society. In addition, it involves integrating environmental, social, and ethical concerns into business processes and connections with investors. Thus, CSR is a corporate concept in which firms integrate social and environmental aspects into their operations and also incorporate them with their stakeholders (Wirba, 2023). The financial sectors and businesses have been implementing and growing their reliance on CSR-based performance to get durable support from nominees that lead them toward long-term sustainable financial growth. The corporate sectors' responsibilities for society were specifically felt during the financial fiasco of 2007–2008 and then after the collapse of the capital markets during the covid-19 pandemic. After that, the market of Islamic finance became attentive around the globe as it is measured as a dissimilar system that focuses more on CSR-based activities such as ethical investment, equitable wealth distribution, and social justice by adhering to Islamic principles (Marzuki et al., 2023). Typically, Islamic finance was introduced to assist the charitable agenda in humanities and businesses. Additionally, Islamic finance contains the Islamic paradigm that focuses more on the development of weak financial groups and societies. Therefore, Islamic corporate governance with its core concepts such as ethical-based investments, risk-sharing, asset-backed transactions, robust governance procedures, etc., integrates with CSR that rely on social and environmental sustainability to deliver utmost sustainable development (Tasnia et al., 2023). For instance, the Islamic Banks that contain sustainable growth involve more in supporting their employees, offering health care for societies, charities, donations, Zakat, education, and natural calamity releases (Zubaidah & Pratiwi, 2024). Thus, by accepting Islamic corporate governance and CSR, firms can foster investors' trust and financial stability.

Fundamentally, CSR adoption by considering Islamic corporate governance can enhance transparency, ethical behavior, and accountability. This not only enhances business market reputation, but it also increases the trust and confidence of investors and raises business operational efficiency that ultimately produces sustainable growth (Emeka-Okoli, 2024). Undoubtedly, CSR-connected initiatives increase a firm's value, reputation, attract socially conscious shareholders, and also contribute to the well-being of humanity. Thus, the integration of Islamic finance governance with CSR creates an inclusive approach that not only offers long-term sustainable financial growth, but it also ensures social and environmental development (Solihati et al., 2023). Visibly, several Islamic financial institutions that are following Islamic corporate governance procedures came up with robust CSR initiatives, involved in ethical-based businesses and truly following ethos-religion-based CSR programs. Hence, it delivers the uppermost financial performance and resources in the best interest of financially weaker societies that also boost social welfare and economic justice (Khan, 2016).

Fig. 1.2 demonstrates the CSR framework of Islamic financial institutes. The core components of the CSR framework for Islamic financial institutes are community-based banking, patrons of poor and weaker economic groups, educational training of staff, market sustainability and efficiency, Islamic governance and compliance, human resources, and development of infrastructure. Definitely, the implementation of a CSR framework in Islamic financial institutions is not only a moral obligation, but it also enhances economic justice and delivers sustainable growth.

3.4. Islamic Corporate Governance, Economic Justice, and Sustainable Growth

The notions of Islamic corporate governance, economic justice, social welfare, and sustainability are closely knitted. Precisely, Islamic corporate governance is rooted in Islamic principles and emphasizes more on ethical-based business procedures that promote fairness, accountability, transparency, and economic justice. Moreover, Islamic corporate governance also stresses on the reasonable, clear, and fair financial treatment to all shareholders, employees, societies, customers, and stakeholders. This unbiased approach and practices of Islamic corporate governance ensure that the financial and economic benefits of business operations are distributed among all justly. Thus, this fair economic benefits distribution among

Fig. 1.2. The Islamic Finance CSR Framework. *Source*: Authors' own elaboration.

all stakeholders eventually promotes economic justice, social welfare of societies, and reduction of inequality. Notably, Islamic finance focuses on some mandatory activities such as the distribution of Zakat, that is, alms giving, prohibition of interest-based activities, risk-sharing, etc., that forces concerns to construct corporate governance procedures in such a way that after executing they foster economic and financial fairness. Also, these corporate governance procedures that are set by considering Islamic rules reduce financial inequality and contribute to the overall well-being of the communities, thus, offer sustainable financial growth.

Remarkably, an exceptional aspect of Islamic corporate governance is emphasis on the fulfillment of social responsibilities via distributing compulsory almsgiving, that is, Zakat and charity, that is, Sadaqah. Characteristically, Zakat works as a catalyst for financial growth by collecting capital from wealthy citizens and distributing it to the people who are less fortunate. The Islamic Banks follow strict Islamic corporate finance procedures to collect Zakat and then provide them as seed capital for microfinancing, the development of social enterprises, skill development, education purposes, etc. Also, for this purpose, Islamic Banks adopted dissimilar methods. Thus, by setting procedures for wealth distribution among the needy and poor, Islamic corporate governance alleviates poverty, contributes to social welfare, and promotes economic justice. In the same vein, some other Islamic finance principles such as Mudarabah and Musharakah, which focus on sharing profit and loss between business and investors, foster an equitable financial system that develops economic justice, reduces unfair practices, and promotes sustainable financial growth.

Notably, the Islamic corporate governance measures for wealth circulation via Zakat and Sadaqah for poverty mitigation, helping individual investors, retired people, low-income class, etc., and enhancing economic justice that is aligned with the United Nations' SDGs.

3.5. Islamic Corporate Governance, SDGs, and the Sustainable Growth

Islamic finance plays a key role in handling and sorting the problems faced by humanity. Similarly, the targets of SDGs such as ending inequality, protecting the globe, ending poverty, etc., are created to ensure that the whole population of the world enjoys justice, prosperity, and health benefits. It is also in line with Islamic finance core objectives. The 2030 Agenda of SDGs for sustainable development was introduced by the United Nations for global transformation and it was unanimously adopted by all United Nations (UN) members. Notably, the SDGs agenda is measured as a new global framework that was endorsed by the UN General Assembly on September 25, 2015. Undeniably, the industry of Islamic finance is supporting the United Nations' SDGs goals as it promotes economic justice, financial growth, social welfare, and socially responsible development. The Islamic finance instruments such as Zakat, waqf, and Sadaqah eventually increased the Islamic finance influence on the SDGs. Fundamentally, Zakat, waqf, and Sadaqah play a main role in meeting the SDGs' main role, that is, mitigating poverty (Ebrahim et al., 2021). Considering all these linkages between Islamic finance and SDGs, the Islamic Development Bank (IDB) and the United Nations development program established the global Islamic finance and impact investing platform (GIFIIP) in 2015. The GIFIIP is raised to place Islamic finance as one of the vital enablers for the SDGs execution around the globe. In the same vein, in 2019, the IDB fully adopted the SDG procedures and launched its new framework that is consistent with the SDG principles (UKIFC, 2020). At the corporate level, regulatory bodies such as the International Federation of Accountants and the Professional Accountancy Organization explain the linkage between Islamic finance corporate governance and SDGs.

The Islamic corporate governance and SDGs both promote sustainable economic growth by inserting ethical, environmental, and social considerations into corporate practices. The Islamic corporate governance procedures are considered best in reducing systemic risks, offering fairness, transparency, risk-sharing, and fostering long-term stability. Thus, all these advantages of Islamic corporate governance bring it in line with the SDGs' key focus goals of utmost economic development, social equity, and eco-friendly sustainability. Therefore, by promoting accountable investment procedures, innovation, and ethical-based governance, both dissimilar frameworks are helping the development of resilient financial systems that generate long-term values and attract sustainable investments to increase corporate reputation. Despite this, the Islamic finance industry is still in the infancy stage of setting the corporate governance measures for implementing SDGs; thus, this may enhance regulatory challenges and investors' pressure on Islamic-tagged financial institutions (Jan et al., 2021; Jan et al., 2023). Therefore, it is important to polish the tools of Islamic Corporate Finance and its procedure for the SDGs implementation before 2030 in Islamic financial institutions.

The 17 SDGs that address the ESG facets of sustainability are included in the 2030 Agenda. These objectives acknowledge that combating poverty requires addressing health and education issues, promoting economic expansion, lowering inequality, and addressing climate change (Priem & Gabellone, 2024; Marmore, 2023). After that, ESG-based activities are rapidly adopted across numerous sectors, more particularly by the banking industry across the globe.

3.6. Islamic Corporate Governance, ESG Goals, and Sustainable Growth

The CSR level of businesses is measured by their ESG-related performance (Ioannou & Serafeim, 2017). Remarkably, Islamic corporate governance and ESG both stress on ethical values, environmental stewardship, and social responsibilities. Thus, when Islamic corporate governance is interconnected with the ESG framework, it offers robust sustainable financial growth for its nominees. The corporate governance mechanisms of Islamic finance and ESG are almost similar. Technically, Islamic finance does not allow its investors to invest in the several businesses that are involved in all those sorts of activities that are forbidden in Islam. For that purpose, the Islamic corporate governance regulatory bodies such as AAOIFI and IFSB involve Shariah supervisory councils which developed numerous screening processes. Also, the Shariah regulatory bodies monitor strictly and do not permit Shariah-tagged businesses to be involved in the interest, weapons, pork, alcohol, pornography, gambling, tobacco, human trafficking, and all other businesses that are deemed illegal in Islam. The Shariah advisory councils' practices of screening business are similar to the ESG investment procedures which also avoid several services and products to construct its portfolio with sustainable, fair, and socially oriented investors. Also, like Islamic Corporate Governance, the ESG procedures do not allow its investors to invest in all those sorts of businesses that harm the environment (see Table 1.6).

Table 1.6 clarifies the similarities and dissimilarities between Shariah finance and ESG investments. Visibly, Shariah finance and ESG-based investments both have numerous similarities; however, their level of engagement in businesses is different. As the adoption of ESG is gaining extra importance for businesses' survival, Islamic financial institutes involve several procedures to adopt its measures.

Table 1.6. Comparison Between Shariah Finance and ESG Investment.

Exercise	Shariah Finance	ESG-based Investment
Efficient ESG combination	Low parameters	Medium parameters
Screening	100% application based on Shariah	High levels of screening, that is, based on client and fund-related screening procedures
Business involvement on social and environmental connected issues	Low parameters	High parameters
Voting	Low parameters	High parameters
Dividends	Dividends should be paid 100 percent	No constraints
Interest/riba earned	Riba is not allowed	No constraints
Security lending	Security-based lending is not allowed. Thus, assets must be possessed, and interest, that is, riba, is not allowed	High ranks with key practitioners applying regulations that guarantee they can vote
Shorting	Shorting is not permitted and assets must be possessed	Low parameters
Restriction on high interest based-leverage	100% application to avoid earning riba, that is, interest	No constraints

Source: Compiled by authors based on Han (2024) and CFA (2019).

Hence, because of the ESG procedures adoption, Islamic financial institutes such as Islamic Banks are now involved in environmental and socially connected governance-based businesses. For instance, Al Barka Banking Group invested USD 197 million from 2019 to 2020 in energy-renewable and energy efficiency-related projects. Likewise, Bank Islam Malaysia increased its funding for green financing and for that purpose allocated an extra RM 800 million in 2020. Also, the IDB is considered the first Islamic Bank that developed a sustainable finance governance framework in 2019 for issuing a green sukuk (Al Ansari & Alanzarouti, 2020). Moreover, the ESG-sukuk has also been introduced, and it has been gaining extensive attention as it allows issuers to combine both Shariah principles and ESG. Basically, the ESG-sukuk integrates an extra layer of Shariah governance that makes sure that funds received from the issuance of bonds are used in those projects that are consistent with ESG and Shariah governance (Hakim, 2024). Principally, green and ESG-Sukuk are Islamic bonds that are issued to finance those projects that are environmentally sustainable and, thus, align with the ESG targets of promoting social, ethical, and environmental stewardship. The AAOIFI-issued GS12 provides guidelines to Islamic finance institutes for the issuance of green Sukuk.

The Islamic corporate governance and ESG are synergistic notions that mutually promote ethical, social, responsible, and sustainable business practices that are also consistent with Shariah rules and regulations. Therefore, by mixing these dissimilar frameworks, businesses can easily target their main aim, that is, long-term financial success while positively contributing to society and the environment. Visibly, according to Refinitiv's EIKON database only in 2022 Shariah-tagged businesses maintained a 6% higher ESG score than those that are the conventional one and not preserving the Shariah screening process (Abdullah & Haron, 2022).

4. Conclusions

The aftershocks of former financial disasters forced financial concerns to reassess the conventional modes they used to allot their investments. Notably, the former financial fiascos are not only measured as failures of traditional financial systems but have also been considered a letdown of conventional corporate governance procedures and frameworks. This rapidly highlighted that Islamic finance offered services and products considered best to tackle all kinds of financial messes. Thus, the Islamic finance governing bodies such as the IFSB and AAOIFI established numerous Shariah-based GSs to develop robust Islamic corporate governance procedures and frameworks. These Islamic finance regulatory bodies' frameworks for Islamic corporate governance elucidate that there must be a vital Shariah board, Shariah supervisory council, internal Shariah compliance, internal Shariah audit, and external independent Shariah audit to certify the Shariah compliance of Islamic finance institutions. Typically, Islamic corporate governance is rooted in Islamic ideologies and stresses more on ethical-based business measures that encourage fairness, accountability, transparency, and economic justice. Therefore, Islamic corporate governance stresses more on ethics in businesses and elucidates that they must function with honesty, morality, and considers social responsibilities. For instance, the Ihsan, that is, benevolence, and Adl, that is, Justice model of AAOIFI, elucidate that to achieve justice, the concerns ought to give priority to Ihsan in all situations. Likewise, Islamic corporate governance stresses on accountability and transparency that build the trust of nominees and also eradicate risk and corruption. By considering the corporate GSs of AAOIF and IFSB, Islamic finance also offers dissimilar risk-sharing products such as mudarabah, musharakah, Takaful, etc. Hence, Islamic corporate governance risk-sharing mechanisms play a key role in fostering sustainable financial growth by injecting crystal clear, socially responsible, and ethical-based performances into financial structures. In the same manner, CSR integration with Islamic corporate governance boosts transparency, accountability, ethical behavior, business reputation in the market. This not only upsurges the trust and confidence of nominees but also develops business operational efficiency that eventually produces sustainable growth. Furthermore, the Islamic corporate governance and SDGs are consistent with each other. Thus, there combination encourages sustainable economic growth by injecting ethical, environmental, and social considerations into corporate practices. Also, Islamic corporate governance is interconnected with the SDGs and ESG frameworks; thus, it offers robust sustainable financial growth. Interestingly, the Shariah advisory councils' procedures for screening businesses are parallel with the ESG investment procedures. By considering ESG adoption, Islamic corporate governance offered several Islamic finance products like Takaful, green Sukuk, and ESG sukuk. The AAOIFI allotted GS12 provides guidelines to Islamic finance institutes for the issuance of green and ESG-Sukuk. Hence, the AAOIFI and IFSB GSs and procedures assist in the development of robust Islamic corporate governance processes that eventually encourage sustainable financial growth by guaranteeing ethical business practices, risk management, social responsibility, and environmental goals, that is, aligned with Sharia principles.

References

AAOIFI. (2015). *Shari'ah standards, accounting and auditing organization for Islamic financial institutions*. Retrieved July 13, 2024, from https://aaoifi.com/?lang=en

AAOIFI. (2019). *AAOIFI issues the final standard on code of ethics for Islamic finance professionals for industry adoption, accounting and auditing organisation for Islamic financial institutions*. Retrieved July 13, 2024, from 00-AAOIFI-Code-of-Ethics-for-Islamic-finance-Professionals-Final-Standard-Issued-CS.pdf

Abdullah, N. A. I. N., & Haron, R. (2022). ESG reporting practices among Islamic banks: A global perspective. *IIUM Law Journal*, *30*(S2), 01–36.

Abdulrahman, Z., Ebrahimi, T., & Al-Najjar, B. (2023). Exploring the nexus between Islamic financial institutions Shariah compliance disclosure and corporate governance: New insights from a cross-country analysis. *International Journal of Finance & Economics*, 29, 4590–4612. https://doi.org/10.1002/ijfe.2891

Agustian, K., Hejazziey, D., Zen, A., Sekarini, R. A., & Wiwin, W. (2023). Comparative analysis of ethical and legal principles in the Islamic business management model. *Journal of Contemporary Administration and Management (ADMAN)*, *1*(2), 101–107.

Alam, A., Fianto, B. A., Ratnasari, R. T., Ahmi, A., & Handayani, F. P. (2023). History and development of Takaful research: A bibliometric review. *SAGE Open*, *13*(3), 1–20. https://doi.org/10.1177/21582440231184852

Al Ansari, R., & Alanzarouti, F. (2020). ESG and Islamic finance: An ethical bridge built on shared values. *Journal of Islamic Financial Studies*, *6*(1), 5–11. http://dx.doi.org/10.12785/jifs/060101

AL-Hawamleh, A., Altarawneh, M., Hikal, H., & Elfedawy, A. (2024). Blockchain technology and virtual asset accounting in the metaverse: A comprehensive review of future directions. *International Journal of Computing and Digital Systems*, *15*(1), 1595–1614.

Ali, M. A., & Hussain, T. (2024). Islamic banking products, services and objectives: A comprehensive analysis of stakeholders' opinions. *GISRAS Journal of Management & Islamic Finance (GJMIF)*, *4*(1), 58–79.

Alkassim Farid, S. (2019). Role of Islamic banking in economic growth. *International Journal of Social Sciences*, *5*(1), 26–41.

Alpen Capital. (2021). *Alpen capital's Islamic finance industry report*. Retrieved September 15, 2024, from https://alpencapital.com/research/2021/alpen-capital-islamic-finance-industry-july-6-2021.php

Asif, M. Z. (2022). The significance of corporate governance in Islamic banking: Enhancing accountability and performance. *Bulletin of Business and Economics (BBE)*, *11*(4), 25–32.

Bhatti, M., & Bhatti, M. I. (2010). Toward understanding Islamic corporate governance issues in Islamic finance. *Asian Politics & Policy*, *2*(1), 25–38.

Broadstock, D. C., Matousek, R., Meyer, M., & Tzeremes, N. G. (2020). Does corporate social responsibility impact firms' innovation capacity? The indirect link between environmental and social governance implementation and innovation performance. *Journal of Business Research*, 119, 99–110.

Capital, A., & Advisors, A. A. (2021). *Islamic finance and wealth management*. DUBAI: Alpen Capital and Alpen Asset Advisors. Retrieved July 8, 2024, from https://argaamplus.s3.amazonaws.com/86f171a0-dcdc-4a26-b7f1-35345c16f250.pdf

CFA. (2019). *Comparison between Islamic finance and ESG investing, PRI (principles for responsible investment)*. Retrieved Accessed July 18, 2024, from https://www.unpri.org/download?ac=9578

Dai, Y. (2024). Sustainable investing and Islamic finance: Evidence from the organization of Islamic cooperation (OIC) countries. *ISRA International Journal of Islamic Finance*, *16*(1), 41–56.

Dharani, M., Hassan, M. K., Rabbani, M. R., & Huq, T. (2022). Does the Covid-19 pandemic affect faith-based investments? Evidence from global sectoral indices. *Research in International Business and Finance*, *59*, 101537.

Drew, S. A., Kelley, P. C., & Kendrick, T. (2006). CLASS: Five elements of corporate governance to manage strategic risk. *Business Horizons*, *49*(2), 127–138.

Ebrahim, R., Abdulla, Y., & Kumaraswamy, S. (2021). *Islamic finance and sustainable development goals in Bahrain*. 2021 International conference on sustainable Islamic business and finance (pp. 8–13). https://doi.org/10.1109/IEEECONF53626.2021.9686329

Emeka-Okoli, S., Nwankwo, T. C., Otonnah, C. A., & Nwankwo, E. E. (2024). Environmental stewardship and corporate social responsibility: A review of case studies from the oil and gas sector. *World Journal of Advanced Research and Reviews*, *21*(3), 069–077.

Franzoni, S., & Ait Allali, A. (2024). Corporate governance of Islamic banks: A sustainable model to protect the participatory depositor? *Journal of Banking Regulation*, *25*(1), 42–48.

Freeman, R. B. (1984). Longitudinal analyses of the effects of trade unions. *Journal of Labor Economics*, *2*(1), 1–26.

Friedman, M. (1962). *Capitalism and freedom*. University of Chicago Press.

Gardezi, S. E. (2023). Ethics and impact of Islamic finance: Exploring the gap between theory and practice. *Journal of Insurance and Financial Management*, *7*(8), 1–12.

Gillan, S. L., Koch, A., & Starks, L. T. (2021). Firms and social responsibility: A review of ESG and CSR research in corporate finance. *Journal of Corporate Finance*, *66*, 101889.

Ginena, K., & Hamid, A. (2015). *Foundations of Shariah Governance of Islamic Banks*. John Wiley & Sons Ltd.

Gwala, R. S., & Mashau, P. (2023). Tracing the evolution of agency theory in corporate governance. In N. Baporikar (Ed.), *Governance as a catalyst for public sector sustainability* (pp. 260–285). IGI Global.

Hakim, A. (2024). Financing green: Exploring Sukuk as a tool for sustainable investment in Islamic finance. Available at *SSRN 4860671*. https://papers.ssrn.com/sol3/papers.cfm?abstract_id=4860671. Accessed on:12-Dec-2024.

Han, T. M. (2024). *Do well by doing good, eastspring*. Retrieved September 13, 2024, from https://www.eastspring.com/myalwarainvestments/insights/thought-leadership/do-well-by-doing-good

Hanif, M., Chaker, M., & Sabah, A. (2024). Islamic finance and economic growth: Global evidence. *Digest of Middle East Studies*, *33*(1), 83–102.

Haqqi, A. R. A. (2014). Shariah governance in Islamic financial institution: An appraisal. *Us-China Law Review*, *11*(112), 112–133.

Haron, R., & Siraj, M. A. (2024). Issues and challenges of sustainable finance in the Islamic capital market. *Islamic Finance and Sustainable Development*, *14*(1), 195–208.

Hasan, Z. (2011). A survey on Shari'ah governance practices in Malaysia, GCC countries and the UK: Critical appraisal. *International Journal of Islamic and Middle Eastern Finance and Management*, *4*(1), 30–51. https://doi.org/10.1108/17538391111122195

Hilmy, H. M. A., & Hassan, R. (2019). Shariah governance structure of Islamic financial institutions in Sri Lanka. *International Journal of Management and Applied Research*, *6*(4), 245–258.

Hossain, M. T., Siwar, C., & Omar, A. R. (2014). Corporate social responsibility as a mean to mitigate risk for Islamic banking industry. *Advances in Environmental Biology*, *8*(9), 466–472.

IFSB. (2006). *Guiding principles on corporate governance for institutions offering only Islamic financial services excluding Islamic insurance (tak āful)*. Institutions and Islamic Mutual Funds, Islamic Financial Service Board, Kuala Lumpur.

IFSB. (2009). *Guiding principles on Shari'ah governance systems for institutions offering Islamic financial services*. Islamic Financial Service Board, Kuala Lumpur.

IFSB. (2023). *Islamic financial services stability report*. Retrieved September 15, 2024, from https://www.ifsb.org/wp-content/uploads/2023/10/Islamic-Financial-Services-Industry-Stability-Report-2023_En.pdf

Ioannou, I., & Serafeim, G. (2017). *The consequences of mandatory corporate sustainability reporting*. Harvard business school research working paper (pp. 11–100).

Jan, A., Mata, M. N., Albinsson, P. A., Martins, J. M., Hassan, R. B., & Mata, P. N. (2021). Alignment of Islamic banking sustainability indicators with sustainable development goals: Policy recommendations for addressing the covid-19 pandemic. *Sustainability*, *13*(5), 2607.

Jan, A., Rahman, H. U., Zahid, M., Salameh, A. A., Khan, P. A., Al-Faryan, M. A. S., & Ali, H. E. (2023). Islamic corporate sustainability practices index aligned with SDGs towards better financial performance: Evidence from the Malaysian and Indonesian Islamic banking industry. *Journal of Cleaner Production*, *405*, 136860.

Jan, A. A., Lai, F. W., & Tahir, M. (2021). Developing an Islamic corporate governance framework to examine sustainability performance in Islamic Banks and Financial Institutions. *Journal of Cleaner Production*, *315*, 128099.

Khan, M. M. (2016). CSR standards and Islamic banking practice: A case of Meezan Bank of Pakistan. *The Journal of Developing Areas*, *50*(5), 295–306.

Ling, D. X., Haron, R., & Hasan, A. (2024). Islamic sustainable finance: The role of Islamic banking standards. In M. M. Billah, R. Hassan, R. Haron, & N. R. M. Zain (Eds.), *Islamic sustainable finance* (pp. 102–116). Routledge.

Marmore. (2023). *Green sukuk an emerging asset class in the GCC*. Retrieved July 17, 2024, from https://www.marmoremena.com/en/insights/green-sukuk–an-emerging-asset-class-in-the-gcc/

Marzuki, M. M., Majid, W. Z. N. A., & Rosman, R. (2023). Corporate social responsibility and Islamic social finance impact on banking sustainability post-COVID-19 pandemic. *Heliyon*, *9*(10), 1–13.

Musaffa. (2020). *Islamic finance in Asia: Rapid growth of the industry in the region*. Retrieved September 15, 2024, from https://academy.musaffa.com/islamic-finance-in-asia-rapid-growth-of-the-industry-in-the-region/

Omar, M. N. (2013). Ethics in Islam: A brief survey. *The Social Sciences*, *8*(5), 387–392.

Priem, R., & Gabellone, A. (2024). The impact of a firm's ESG score on its cost of capital: can a high ESG score serve as a substitute for a weaker legal environment. *Sustainability Accounting, Management and Policy Journal*, *15*(3), 676–703.

Rashid, A., Akmal, M., & Shah, S. M. A. R. (2024). Corporate governance and risk management in Islamic and convectional financial institutions: Explaining the role of institutional quality. *Journal of Islamic Accounting and Business Research*, *15*(3), 466–498.

Ricoeur, P. (1973). Ethics and culture. *Philosophy Today*, *17*(2), 153.

Saeed, A. (2016). Sharia and finance. In J. E. Lowry (Ed.), *The Ashgate research companion to Islamic law* (pp. 249–259). Routledge.

Sarib, S., Komaruddin, K., Chairunnisa, M. D., Majdi, A. L., & Mokodenseho, S. (2023). Qualitative study of the role of Islamic law in shaping Muslim identity and business ethics. *Sanskara Hukum dan HAM*, *2*(01), 58–65.

Sekreter, A. (2011). Sharing of risks in Islamic finance. *IBSU Scientific Journal*, *5*(2), 13–20.

Setiawan, I. (2023). The significance of corporate social responsibility in sustainable development: An analysis from an Islamic law perspective. *Journal of Law and Sustainable Development*, *11*(9), 1–23.

Sherif, M. (2020). The impact of coronavirus (COVID-19) outbreak on faith-based investments: An original analysis. *Journal of Behavioral and Experimental Finance*, *28*, 100403.

Siregar, E. S., & Irmayuliana, I. (2024). The effect of Murabahah, Mudharabah, and Musharakah financing on net profit growth in bank Muamalat Indonesia. *Journal BAABU AL-ILMI: Ekonomi dan Perbankan Syariah*, *7*(1), 86–95.

Solihati, G. P., Suhardiyanto, H., Hakim, D. B., & Irawan, T. (2023). Integrating good corporate governance, Islamic corporate social responsibility, Zakat, Syariah governance, and Syariah compliance: Exploring their interconnected impact on the financial health of Islamic commercial banks. *Journal of Contemporary Administration and Management (ADMAN)*, *1*(3), 271–277.

Tahir, A. R., & Sohail, M. (2012). The concepts of ethical life in Islam. *Interdisciplinary Journal of Contemporary Research in Business*, *3*(9), 1360–1369.

Tasnia, M., Syed Jafaar Alhabshi, S. M., & Rosman, R. (2023). Corporate social responsibility and Islamic and conventional banks performance: A systematic review and future research agenda. *Journal of Sustainable Finance & Investment*, *13*(4), 1711–1731.

UKIFC. (2020, May). *Islamic finance and the SDGs: Framing the opportunity through leadership series part 1*. Retrieved July 9, 2023, from https://www.ukifc.com/wp-content/uploads/2020/05/ISLAMIC-FINANCE-AND-THE-SDGS-%E2%80%93-THOUGHT-PAPER-13052020.pdf?_gl=1*1ynob8g*_ga*NjQ1NzEzNzczLjE3MjA1MzE3MzU.*_ga_RTFMMZCKEY*MTcyMDUzMTczNS4xLjEuMTcyMDUzMTg0OC4wLjAuMA

Wahyono, B. (2022). The value of political connections and Sharia compliance during the COVID-19 pandemic. *Eurasian Economic Review, 12*(1), 1–28.

Wirba, A. V. (2023). Corporate social responsibility (CSR): The role of government in promoting CSR. *Journal of the Knowledge Economy, 15*(2), 1–27. https://doi.org/10.1007/s13132-023-01185-0

Yusuf, M., Dasawaty, E., Esra, M., Apriwenni, P., Meiden, C., & Fahlevi, M. (2024). Integrated reporting, corporate governance, and financial sustainability in Islamic banking. *Uncertain Supply Chain Management, 12*(1), 273–290.

Zubaidah, S., & Pratiwi, P. D. (2024). Islamic corporate governance, profitability, corporate social responsibility, and sustainability report disclosure. In R. I. Robbie, A. Roziqin, S. M. Deniar, A. Praharjo & K. Roz (Eds.), *Environmental issues and social inclusion in a sustainable era* (pp. 263–272). Routledge.

Zuki, M. F. M., Ishak, M. A. F., & Roja, M. I. H. (2024). Takaful business model and business performance: A comparative evidence from the global Takaful industry. *International Journal of Islamic Business*, *9*(1), 1–29.

Chapter 2

Framework for Measuring the Impact of Islamic Corporate Governance on Sustainable Growth

Sonali Srivastava[a], *Manisha Singh*[b] *and Sachin Prakash Srivastava*[c]

[a]*Jaypee Business School, Jaypee Institute of Information Technology, Noida, India*
[b]*VIT Business School, VIT Bhopal University, Bhopal, India*
[c]*School of Business, Dr. Vishwanath Karad MIT World Peace University, Pune, India*

Abstract

Islamic corporate governance (CG) plays a significant role in ensuring the sustainability of organizations' growth by aligning it with the objectives of Shariah. It promotes Shariah values and fosters a culture of trust that safeguards against wastage, extravagance, fraud, and misuse of power by those in governance. This chapter reviews Islamic CG, highlighting its differences from conventional CG and its relevance to sustainable growth. The principle of socially responsible behavior in religious-based economic systems is employed to interpret how contemporary organizations should be governed, and the objectives of stakeholders are considered in business operations and spiritual obligations. The Islamic economic model has great potential to encourage a unique perspective on the role of stakeholders, which is implemented through the inclusive process of CG. Responsible investing is based on the ethical core principles of faith and connection between capitalism and religions. The Islamic world distinguishes between capitalism and material success and capitalism and moral management. The study establishes the impact of Islamic CG on the dynamics of sustainable growth and development of a company from a wide array of measures so as to overshadow corporate growth, employees' involvement, ethical and transparency issues,

Islamic Finance and Corporate Governance: Synergies for Sustainable Growth, 23–42

doi:10.1108/978-1-83662-346-520251005

tackling macroeconomic issues to promote smooth state balance sheet formation, and much more. Behavioral CG relies upon credible ethical practices that align all stakeholders and shareholders in a company's business, a sound corporate infrastructure, social cooperation, and a high-quality legal framework.

Keywords: Islamic CG; sustainable growth; Shariah compliance; risk management; environmental sustainability; ethical investment

1. Introduction

CG is essential for firms to achieve and maintain sustainable growth. In recent years, Islamic CG has emerged as an important discipline due to the growing importance of Islamic economics and finance in the area of corporate finance worldwide (Aslam & Haron, 2020; Jan et al., 2021). It is vital as well as challenging to evaluate and analyze the Islamic CG while focusing on its defining characteristics and its main differences with (non-Islamic) CG (Ullah et al., 2023). This comprehensive guide provides a comparative analysis of the classical principles of CG based on the Holy Quran and Sunnah and the contemporary CG framework (Bin Hagshah, 2022). Demands for greater equity in terms of both economic and social well-being of the less fortunate and the empowerment of the workforce of today by way of increased access to capital, observance of international labor standards, distribution of wealth, and a just and equitable system of remuneration have been made. These ideals resonate fully with the Islamic principles and practices of CG (Kader, 2021; Setiawan, 2023). Profit maximization is not only seen as the primordial goal of the corporation. In the Islamic system of values, the inequalities arising from such objectives can trigger socioeconomic imbalances and powerful vested interest groups that can impede sustainable growth and the rule of law (Anjum, 2022; Ismail et al., 2020).

Corporation should operate on the premise of fulfilling its obligations to the overall stakeholders regardless of their positions, based on a philosophy condoning firm integrity, utilizing resources with responsibility, and an emphasis on corporate accountability (Badshah, 2020; Jan et al., 2021). The differences in the principles between conventional business and Islamic business, showing distinct financial management principles, have significant implications on the objectives of a corporation and the roles of stakeholders (Khan & Zahid, 2020; Muhammad et al., 2021). Nonetheless, the absence of an authentic Islamic financial model cascades in success toward developing a serious conflict resolution pattern conforming to the needs of the Islamic corporation. Cost-effective Islamic business, Islamic principles in business, and the Islamic organizational framework describe the objectives and culture of Islamic business within an Islamic perspective (Mergaliyev et al., 2021; Tarique et al., 2021).

A regulation by the Shari'ah supervisory board, who advises the Islamic corporation, is an additional supervisory arrangement to ensure compliance with the

Shari'a. The inclusion of the Shari'ah supervision reflects the Islamic corporation to be different from the conventional business corporation since the former is under obligation to manage and operate based on the absolute Shari'ah principles, while the manager's job in universal business enterprise is to broaden the investor's benefit with an objective to maximize returns on investment (Muslihun, 2023; Sriani & Habibah, 2024). The former represents the shareholders and regards as a stakeholder who has an interest in deliberating issues related to the Islamic business, while the manager of conventional business actively manages corporate business operations with an objective aimed at wealth maximization (Abdullah & Asutay, 2021; Badshah, 2020).

Islamic corporation is that of a trustee holding responsibility for an advertisement of strong moral values such as fairness, justice, responsible usage of resources, accountability, transparency, and good governance. The main concern differs greatly from the corporate perspective under the capitalist view (Abdullah & Asutay, 2021; Hirsanudin & Martini, 2023; Sapuan et al., 2020). Instead of concentrating on the wealth maximization objective as stated in conventional theories, the Islamic corporation appointed as khilafah (leader or custodian) for the creator's wealth is required to internalize commercial actions with an obligation to illustrate business expertise (Abdullah & Asutay, 2021; Azizah, 2024). In order to lead and manage a fully Islamic corporation, the Islamic organizational framework projects specific traits and principles. The organizational stakeholders, particularly those who take part in business operations whether employed, service providers, or consumers, are ensured and guaranteed with their inherent roles and responsibilities (Koleva, 2021; Salin et al., 2020). The employees' rewards for their contributions comply with the universal principles of Shari'ah. These rewards encompass the core element, which includes a fair wage based on a distinct freedom agreement, benefits on productivity, and team rewards. All liability, risk, and profit should be fairly distributed to ensure trust, commitment, and shared value (Alduaij, 2020; Muliansyah & Hermawan, 2024; So et al., 2021).

This chapter presents an overview of CG within the Islamic organizational framework. It is essential to comprehend the organizational framework in Islam. Islam is a way of life and governs all aspects of human life, including social, political, economic, cultural, as well as organizational aspects. Islamic organization is one of the unique characteristics that separates Islam from other religions. Islamic corporations or organizations are mandated to operate on the basis of the teachings of the Qur'an and Sunnah (Jubba et al., 2021; Riinawati, 2022).

1.1. Objectives and Rationale of the Study

The concept of CG has assumed increasing significance of the collapses of big corporations across the world due to the rising practices of business malpractices and sharp practices. CG has been defined as the process and structure used to direct and define the financial and human resources of an organization toward the achievement of its business objectives, transparently and responsibly. Thus, CG often refers to the mechanisms and structures surrounding the organization of business and the ongoing relations between both management and the board and those people who have an influence in how the business is run. It is a system of laws, regulations, and customs affecting the control and fair treatment in the conduct of legal entities within a nation. Islamic CG refers to the culture, customs, regulations, and laws that affect the proper and ethical conduct of business within any Islamic society or nation.

This study explores the impact that Islamic CG has on the sustainable growth of Islamic banks. The impact of Islamic governance, drawing on prior studies and focusing on three key aspects of Islamic governance: the role of the Islamic supervisory board, its composition, and the Islamicity of the business model. Explore governance TO cover a unique setting, Iran, where explicit Shari'ah compliance is mandated by law, and address several shortcomings of prior studies by looking at the ex-post impact on the bank's sustainable banking activities, the degree of interaction between different stakeholders, and use data-driven metrics. This study aims to examine the impact of ICG on sustainable corporate growth, by considering the moderating role of corporate social responsibility (CSR) on the relationship. CSR dissatisfaction can greatly influence corporate growth if stakeholders believe that a company's profits are earned unethically or at the expense of society. This study utilizes the earnings-based growth model of Dechow et al. (1995) as a firm's growth proxy. The level of CSR disclosures is included in the empirical model as the moderating variable. Since stakeholders suggest that a high quality of CSR disclosure can create long-term sustainable growth, higher CSR disclosures may help facilitate sustainable growth and guide a firm's behavior to become more socially responsible.

The environment in which the economic agents gain greater transparency, the flow of information has become more efficient, and the businesses are not immune to significant impacts on these rapid changes in the areas of CG. On the contrary, companies from many other countries, especially Islamic countries, have established their CG practices and the concept of social environmental initiatives to enhance their use and diffuse in the organizations. The main concept behind the unique CG system of Islam is to establish a moral, ethical, and social discipline in the organization. This uniqueness encompasses many elements, which are far more different and transcend the structure and function compared with the CG model of the Western world. Although there are similarities between the conventional and Islamic CG model, such as transparency, accountability, and fairness, the model of Islamic corporate. Islamic financial intermediation regulations and Shariah compliance are critical determinants of associate investment risk in determining shareholders. Therefore, it is recommended that the CG framework promulgated by each Islamic financial authority must set out its CG guidelines for each system it oversees.

1.2. Theoretical Foundations of Islamic CG

The Islamic approach also mandates the establishment of guidelines for all kinds of financial transactions and the introduction of governance mechanisms that will align the interests of the management and external interests in minimizing the agency problem (Adekoya, 2022; Arifin, 2021). Given the recent dramatic changes in CG, the role of institutional investors and the dynamics of capital flows over the last decade are crucial to the global and Islamic perspective. The increasing role of Islamic companies in expanding the Islamic approach to global financial markets cannot be ignored. With the Islamic world controlling a large share of global energy sources, the development of its own unique alternative financial system is neither an accident nor happenstance. As Islamic finance is being embraced by Muslim investors, it cannot be overlooked (Anggadwita et al., 2021; Jan et al., 2021; Murphy & Smolarski, 2020; Rabbani et al., 2021). Policy-makers, therefore, must be mindful of the nexus between CG and the efficiency of these providers of vital products and services, as well as the CG issues that emerge with the increasing interest in Islamic alternative investment vehicles proposed by large institutional investors (Hasan et al., 2022; Mundi & Kumar, 2023). With an improved understanding of the CG dimensions of Islamic finance and the efficient tools that are used in its conduction, it is hoped that such a nexus shall enhance aspirations in building knowledge from an area that is largely obscure to date (Nomran & Haron, 2020; Shahar et al., 2020).

In respect of corporate stakeholders' value, Islamic teachings and texts offer a combination of both spirit and rationale. Contrary to the practice today, particularly with respect to the Anglo-Saxon model of CG which conceals self-serving interests that primarily serve the interest of the few (the capital), the Islamic principles substantially place obligations on the agents who are entrusted with responsibilities over the capital and the profits (El & Ben, 2023; Hassan et al., 2022; Hirsanudin & Martini, 2023; Nouman et al., 2021). Islamic rules and regulations are a guide to the governance of public as well as private institutions. The current global economic crisis also provides an opportunity to place the obligations of the market and systemic risk-taking into regulatory and CG environments. To ensure the effectiveness of the CG model adopted, the governance model adopted has to be vis-a-vis the values of the stakeholders (Li et al., 2023; Meier et al., 2021; Zattoni & Pugliese, 2021).

2. Regulatory Framework and Compliance of Islamic CG

Islamic CG brings uniqueness to the Islamic banking community and contributes to CG knowledge. Islamic and general banks have many similarities but differ in terms of product and service offerings, service and regulatory demands of the Shari'ah board, organizational structure, and corporate boards (Khokhar et al., 2020; Shamsudheen et al., 2021). Islamic banks follow the conventional principles of CG, and all UAE commercial banks apply the same rules set by the UAE central bank or its other regulations (Anwer et al., 2020; Reyad et al., 2022). Sharjah Islamic banks (SIBs) are chosen to focus on Shari'ah governance because they have proven to be the best Islamic commercial bank in the UAE and also have strategic interests, values, and a high-level commitment to Shari'ah compliance practices (Kapur et al., 2020; Sidaoui et al., 2022).

Regulatory framework should be built upon the importance of the inner quality and sincerity of the entity itself. The implementation of mandatory Islamic CG in spiritual behavior should be more persuasive. It should be implemented based on spiritual guidance and reference that holds consensus among highly reputable (Ayub et al., 2023; Olorogun & Othman, 2021). However, before the procedures can be determined and embedded into business practices, a rich understanding about what constitutes the acceptable good behavior and conviction pathways to the promised remunerations should be well comprehended and believed (Ramli et al., 2022; Riaz et al., 2023). However, this should not turn into a condition to allow the capital market to promote poor-minded managers that ignore the future welfare. It may be very significant to develop a genuinely required set of spiritual corporate porousness that reflects Islamic value (Ng, 2020; Sani & Maharani Ekowati, 2020). The application can be strictly applied for Muslim investors, but should not undermine the liability to follow certain ethics, as long as the values do not disrupt public policy, security, and the country's economic progress as an integrated society (Jan et al., 2021; Tabash et al., 2022). Compliance, as in, most regulated-beyond-company-law business activities requires to have a similar principle, such as implementing Shari'ah's law. Concerns related to judgment in unpredictable business situations such as the legitimacy of these availabilities should quickly be resorted to Shari'ah compliance monitoring. Compliance with Islamic CG should be able to bring a meaning and moral to life in a full wrath of reconciliation (Basiruddin & Ahmed, 2020; Hobvi et al., 2022).

Sharjah Islamic Bank in Sharjah, UAE, is recognized as the best Islamic cooperative with a strategic vision, sustainable growth, and a high-level management commitment to Shari'ah compliance rules and values (Amin et al., 2020). In principle, Islamic CG policies, legal practices, and company strategies promote collaboration in social responsibility, providing value to all interested parties. The Sharjah Islamic Bank has identified that these governance challenges can be addressed through Shari'ah practices. The organization aims to lead growth by considering the social, moral, and ethical aspects of stakeholders and investor confidence. With Sharjah Islamic Bank as an Islamic CG leader, focused on the subject and committed to compliance, this chapter seeks to foster international CG scholarship, resulting in advancements beyond real-world expertise (Jan et al., 2021; Murphy & Smolarski, 2020; Rashid et al., 2022).

3. Comparison with Conventional CG

CG deals with two sets of stakeholders: the employees and the shareholders. Conventional CG, however, can also deal with providers of credit to a company and the business partners with whom it has a relationship (Hirsanudin & Martini, 2023; Sadek et al., 2020). The responsibilities are derived from legislation or accepted rules that govern the way business is done. These responsibilities include discharging their obligations of due care and disclosure, protecting the firm, mitigating its problems, acting in good faith and in the best interests of the firm, and preserving the interests of the firm within their domain of authority to advance the interests of shareholders and the firm collectively (Hirsanudin & Martini, 2023; Mukhibad et al., 2022). Additionally, the board of directors has to ensure that the company has an effective and efficient control and operating system to protect the organization's assets. It also has the responsibility of determining whether the necessary internal controls and audit and reporting procedures are in place. Finally, the board is expected to be efficient in designing the organizational structure and regulatory system to create and preserve the company's value (Abiodun, 2020; Al-Matari, 2020). The unique features of ICIG conform to the prescriptions and recommendations on CSR, CG codes, and corporate best practice. Conventional CG is criticized by many researchers for being responsible for the wide-ranging financial and economic problems. Many companies reported unethical behavior, which has a negative implication on corporate behavior (Khan et al., 2021; Safari & Parker, 2023). Conventional CG is reinforced by the increasing demand for more transparent, responsible, and accountable business practices in the world of business and finance. CSR is increasingly used and has become an important term to describe how corporations should behave (Hanif & Haron, 2022; Harun et al., 2020).

Conventional CG has faced substantial criticism from numerous researchers who argue that it is responsible for a range of financial and economic problems. This criticism stems from various reports of unethical behavior within companies, which have significant negative implications for corporate conduct (Khan et al., 2021; Safari & Parker, 2023). The demand for more transparent, responsible, and accountable business practices has intensified, further reinforcing the need for robust conventional CG in the realms of business and finance.

In response of these issues, CSR has gained prominence as an essential framework that outlines how corporations should behave. CSR is increasingly recognized as vital for ensuring that companies operate in a manner that is not only profitable but also ethical and beneficial to society (Hanif & Haron, 2022; Harun et al., 2020). This shift toward greater corporate responsibility highlights the evolving expectations placed on businesses to contribute positively to their community and the broader environment.

Shari'ah supervisory boards (SSBs) can play rules similar to those of ethics committees or audit committees providing legitimacy on Islamic matters (Almutairi & Quttainah, 2020; Islam & Islam, 2023). Their work involves, for example, laying down informal guidelines for the terms and conditions of new products and services based on Islamic principles, tracking down Islamic transactions that conflict with the rules laid down. SSBs are a key intrinsic component of any Islamic financial institution (IFI). Their primary role is to ensure that the institution operates in strict accordance with Islamic Shari'ah principles. The Islamic concept of profit-sharing through risk and wealth-sharing, which is the opposite of the conventional process during which there is a guaranteed rate of fixed payment in exchange for deposit funds or capital facilities, is discussed in the Quran (Alam & Miah, 2021; Rusydiana, 2021; Sriani & Habibah, 2024). SSBs apply Islamic principles to the financial activities of the institution. Their function is, therefore, to ensure the transparency, compliance, and ethical appropriateness of the institution's activities and, thus, enhance the credibility and reputation of the Islamic institution (Alam & Miah, 2022; Gusrianti & Sari, 2023).

Some of the suggested main characteristics that the corporate governance indicators should satisfy include the need to be widely available, comparable, reliable, and sensitive to differences between countries. Both input and output indicators should be designed with the principle that each indicator should capture governance (Black et al., 2023; Hundal, 2021). They should measure the operations or mechanisms that ensure the existence of good governance. These outputs will need to have measures that should be applied to the outcomes and impacts of governance practices. Metrics should provide greater clarity and quality about the decision-making process to arrive at a conclusion (Belita et al., 2020; Jagannathan et al., 2021; Sovrano et al., 2022). To measure the transparency in the performance of CG, a set of key CG indicators is needed. These indicators should provide transparency in both financial and non-financial issues. The development of these key CG indicators is considered extremely fundamental for reliable monitoring of CG and for achieving the objective of CG through these established indicators (Almagtome et al., 2020; Li et al., 2021; Tjahjadi et al., 2021). The more transparently financial and non-financial issues are presented, the more adequate picture of the firm will be available to the interested stakeholders (Hadro et al., 2022; Romito & Vurro, 2021; Turzo et al., 2022).

4. The Relationship Between CG and Sustainable Growth

The governance–performance relationship within this broader framework is complex for a number of reasons. First, there are numerous but often distinct albeit correlating mechanisms through which CG ostensibly influences corporate outcomes. Second, many factors contribute to performance, not all of which relate to CG (Awais et al., 2022; Kateb et al., 2023; Sari & Hussien, 2024). As a result, it is difficult to identify the precise nature of the effect of CG on sustainable business activities. There are important interdependencies between CG mechanisms, too. One governance mechanism cannot be fully effective if others are under designed or fail to act as complements, rather than necessitating trade-offs. And making trade-offs is sensitive to the prevailing institutional framework (Aguilera et al., 2021; Costa et al., 2022; Zaman et al., 2022). The institutional environment defines the distance between corporate insiders (owners and managers) and corporations. It also defines the distance between corporate outsiders and corporations (Beason et al., 2022; Bueno-Garcia et al., 2021; Wu et al., 2023). Although the general notion and consistency of the agency theory are flawed, and the accumulation of empirical evidence provides mixed results on the impact of CG mechanisms and performance measures, the relationship remains at the center stage of CG (Al-Ahdal et al., 2020; Wang et al., 2020). The failure of the agency theory has led to the exploration and use of other frameworks and theories to understand the complex relationship between CG and corporate performance and other business activities: sustainability, CSR, social justice, etc. Despite the growing interest and increasing body of research in this area, however, still some distance from establishing the precise nature and direction of this relationship (Aksom & Tymchenko, 2020; Boivie et al., 2021; Jan et al., 2021). An excellent system of Islamic CG is that which upholds trust, morals, and equity in human affairs. Islamic CG is more than the structure and operations of a board of directors and a committee of senior managers and the obligation of business operations as it includes the responsibilities and relations within the company, as well as the several rights of the stakeholders that have a proper interest in it. (Jan et al., 2021; Murphy & Smolarski, 2020). The business company is seen as a tool of faith dominated by the Islamic worker ethos which has a social liability and good faith.

Islamic CG is a system that consists of a series of relations and regulations which connect the actions of all engaged in the corporation and determining its control according to the objectives of shari'at (Hirsanudin & Martini, 2023; Jamaludin, 2021). The principles of CG according to Islam are based on the teachings of the Qur'an, hadiths (Sunnah), ijtihad (ijma'), and Islamic and are in line with the aims of the Shari'ah. The organization of disposals and the role of companies are not detached matters simply connected with consideration of monetary problems (Ermawati et al., 2021; Riinawati, 2022; Syah, 2021). In order to make sure that companies with key goods and services to employees, shareholders, and other connected parties meet their aims and global aims, capable methods of organization are within reason requested. The discussion on governance has obsessed on particular troubles in part procedure schemes which may not be capable to underprop the prosperity of companies in arranging effectively with social demands (Clauß et al., 2022; Kimmitt et al., 2020).

4.1. Impact of Islamic CG on Financial Performance

The concurrent framework of CG in a company should be a complete complex desire. This word will obtain an overview of the most significant and most applicable matter, including the pressures of both the appropriate environment, such as certainty toward the quality agricultural products, the society, the duties of the owners, the controls of administration, the connections that obtain the contracts, the product which finally performs (Jan et al., 2021; Karbhari et al., 2020). CG is an actual element of the building of an Islamic company. CG is the attendance of really practical devices and participating securities in the variety of higher stakes of a worker, contributing to a more profitable level in power, which is devolved to leading-stage administration (Hassan et al., 2022; Jan et al., 2021; Zadjuli & Shofawati, 2020). The method of CG by independent supervisory is generally linear against the desires. Refer to the personal and institutional owners, who make sure that the role of the administration is to admit the goals of the institution (Hirsanudin & Martini, 2023; Muhammad et al., 2021).

4.2. Impact of Islamic CG on Social Responsibility

Corporate development elements in an Islamic system do not only involve businesses and physical contacts but also broadly involve social and human aspects. Paying attention to social aspects, the fulfillment of stakeholders, responsibility over stakeholders and government, workers, and environmental development are part of the elements which have significance for Islamic corporate development (Indriastuti & Najihah, 2020; Koleva, 2021). CG can be used to reach sustainable growth for Islamic companies and can also be used to direct the company toward social responsibility awareness in the religious ethical context. With the development of the Islamic region as its basic principle, Islamic CG must be considered to motivate it to include more social responsibility in the company's market directions and achieve long-term priority company commitment (Jan et al., 2021; Probohudono et al., 2022; Setiawan, 2023). Executives, governance-oriented corporate power represents the subject of society's highest expectations and requests. It prevents and calculates good corporate activities to be responsible and accountable for all entities who have the power of CG in all companies (Hirsanudin & Martini, 2023; Jan et al., 2021; Mukhibad et al., 2022). Companies that retain the governing of their own operations have a commitment to the corporate power of the securities market; shareholders only entrust the ruling party and the assignment of the running daily affairs are usually helped by legislatures (Ahmed & Yahaya, 2024; Rock, 2020). Regulatory authorities have the right to create a frame for national levels of CG, but the primary responsibility lies with companies themselves. Influences on companies and markets in advanced countries in recent years indicated that a combination of items such as cultural expression, integrity, and ethics affects the decisions and behavior of people engaged in these companies (Hopt, 2024; Scherer & Voegtlin, 2020). Companies have been deciding to run based on more monetary factors for the cost of competitive need. However, on the majority level, authenticated consequences are observed when virtuous decisions are made (Kamaruddin et al., 2021; Sapuan et al., 2020; Sulaiman et al., 2022), value enhancing an organization to act in a virtuously responsible manner. The actual responsibility of the company is to work with applied leadership in preserving a secure and healthy culture. To create the necessary conditions under which people are anxious to operate properly, this commission must assist not only the corporation reach success but also the economy act to its entire advantage (El & Ben, 2023; Hassan & Noor, 2020; Rochayatun & Andriyani, 2023).

4.3. Impact of Islamic CG on Environmental Sustainability

Efficient and effective management of environmental resources within an Islamic CSR framework creates a focus on environmental stewardship that sustains. According to Islamic teachings, humans are entrusted as stewards of the earth by God, and therefore, the earth is maintained and protected for future generations (Ali & Agushi, 2024; Thohir, 2023). Islamic CSR is wider than compliance with rules and regulations. Islamic teaching requires not only avoiding harming others but also preventing harm from happening to others (Hendar, 2023; Shu et al., 2021). The transactional governance agencies consist of shareholders and external stakeholders such as labor, suppliers, customers, and local communities. In practice, these constituencies may not have the resources or economic power to internalize the negative consequences of a firm's strategy for wealth creation or depletion of natural resource (Acebo et al., 2021; Lehtinen & Aaltonen, 2020). When perceived to be outside the boundary, avoiding regulation expense of management, it is easy for managers to permit negative social development in outlying areas. Business practices that directly and indirectly degrade the earth's natural resources clearly go against Islamic teachings (Gulzar et al., 2021; Sabrina, 2020) conventional CSR guidelines, the MHC expects the annual report of a company that incorporates worldly religious activities to reflect the practices that produce these numbers, including environmental metrics consistent with the Quran and Sunnah as well as the regulations of the host government (Faza' et al., 2023; Zuhroh, 2022). As there are no reporting guidelines within Islamic teachings concerning financial metrics, MHC relies on secular rules and regulations together with commonly accepted financial principles that are free from usury to ensure the integrity of MHC-sponsored transactions (Al-Sartawi, 2020; Musleh Alsartawi et al., 2022). Although reducing harm is relatable to quantification and regulation, the primary values dimension is qualitative, representing reputation capital. Effective disclosure of the company's reputation capital is a function of management judgment about the corporate philosophy (Baumgartner et al., 2020; Pham & Tran, 2020; Zhang et al., 2021). Disclosures would extend to include the company's situation concerning the sacred covenant, as well as details of the governance framework applied for managing company-stakeholder relations (Aniefor & Ekwueme, 2021; Buhmann, 2021; Wielga & Harrison, 2021).

5. Challenges and Opportunities in Implementing Islamic CG for Sustainable Growth

The concept of the Quran, Sunnah, as well as Ijma is laws that traditionally have been used to measure CSR and governance closely and have been embedded in Islamic ethical principles and legal preferences that qualify Islamically driven activities as best conducive practices (Al-Doseri & Aldhmour, 2024; Muhammad et al., 2021; Murphy & Smolarski, 2020). This study has discussed the potential benefits in shaping behavior by enhancing the disclosure practice and voluntary adoption of Islamic financial characteristics. This study observes that different perceptions, sociocultural understanding, views, expected benefits, underlying factors, relational consequences, practicability, management, and regulatory implications are key to embracing the challenge (Mohd Zain et al., 2021; Salem et al., 2023; Ur Rehman et al., 2020). Finally, taking on this challenge is about searching for the paradigmatic good that gives GCC-OIC countries and their transnational potentials the strategic merit to compete and compete sustainably in the current geopolitical state of affairs (Bettis & Malley, 2021; Seyfi & Hall, 2020).

The concepts, processes, regulations, enforcement, and the desired outcomes of Islamic CG present several challenges to GCC-OIC corporations. The opportunities are meaningful management, transparency in disclosure, ethical behavior, and good organizational citizenship that is necessary to grow and prosper in the global market (Ali et al., 2023; Cezarino et al., 2022; Yuwono et al., 2023). Some potential benefits of affiliating with the Islamic CG label can position the GCC and some OIC corporations in attracting responsible investors. Some OIC international corporations can be provided an innovative strategic good that can foster certain CSRs, impact green growth, wealth creation, global collaboration, and regional business obligation compliance, including employment commitments in the Islamic market (Aslam et al., 2024; Mousa, 2021).

6. Future Trends and Innovations

This section identifies the trends and future areas for innovations that may shape Islamic governance, which could impinge on the future growth of firms across Islamic nations. Research on Islamic governance, the field will benefit greatly from the proposed issues, which managers should aspire to address. Anticipate that there would be an increase in stakeholder orientation based on Quranic justice, modesty, and avoidance of extravagance. The more responsible and fair corporate behaviors and management supremacy could push Islamic governance to new moral and ethical underpinnings that address minority shareholders and wider stakeholder interests. A roadmap to boards and managers of public limited responsibility firms on conducting business according to Shari'ah principles. The narrow empirical study toward Islamic CG anticipates that the future will see a heightened awareness of stakeholders to embed a greater number of Shari'ah governance requisites into the governance literature and also contribute to firm sustainability and their financing role within the entire economy. The future is imperative the right environment and mindset for stakeholders nestled and operating under Islamic governance.

7. Conclusion

Good governance practices in Islamic finance can be achieved by adopting the tenets of Shari'ah, which are designed to protect the interests of all stakeholders (Binti Nazmi et al., 2022; Hirsanudin & Martini, 2023). In Islamic finance, the mudarib (fund manager) is only entitled to earn an agreed sum or percentage as a business income; any additional monetary amount or item ex post sharing is strictly prohibited. In the traditional banking model worldwide, more focus is placed on fighting the "war" between depositors and managers over the surplus in the form of excessive executive compensation and generous bonuses that are associated with greater risk-taking activities and fees influence (Ali et al., 2023; Ryandono et al., 2021). It could be significant according to modern capitalist-oriented corporate strategists, and this may create a lack of consistency in determining partnership property rules in Islamic capital markets according to Shari'ah. The dual character of the Shari'ah, as both a legal and religious duty, offers a major disadvantage in the relation of state and religion. It is difficult to judge whether ethical investments respect the Shari'ah or Islamic principles when foreign funds invest in any company, and ethical investments may be withheld compared to conventional investments due to this mistrust.

References

Abdullah, H., & Asutay, M. (2021). Constituting Islamic corporate governance theory through Islamic moral economy. In T. Azid, M. Mukhlisin, N. Akbar, & M. Tahir (Eds.), *Monetary policy, Islamic finance, and Islamic corporate governance: An international overview* (pp. 13–35). Emerald Publishing Limited.

Abiodun, E. A. (2020). Internal control procedures and firm's performance. *International Journal of Scientific & Technology Research*, *9*(2), 6407–6415.

Acebo, E., Miguel-Dávila, J. Á., & Nieto, M. (2021). External stakeholder engagement: Complementary and substitutive effects on firms' eco-innovation. *Business Strategy and the Environment*, *30*(5), 2671–2687.

Adekoya, A. A. (2022). Islamic banking and finance in developing countries: The goals, challenges and prospects. *International Journal of Economics, Commerce and Management*, *10*(5), 348–369.

Aguilera, R. V., Aragón-Correa, J. A., Marano, V., & Tashman, P. A. (2021). The corporate governance of environmental sustainability: A review and proposal for more integrated research. *Journal of Management*, *47*(6), 1468–1497.

Ahmed, A., & Yahaya, O. A. (2024). Unlocking the power of corporate governance and its impact on financial stability. *Governance and Management Review*, *9*(1), 71–109.

Aksom, H., &Tymchenko, I. (2020). How institutional theories explain and fail to explain organizations. *Journal of Organizational Change Management*, *33*(7), 1223–1252.

Al-Ahdal, W. M., Alsamhi, M. H., Tabash, M. I., & Farhan, N. H. (2020). The impact of corporate governance on financial performance of Indian and GCC listed firms: An empirical investigation. *Research in International Business and Finance*, *51*, 101083.

Alam, M. K., & Miah, M. S. (2021). Independence and effectiveness of Shariah supervisory board of Islamic banks: Evidence from an emerging economy. *Asian Review of Accounting*.

Al-Doseri, F., &Aldhmour, F. M. (2024). The role of corporate social responsibility from an Islamic economy perspective in times of crisis: Literature review study. *The AI Revolution: Driving Business Innovation and Research*, *2*, 803–817.

Alduaij, D. (2020). *Ensuring Shariah compliance in Islamic financial institutions as an essential interest of shareholders*. https://orca.cardiff.ac.uk/id/eprint/138603/1/2021 AlduaijDPhD.pdf

Ali, H., Yin, J., Manzoor, F., & An, M. (2023). The impact of corporate social responsibility on firm reputation and organizational citizenship behavior: The mediation of organic organizational cultures. *Frontiers in Psychology*, *13*, 1100448.

Ali, M., &Agushi, M. (2024). Eco-Islam: Integrating Islamic ethics into environmental policy for sustainable living. *International Journal of Religion*, *5*(9), 949–957.

Almagtome, A., Khaghaany, M., & Önce, S. (2020). Corporate governance quality, stakeholders' pressure, and sustainable development: An integrated approach. *International Journal of Mathematical, Engineering and Management Sciences*, *5*(6), 1077.

Al-Matari, E. M. (2020). Do characteristics of the board of directors and top executives have an effect on corporate performance among the financial sector? Evidence using stock. *Corporate Governance: The International Journal of Business in Society*, *20*(1), 16–43.

Almutairi, A. R., & Quttainah, M. A. (2020). Foreign directors and corporate governance in Islamic banks. *Journal of Islamic Accounting and Business Research*, *11*(4), 765–791.

Al-Sartawi, A. M. A. M. (2020). Shariah disclosure and the performance of Islamic financial institutions. *Asian Journal of Business and Accounting*, *13*(1), 133–160.

Amin, M. F. B., Khokhar, I., & Khan, M. N. (2020). Examining the comparative efficiency of GCC Islamic banking. *Journal of Islamic Banking & Finance*, *37*(4).

Anggadwita, G., Dana, L. P., Ramadani, V., & Ramadan, R. Y. (2021). Empowering Islamic boarding schools by applying the humane entrepreneurship approach: The case of Indonesia. *International Journal of Entrepreneurial Behavior & Research*, *27*(6), 1580–1604.

Aniefor, S. J., & Ekwueme, C. M. (2021). Board experience and environmental reporting: Evidence from quoted manufacturing firms in Nigeria. *International Journal of Advanced Academic Research*, *7*(11), 1–21.

Anjum, M. I. (2022). An Islamic critique of rival economic systems' theories of interest. *International Journal of Ethics and Systems*, *38*(4), 598–620.

Anwer, Z., Khan, S., & Abu Bakar, M. (2020). Sharīʿah-compliant central banking practices: Lessons from Muslim countries' experience. *ISRA International Journal of Islamic Finance*, *12*(1), 7–26.

Arifin, M. (2021). The influence of Islamic law and economic principles on banking industry in Indonesia. *Journal of Legal, Ethical and Regulatory Issues*, *24*(S3), 1–11.

Ashraf, M. S., Aslam, E., Ali, J., & Iqbal, A. (2024). Mediating effect of corporate image towards Islamic bank loyalty: The role of religiosity, collectivism, sight cues, and CSR. In H. M. Qadri & M. I. Bhatti (Eds.), *Islamic finance in the modern era* (pp. 161–178). Routledge.

Aslam, E., & Haron, R. (2020). Does corporate governance affect the performance of Islamic banks? New insight into Islamic countries. *Corporate Governance: The International Journal of Business in Society*, *20*(6), 1073–1090.

Awais, M., Ullah, N., Sulehri, N. A., Thas Thaker, M. A. B. M., & Mohsin, M. (2022). Monitoring and efficiency in governance: A measure for sustainability in the Islamic banking industry. *Frontiers in Psychology*, *13*, 884532.

Ayub, M., Hassan, M. K., & Saba, I. (2023). Revisiting the paradigm of Sharīʿah governance of Islamic financial institutions. *Journal of Islamic Accounting and Business Research*, *15*(8), 1245–1265.

Badshah, W., & Bulut, M. (2020). A Turkish perspective of Islamic corporate governance for a sustainable financial performance. *International Journal of Business and Management*, *5*(12), 32–41.

Basiruddin, R., & Ahmed, H. (2020). Corporate governance and Shariah non-compliant risk in Islamic banks: Evidence from Southeast Asia. *Corporate Governance: The International Journal of Business in Society*, *20*(2), 240–262.

Baumgartner, K. T., Ernst, C. A., & Fischer, T. M. (2020). Corporate reputation disclosures affect stakeholders' behavioral intentions: Mediating mechanisms of perceived organizational performance and corporate reputation. *Journal of Business Ethics*, *175*(2), 361–389.

Beason, T., & Schreindorfer, D. (2022). Dissecting the equity premium. *Journal of Political Economy*, 130(8), 2203–2222.

Belita, E., Squires, J. E., Yost, J., Ganann, R., Burnett, T., & Dobbins, M. (2020). Measures of evidence-informed decision-making competence attributes: A psychometric systematic review. *BMC Nursing*, *19*, 1–28.

Bin Hagshah, A. F. (2022). *The new Saudi Corporate Governance Framework: A comparative legal study with the UK and Delaware*. https://theses.gla.ac.uk/83009/3/2022BinHagshahPhD.pdf

Binti Nazmi, N. A., Hassan, R., & Rahim Abdul Rahman, A. (2022). Measuring good governance for Islamic financial institutions for achieving Islamic social finance objectives: The need for Shariah governance index. In M. K. Hassan, A. Muneeza, & A. M. Sarea (Eds.), *Towards a post-covid global financial system: Lessons in social responsibility from Islamic finance* (pp. 91–102). Emerald Publishing Limited.

Black, B., de Carvalho, A. G., Kim, W., & Yurtoglu, B. B. (2023). How useful are commercial corporate governance ratings? Evidence from emerging markets. *Journal of Corporate Finance*, *80*, 102405.

Boivie, S., Withers, M. C., Graffin, S. D., & Corley, K. G. (2021). Corporate directors' implicit theories of the roles and duties of boards. *Strategic Management Journal*, *42*(9), 1662–1695.

Bueno-Garcia, M., Ortiz-Perez, A., & Mellado-Garcia, E. (2021). Shareholders' environmental profile and its impact on firm's environmental proactivity: An institutional approach. *Business Strategy and the Environment*, *30*(1), 374–387.

Buhmann, A., & Fieseler, C. (2023). Deep learning meets deep democracy: Deliberative governance and responsible innovation in artificial intelligence. *Business Ethics Quarterly*, *33*(1), 146–179.

Cezarino, L. O., Liboni, L. B., Hunter, T., Pacheco, L. M., & Martins, F. P. (2022). Corporate social responsibility in emerging markets: Opportunities and challenges for sustainability integration. *Journal of Cleaner Production*, *362*, 13224.

Clauß, T., Kraus, S., & Jones, P. (2022). Sustainability in family business: Mechanisms, technologies and business models for achieving economic prosperity, environmental quality and social equity. *Technological Forecasting and Social Change*.

Costa, A. J., Curi, D., Bandeira, A. M., Ferreira, A., Tomé, B., Joaquim, C., & Marques, R. P. (2022). Literature review and theoretical framework of the evolution and interconnectedness of corporate sustainability constructs. *Sustainability*, *14*(8), 4413.

Dechow, P. M., Hutton, A. P., & Sloan, R. G. (1996). Economic consequences of accounting for stock-based compensation. *Journal of Accounting Research*, *34*, 1–20.

El Melki, A., & Ben Salah Saidi, H. (2023). Ethical and socially responsible investments in the Islamic banking firms: Heart, mind, and money: Religious believes and financial decision-making in the participatory financing contracts: Charitable donation announcement effect on agents' level of effort and commitment. In N. Naifar & A. Elsayed (Eds.), *Green finance instruments, FinTech, and investment strategies: Sustainable portfolio management in the post-COVID era* (pp. 81–123). Springer.

Ermawati, E., Musyahidah, S., & Nurdin, N. (2021). Muslim society perspective on Islamic banking corporate social responsibility in Indonesia (based on Qur'an and Hadits economic themes). *International Journal of Business and Management Review*, *9*(3), 29–40.

Faza', M., Badwan, N., & Hamdan, M. (2023). Determinants of effective Shariah compliance auditing in Palestine: A theoretical and conceptual analysis. *Journal of Money Laundering Control*, *27*(5), 845–857.

Gulzar, A., Islam, T., Hamid, M., & Haq, S. M. (2021). Environmental ethics towards the sustainable development in Islamic perspective: A brief review. *Ethnobotany Research and Applications*, *22*, 1–10.

Gusrianti, G., & Sari, P. H. (2023). *Transparency of Shariah supervisory board information in Islamic Banks of Indonesia and Malaysia: The effect of Islamic corporate governance*.

Hadro, D., Fijałkowska, J., Daszyńska-Żygadło, K., Zumente, I., & Mjakuškina, S. (2022). What do stakeholders in the construction industry look for in non-financial disclosure and what do they get? *Meditari Accountancy Research*, *30*(3), 762–785.

Hanif, M. F., & Haron, R. (2022). Corporate governance and corporate social responsibility in Islamic banks: A systematic literature review. *IIUM Law Journal*, *30*(S2), 57–92.

Harun, M. S., Hussainey, K., Mohd Kharuddin, K. A., & Farooque, O. A. (2020). CSR disclosure, corporate governance and firm value: A study on GCC Islamic banks. *International Journal of Accounting & Information Management*, *28*(4), 607–638.

Hasan, R., Velayutham, S., & Khan, A. F. (2022). Socially responsible investment (SRI) Sukuk as a financing alternative for post COVID-19 development project. *International Journal of Islamic and Middle Eastern Finance and Management*, *15*(2), 425–440.

Hassan, A., Sohail, M. S., & Munshi, M. M. R. (2022). Sharīʿah governance and agency dynamics of Islamic banking operations in the Kingdom of Saudi Arabia. *ISRA International Journal of Islamic Finance*, *14*(1), 89–106.

Hendar, J. (2023). Maqashid shari'ah as the basis for decision making of corporate social responsibility based on a prophetic legal paradigm. *Prophetic Law Review*, *5*(1). https://doi.org/10.20885/PLR.vol5.iss1.art6.

Hirsanuddin, H., & Martini, D. (2023). Good corporate governance principles in Islamic banking: A legal perspective on the integration of TARIF values. *Journal of Indonesian Legal Studies*, *8*(2), 935–974.

Hobvi, A. L. J., Zunaidi, A., & Fikriyah, A. (2022). Implementation of compliance management in the sharia banking sector. *Proceedings of Islamic Economics, Business, and Philanthropy*, *1*(2), 346–362.

Hopt, K. J. (2024). *Groups of companies – A comparative study on the economics*. Law and Regulation of Corporate Groups.

Hundal, S. (2021). *Corporate governance-theoretical perspectives and measurement of good governance through corporate governance index*.

Indriastuti, M., & Najihah, N. (2020). Improving financial performance through Islamic Corporate social responsibility and Islamic corporate governance. *Jurnal Riset Akuntansi Dan Bisnis Airlangga*, *5*(1), 818.

Islam, M. M., & Islam, M. A. (2023). Effectiveness of Shariah supervisory board and performance of Islamic banks: The mediating role of board of directors. *Journal of Islamic Banking & Finance*, *40*(2), 82–101.

Ismail, A. Y., Hameed, L. B. M., Suhaimi, A. F. M., Jamaludin, N. I., & Shahimi, S. (2020, July). Value based intermediation and interconnection of sustainable development goals in Islamic banking framework. *International Journal of Islamic Economics and Finance Research*, *3*(1), 45–56.

Jagannathan, K., Jones, A. D., & Ray, I. (2021). The making of a metric: Co-producing decision-relevant climate science. *Bulletin of the American Meteorological Society*, *102*(8), 1579–1590.

Jamaludin, A. (2021). The Islamic models of corporate governance. *Turkish Journal of Computer and Mathematics Education (TURCOMAT)*, *12*(11), 874–878.

Jan, A. A., Lai, F. W., & Tahir, M. (2021). Developing an Islamic corporate governance framework to examine sustainability performance in Islamic banks and financial institutions. *Journal of Cleaner Production*, *315*, 128099.

Jubba, H., Awang, J., & Sungkilang, S. A. (2021). The challenges of Islamic organizations in promoting moderation in Indonesia. *Wawasan: JurnalIlmiah Agama Dan Sosial Budaya*, *6*(1), 43–54.

Kader, H. (2021). Human well-being, morality and the economy: An Islamic perspective. *Islamic Economic Studies*, *28*(2), 102–123.

Kamaruddin, M. I. H., Auzair, S. M., Rahmat, M. M., & Muhamed, N. A. (2021). The mediating role of financial governance on the relationship between financial management, Islamic work ethic and accountability in Islamic social enterprise (ISE). *Social Enterprise Journal*, *17*(3), 427–449.

Kapur, M., Banerjee, A., & Malik, K. (2020). Qualitative assessment of Basel III liquidity standards and its application in the UAE. *Indian Journal of Finance and Banking*, *4*(2), 118–129.

Karbhari, Y., Alam, M. K., & Rahman, M. M. (2020). Relevance of the application of institutional theory in Shariah governance of Islamic banks. *PSU Research Review*, *5*(1), 1–15.

Kateb, I., Nafti, O., & Zeddini, A. (2023). How to improve the financial performance of Islamic banks in the MENA region? A Shariah governance perspective. *International Journal of Emerging Markets*. Vol. ahead-of-print No. ahead-of-print. https://doi.org/10.1108/IJOEM-03-2023-0434

Khan, A. A., Ghias, S., & Hyder, S. I. (2021). Islamic banking prospects, challenges and criticism: A systematic literature review. *Journal of Accounting and Finance in Emerging Economies*, *7*(4), 921–930.

Khan, I., & Zahid, S. N. (2020). The impact of Shari'ah and corporate governance on Islamic banks performance: Evidence from Asia. *International Journal of Islamic and Middle Eastern Finance and Management*, *13*(3), 483–501.

Khokhar, I., Hassan, M. U., Khan, M. N., Amin, M. F. B., & Center, I. B. (2020). Investigating the efficiency of GCC banking sector: An empirical comparison of Islamic and conventional banks. *International Journal of Financial Research*, *11*(1), 220–235.

Koleva, P. (2021). Towards the development of an empirical model for Islamic corporate social responsibility: Evidence from the Middle East. *Journal of Business Ethics*, *171*(4), 789–813.

Lehtinen, J., & Aaltonen, K. (2020). Organizing external stakeholder engagement in inter-organizational projects: Opening the black box. *International Journal of Project Management*, *38*(2), 85–98.

Li, T., Trinh, V. Q., & Elnahass, M. (2023). Drivers of global banking stability in times of crisis: The role of corporate social responsibility. *British Journal of Management*, *34*(2), 595–622.

Li, Z., Crook, J., Andreeva, G., & Tang, Y. (2021). Predicting the risk of financial distress using corporate governance measures. *Pacific-Basin Finance Journal*, *68*(4), 101334.

Meier, S., Gonzalez, M. R., & Kunze, F. (2021). The global financial crisis, the EMU sovereign debt crisis and international financial regulation: Lessons from a systematic literature review. *International Review of Law and Economics*, *65*, 105945.

Mergaliyev, A., Asutay, M., Avdukic, A., & Karbhari, Y. (2021). Higher ethical objective (Maqasid al-Shari'ah) augmented framework for Islamic banks: Assessing ethical performance and exploring its determinants. *Journal of Business Ethics*, *170*(1), 797–834.

Mohd Zain, F. A., Wan Abdullah, W. A., & Percy, M. (2021). Voluntary adoption of AAOIFI disclosure standards for takaful operators: The role of governance. *Journal of Islamic Accounting and Business Research*, *12*(4), 593–622.

Mousa, G. (2021). Can conventional governance mechanisms be a matter for financial performance in Islamic countries? Conventional governance mechanisms. *Journal of Islamic Business and Management*, *11*(02), 286–313.

Muhammad, R., & Nugraheni, P. (2021). The effect of internal factors on the mudharabah financing of Indonesian Islamic banks. *Journal of Sustainable Finance & Investment*, 1–17.

Mukhibad, H., Nurkhin, A., Waluyo Jati, K., & YudoJayanto, P. (2022). Corporate governance and Islamic law compliance risk. *Cogent Economics & Finance*, *10*(1), 2111057.

Muliansyah, E., & Hermawan, M. S. (2024). The concept of good corporate government (GCG) Amil Zakat Institution (LAZ) in the Sharia perspective of enterprise theory (set): Literature review. *Educational Administration: Theory and Practice*, *30*(6), 1046–1058.

Mundi, H. S., & Kumar, D. (2023). The potential of alternative investments as an asset class: A thematic and bibliometric review. *Qualitative Research in Financial Markets*, *15*(5), 119–141.

Murphy, M. J., & Smolarski, J. M. (2020). Religion and CSR: An Islamic "political" model of corporate governance. *Business & Society*, *59*(5), 823–854.

Musleh Alsartawi, A., Reyad, S., & Madbouly, A. (2022). Shariah, presentation and content dimensions of Web 2.0 applications and the firm value of Islamic financial institutions in the GCC countries. *Journal of Islamic Marketing*, *13*(9), 1988–2005.

Muslihun, M. (2023). *The active role of Sharia supervisory board in Sharia compliance and risk mitigation: A case study of Bank NTB Syariah*. Quality-Access to Success.

Nomran, N. M., & Haron, R. (2020). A systematic literature review on Sharī'ah governance mechanism and firm performance in Islamic banking. *Islamic Economic Studies*, *27*(2), 91–123.

Nouman, M., Siddiqi, M. F., Ullah, K., & Jan, S. (2021). Nexus between higher ethical objectives (Maqasid Al Shari'ah) and participatory finance. *Qualitative Research in Financial Markets*, *13*(2), 226–251.

Olorogun, L., & Othman, J. (2021). Exploring ethical dimensions of Islamic insurance: Implications for market acceptance in Malaysia. *Journal of Business and Economic Options*, *4*(1), 25–31.

Pham, H. S. T., & Tran, H. T. (2020). CSR disclosure and firm performance: The mediating role of corporate reputation and moderating role of CEO integrity. *Journal of Business Research*, *120*, 127–136.

Probohudono, A. N., Nugraheni, A., & Nurrahmawati, A. (2022). Comparative analysis of QISMUT+ 3's Islamic corporate social responsibility. *Journal of Islamic Marketing*, *13*(7), 1436–1456.

Rabbani, M. R., Ali, M. A. M., Rahiman, H. U., Atif, M., Zulfikar, Z., & Naseem, Y. (2021). The response of Islamic financial service to the COVID-19 pandemic: The open social innovation of the financial system. *Journal of Open Innovation: Technology, Market, and Complexity*, *7*(1), 85.

Ramli, N. A., Abdul Mohsin, A. M., Salleh, A., & Mat Akhir, N. S. (2022). Human governance a pathway to integrity in counteracting corruption. *International Journal of Islamic and Middle Eastern Finance and Management*, *15*(5), 903–923.

Reyad, S., Chinnasamy, G., & Madbouly, A. (2022). Risk management and corporate governance of Islamic banks: Evidence from GCC countries. *Corporate Governance: The International Journal of Business in Society*, *22*(7), 1425–1443.

Riaz, U., Burton, B., & Fearfull, A. (2023). Emotional propensities and the contemporary Islamic banking industry. *Critical Perspectives on Accounting*, *94*, 102449.

Riinawati, R. (2022). The concept of Islamic education management from the perspective of the Qur'an and Al-Hadith. *Tafkir: Interdisciplinary Journal of Islamic Education*, *3*(2), 148–162.

Rochayatun, S., & Andriyani, F. (2023). Corporate social responsibility and spirituality: Islamic perspective. *Maliki Islamic Economics Journal*, *3*(2), 139–155.

Romito, S., & Vurro, C. (2021). Non-financial disclosure and information asymmetry: A stakeholder view on US listed firms. *Corporate Social Responsibility and Environmental Management*, *28*(2), 595–605.

Rusydiana, A. S. (2021). Sharia supervisory board: A review and some finding. *Review on Islamic Accounting*, *1*(1), 1–10.

Ryandono, M. N. H., Kusuma, K. A., & Prasetyo, A. (2021). The foundation of a fair Mudarabah profit sharing ratio: A case study of Islamic banks in Indonesia. *The Journal of Asian Finance, Economics and Business*, *8*(2), 329–337.

Sadek, D. M., Abas, Z., Abd Rahim, K., Anuar, A., & Abd Rahim, M. A. (2020). The practices of corporate governance and Shariah governance in Islamic financial institutions. In I. Saidon & R. Said (Eds.), *Ethics, governance and risk management in organizations. Accounting, finance, sustainability, governance & fraud: Theory and application* (pp. 131–147). Springer.

Safari, M., & Parker, L. D. (2023). Understanding multiple accountability logics within corporate governance policy discourse: Resistance, compromise, or selective coupling? *European Accounting Review*.

Salem, R., Ezeani, E., & Song, X. (2023). The relationship between religiosity and voluntary disclosure quality: Cross-country evidence from the banking sector. *Review of Quantitative Finance and Accounting*, *60*(3), 983–1023.

Salin, A. S. A. P., Manan, S. K. A., & Kamaluddin, N. (2020). Ethical framework for directors – Learning from the prophet. *International Journal of Law and Management*, *62*(2), 171–191.

Sani, A., & Maharani Ekowati, V. (2020). Spirituality at work and organizational commitment as moderating variables in relationship between Islamic spirituality and OCB IP and influence toward employee. *Journal of Islamic Marketing*, *11*(6), 1777–1799.

Sapuan, N. M., Wahab, N. A., Sholihin, M., & Sawaluddin, S. (2020). Human governance and firm success from western and Islamic perspectives. *Journal of Governance and Integrity*, *4*(1), 56–63.

Sari, W., & Hussien, M. (2024). Corporate governance and financial performance in Sharia banks: An analysis in Islamic finance. *Cebong Journal*, *13*(2), 75–84.

Scherer, A. G., & Voegtlin, C. (2020). Corporate governance for responsible innovation: Approaches to corporate governance and their implications for sustainable development. *Academy of Management Perspectives*, *34*(2), 182–208.

Setiawan, I. (2023). The significance of corporate social responsibility in sustainable development: An analysis from an Islamic law perspective. *Journal of Law and Sustainable Development, 11*(9), 1–23.

Seyfi, S., & Hall, C. M. (Eds.) (2020). Cultural heritage tourism in the MENA: Introduction and background. In *Cultural and heritage tourism in the Middle East and North Africa* (pp. 1–33). Routledge.

Shahar, N. A., Nawawi, A., & Salin, A. S. A. P. (2020). Shari'a corporate governance disclosure of Malaysian IFIS. *Journal of Islamic Accounting and Business Research, 11*(4), 845–868.

Shamsudheen, S. V., Mahomed, Z., & Mohamad, S. (2021). Reconciling selection criteria of Islamic banking services: A survey on perception of Islamic bankers, institutional clients and retail customers in UAE. *Journal of Islamic Accounting and Business Research, 12*(1), 112–130.

Shu, H., & Duan, J. (2023). The relationship between social responsibility fulfilment and industry competitiveness: Empirical evidence from construction industry in China. *Plos One, 18*(11), e0295181.

Sidaoui, M., Ben Bouheni, F., Arslankhuyag, Z., & Mian, S. (2022). Fintech and Islamic banking growth: New evidence. *The Journal of Risk Finance, 23*(5), 535–557.

Soelton, M., Apriani, F., Wahyono, T., Arief, H., Saratian, E. T. P., Nugrahati, T., …, & Syah, T. Y. R. (2021). Conceptualizing the role of organizational performance and good corporate governance in Social Welfare Institutions Banten–Indonesia. *International Journal of Innovative Science and Research Technology, 6*(3), 982–992.

Sovrano, F., Palmirani, M., & Vitali, F. (2022). Combining shallow and deep learning approaches against data scarcity in legal domains. *Government Information Quarterly, 39*(3), 101715.

Sriani, E., & Habibah, I. (2024). The role of the sharia supervisory board in ensuring contract compliance in sharia financial institutions'financing practices. *Jurnal Ilmiah Mizani: Wacana Hukum, Ekonomi Dan Keagamaan, 10*(2), 198–207.

Sulaiman, R., Toulson, P., Brougham, D., Lempp, F., & Haar, J. (2022). The role of religiosity in ethical decision-making: A study on Islam and the Malaysian workplace. *Journal of Business Ethics, 179*(1), 297–313.

Tabash, M. I., Alam, M. K., & Rahman, M. M. (2022). Ethical legitimacy of Islamic banks and Shariah governance: Evidence from Bangladesh. *Journal of Public Affairs, 22*(2), e2487.

Tarique, K. M., Islam, R., & Mohammed, M. O. (2021). Developing and validating the components of Maqasid al-Shari'ah-based performance measurement model for Islamic banks. *International Journal of Islamic and Middle Eastern Finance and Management, 14*(2), 366–390.

Thohir, U. F., Gunaryo, A., Suwandaru, A., & Raharjo, R. (2023). Islamic environmental conservation: Navigating the challenges and demands of globalization. *ESENSIA: Jurnal Ilmu-Ilmu Ushuluddin, 24*(1), 41–50.

Tjahjadi, B., Soewarno, N., & Mustikaningtiyas, F. (2021). Good corporate governance and corporate sustainability performance in Indonesia: A triple bottom line approach. *Heliyon, 7*(3), e06453.

Turzo, T., Marzi, G., Favino, C., & Terzani, S. (2022). Non-financial reporting research and practice: Lessons from the last decade. *Journal of Cleaner Production, 345*, 131154.

Ullah, S., Haroon, M., Hussain, S., & Rehman, A. U. (2023). Islamic labelling and corporate governance: A perspective of Shariah compliance firms. *Journal of Islamic Accounting and Business Research, 14*(6), 849–867.

Ur Rehman, Z., Zahid, M., Rahman, H. U., Asif, M., Alharthi, M., Irfan, M., & Glowacz, A. (2020). Do corporate social responsibility disclosures improve financial performance? A perspective of the Islamic banking industry in Pakistan. *Sustainability, 12*(8), 3302.

Wang, R., Zhou, S., & Wang, T. (2020). Corporate governance, integrated reporting and the use of credibility-enhancing mechanisms on integrated reports. *European Accounting Review*, *29*(4), 631–663.

Wielga, M., & Harrison, J. (2021). The effectiveness of non-state-based grievance mechanisms in providing access to remedy for rightsholders: A case study of the roundtable on sustainable palm oil. *Business and Human Rights Journal*.

Wu, X., Adbi, A., & Mahmood, I. P. (2023). The social structure of insiders and outsiders: Toward a network community perspective on firm performance. *Academy of Management Journal*, *67*(4), 903–932.

Yuwono, H., Kurniawan, M. D., Syamsudin, N., Eliyana, A., Saputra, D. E. E., Emur, A. P., & Jalil, N. I. A. (2023). Do psychological capital and transformational leadership make differences in organizational citizenship behavior? *Plos One*, *18*(12), e0294559.

Zadjuli, S. I., & Shofawati, A. (2020). Implementing good corporate governance in zakat institution. *Bussecon Review of Social Sciences (2687–2285)*, *2*(1), 27–37.

Zaman, R., Jain, T., Samara, G., & Jamali, D. (2022). Corporate governance meets corporate social responsibility: Mapping the interface. *Business & Society*, *61*(3), 690–752.

Zattoni, A., & Pugliese, A. (2021). Corporate governance research in the wake of a systemic crisis: Lessons and opportunities from the COVID-19 pandemic. *Journal of Management Studies*.

Zhang, L., Shan, Y. G., & Chang, M. (2021). Can CSR disclosure protect firm reputation during financial restatements? *Journal of Business Ethics*, *173*, 157–184.

Zuhroh, I. (2022). Mapping Islamic Bank Governance studies: A systematic literature review. *Cogent Business & Management*, *9*(1), 2072566.

Chapter 3

Ethical Investment in Islamic Finance: The Role of ESG Toward Sustainable Growth

Premagowrie Sivanandan and Rosimah Ahmad

School of Accounting and Finance, Taylor's University, Malaysia

Abstract

The concept of sustainable growth has gained lots of traction in recent years especially due to the aftershock of the Covid-19, which has left individuals and businesses reeling from the adverse consequences such as loss of livelihood, poverty, and bankruptcy. Hence, sustainable growth has become a necessary long-term goal for individuals and businesses alike to be able to attain financial success combined with the ability to meet environmental, social, and governance (ESG) needs. In this context, Islamic finance, which centers on the principles of Shari'ah law, is expected to help individuals and businesses from the financial and nonfinancial perspectives (i.e., ESG), to attain sustainable growth through ethical investments. The interaction between ESG and ethical investment in Islamic finance is expected to build a sustainable future for potential investors, shareholders, and other stakeholders, such as the public, customers, and employees, in alignment with the United Nation's (UN) Agenda 2030 and the sustainable development goals (SDGs). This chapter, first, provides an overview of Islamic finance followed by discussion on the foundations of Islamic finance and ethical investment. Next, this chapter explains the origin, definition, and role of ESG in modern investment practices. This chapter also reviews the synergy between ESG

Islamic Finance and Corporate Governance: Synergies for Sustainable Growth, 43–56

doi:10.1108/978-1-83662-346-520251006

and ethical investment in Islamic finance and sustainable growth. Finally, the integration of ESG in Islamic investment is examined in this chapter.

Keywords: Islamic finance; ESG; sustainable growth; ethical investment; UN SDGs

1. Introduction

Islamic finance refers to financing activities such as investments that are permissible under the Islamic law, that is, *Shari'ah* law, which does not make a distinction between religious beliefs and the normal aspects of life. The establishment of formal practices of Islamic finance only occurred in the 20th century even though the concept of Islamic banking and finance came into existence with the foundation of *Islam* (Corporate Finance Institute, 2024). Islamic banking and finance, which has been around for more than 40 years, incorporates moral and ethical elements that can advance better economic justice and fairness in contrast to conventional banking and finance (Ash-Shiddiqy et al., 2023). Similarly, Safiullah (2021) asserts that conventional banking and finance focuses on profit-making and regards payment of interest as an integral part of its operations. Izzeldin et al. (2021) affirm that Islamic finance is governed by strict Islamic religious laws, whereas conventional banking and finance is regulated by secular laws.

Hussain et al. (2015) state that the three governing principles of Islamic finance are equity, ownership, and participation. In addition, prohibitions outlined under Islamic finance include speculation/gambling (*maysir*), risk and uncertainty (*gharar*), investment in prohibited (*haram*) activities such as production and sale of alcohol, and interest payments. Due to this, Islamic finance allows specific types of financing activities that are aligned with *Shari'ah* law consisting of profit-and-loss sharing (PLS), non-profit-and-loss-sharing (non-PLS), and fee-based products (*wakalah*, *kafalah*, or *ju'ala*) (Hussain et al., 2015). PLS financing products include PLS partnership (*mudarabah*) and PLS joint venture (*musharakah*). On the other hand, non-PLS financing products consist of cost-plus financing (*murabahah*), leasing (*ijarah*), forward financing transaction (*salam*), and short-term financing (*istisna'a*). Furthermore, the two primary investment options allowable under Islamic finance principles are equities and fixed-income instruments (Hussain et al., 2015).

2. Foundations of Islamic Finance and Ethical Investment

Islamic finance is guided by several core principles that distinguish it from conventional finance. These principles are derived from *Shari'ah* law (Islamic law) and aim to ensure ethical conduct, social justice, and the promotion of economic well-being while adhering to religious beliefs (Yasin et al., 2024). The core principles of Islamic finance are given below.

*2.1. Prohibition of Interest (*Riba*)*

Riba refers to usury or interest charged on loans. In Islamic finance, earning or paying interest is strictly prohibited as it is viewed as exploitative and unjust (Khan et al., 2018). Instead, Islamic finance promotes profit-sharing arrangements where risks and rewards are shared between parties.

*2.2. Risk-sharing (*Mudarabah *and* Musharakah*)*

Islamic finance encourages risk-sharing between parties involved in financial transactions. Mudarabah refers to a partnership where one party provides capital (*Rab al-Maal*) and the other party provides expertise and labor (*mudarib*) and profits are shared according to a pre-agreed ratio (Zaker, 2019). *Musharakah* is a joint venture where all partners contribute capital and share profits and losses according to a pre-agreed ratio.

2.3. Asset-backed Financing (Tangible Asset)

Islamic finance requires that transactions be supported by tangible assets or services. This principle prohibits purely speculative transactions and emphasizes the real economy over financial engineering (Alam et al., 2017).

*2.4. Prohibition of Speculation (*Gharar*)*

Gharar refers to excessive uncertainty or ambiguity in contracts. Islamic finance discourages transactions that involve uncertainty or risk that is disproportionate to the value of the goods or services being traded (Nordin et al., 2014). Based on this Islamic principle, contracts must be clear and transparent.

3. Ethical Standards (Adherence to Shari'ah)

All financial transactions in Islamic finance must be complied with *Shari'ah* law and principles mentioned above in addition to ethical standards and moral values. This ensures that financial activities contribute positively to society without harming individuals or the community.

3.1. Zakat *(Charity or Almsgiving)*

Zakat is an obligatory form of charity in Islam, where a portion of wealth is given to the needy. In Islamic finance, institutions often collect and distribute *zakat* as means to redistribute wealth and promote social justice.

3.2. Prohibition of Haram Activities

Islamic finance prohibits investment in activities considered harmful or forbidden in Islam, such as gambling, alcohol, pork, and other unethical or socially damaging industries.

These principles form the foundation of Islamic finance, guiding financial institutions and transactions to operate in a manner that promotes fairness, ethical conduct, and social responsibility within the framework of *Shari'ah* law.

3.3. Prohibition of Riba *(Interest)*

Islamic economics fundamentally emphasizes a set of fundamental ethical concepts that distinguish it from other economic systems such as capitalism and socialism. One of the central tenets is the prohibition of interest (*riba*), which is seen as exploitative and socially damaging. Instead of interest-based transactions, Islamic finance promotes profit-sharing and equity-based financing, which align economic activities with ethical principles and encourage economic justice (Khalidin, 2024).

Moreover, Islamic economics places a strong emphasis on ethical considerations to discourage practices deemed harmful to individuals and society. Activities such as speculation, gambling, and the production of alcohol and pork are prohibited because they are perceived as detrimental to social cohesion and individual well-being. By advocating for ethical behavior and appropriate economics and finance practices, it aims to foster a system that prioritizes the welfare of society and minimizes exploitation.

In essence, Islamic finance which forms an essential part in Islamic economics integrates ethical values into its framework to ensure that economic activities which require Islamic financing are conducted in a manner that respects societal norms and promotes communal well-being. This ethical foundation not only guides financial transactions but also influences broader economic policies and practices such as wealth redistribution within Islamic societies.

4. Wealth Redistribution (Zakat)

Wealth redistribution and prioritizing tangible, productive economic activities are, indeed, distinctive features of Islamic economics. Islamic economics places a significant emphasis on wealth redistribution through *zakat*, which is a mandatory form of charity or almsgiving (Razak, 2020). Muslims who meet a certain threshold of wealth are required to donate a portion of their assets annually to help those in need. This system aims to reduce income inequality and ensure that wealth circulates within society rather than concentrating among a few individuals or groups (Herianingrum et al., 2024). *Zakat* funds typically support the poor, needy, orphans, widows, and other vulnerable members of society, contributing to social welfare and cohesion.

4.1. Investment in Tangible Assets and Productive Activities

Islamic economics promotes investments in tangible assets and productive economic activities over speculative or purely financial transactions. This preference is rooted in the principle of promoting real economic growth and development rather than speculative gains. Tangible assets include physical assets such as land, buildings, machinery, and infrastructure, as well as investments in sectors like industry, agriculture, and infrastructure development. By prioritizing these sectors, Islamic economics aims to generate sustainable economic growth, create employment opportunities, and enhance the overall welfare of society (Soemitra, 2021).

4.2. Sustainable Growth and Societal Benefits

By focusing on tangible and productive investments, Islamic finance seeks to foster sustainable economic growth that generates tangible benefits for society. Investments in productive sectors contribute to job creation, technological advancement, and the development of essential infrastructure, which are critical for improving living standards and enhancing the quality of life for individuals and communities (Imam & Kpodar, 2016). S&P Global Ratings (2022) also assert that through its leveraging with ESG values, the Islamic finance industry is headed toward enhanced sustainable growth due to the issuance of more dedicated social Islamic finance instruments and green *sukuk*, and this can be further strengthened through fintech collaborations and higher digitalization.

In summary, Islamic finance integrates principles of wealth redistribution through zakat and prioritizes investments in tangible assets and productive economic activities. These principles aim to promote economic justice, reduce income inequality, and achieve sustainable growth that benefits society. By emphasizing real economic activities and discouraging speculative practices, Islamic economics aligns financial activities with ethical values and societal welfare (Khan, 2019).

Islamic economics also recognizes the ethical and spiritual aspects of commerce. It highlights the value of moral conduct, justice, and compassion in business dealings. Islamic ideas serve as a framework for economic conduct, attempting to harmonize it with moral principles and encouraging a sense of obligation to one's fellow human beings and to society at large (Rahim, 2013). This all-encompassing approach to economics recognizes that ethical issues shouldn't be sacrificed for economic growth to achieve material well-being and spiritual fulfillment.

5. ESG: Origin, Definition, and Role in Modern Investment Practices

Since its inception, the concept of ESG has garnered popularity due to the importance of sustainability and corporate social performance in the modern business ecosystem. The term "ESG" was officially adopted in 2004 following its initial public appearance in a report named *Who Cares Wins* by the UN, which outlined three fundamental components of Environmental (E), Social (S), and Governance (G) and provided examples of how to incorporate these factors into a company's operations (IBM, 2024) and investment practices. The report with an emphasis on the environmental angle was crafted because of the then UN Secretary-General, the late Kofi Annan's realization that, the UN's peacekeeping and human rights goals will not be achievable without the participation of the business community (The Edge Malaysia, 2023). The UN's move to embrace the business community in its global agenda arose from the fact that businesses have utilized and, to some extent, exploited natural resources and human capital to flourish, which has had negative consequences on the environment and society due to the impact of adversities such as global warming, deforestation, and poverty. Thus, the UN empowered banks and institutional investors to push forward the ESG agenda within the business community due to the control banks hold over companies' funds and the ability of institutional investors to influence companies' decision-making through their shareholdings (The Edge Malaysia, 2023). Over time, ESG measures have gained significant traction in the investment decision-making process as a means of assessing an organization's impact on the environment and society (IBM, 2024). Nik Abdullah (2022) defines ESG (also referred to as "sustainability reporting") as the process of measuring, reporting, and being accountable to internal and external stakeholders who are responsible for organizational performance in the context of sustainable development. In the same vein, Li et al. (2021) define the "E" in environmental as environmental aspects that may pose a positive or negative impact on financial performance, the "S" in social as social matters that could have a positive or negative effect on financial performance, and the "G" in governance as governance factors that may influence financial performance, either positively or negatively. To elucidate the concept of ESG further, the "E" captures energy efficiencies, carbon footprints, greenhouse gas emissions, deforestation, biodiversity, climate change and pollution mitigation, waste management, and water usage. On the other hand, the "S" covers labor standards, wages and benefits, workplace and board diversity, racial justice, pay equity, human rights, talent management, community relations, privacy and data protection, health and safety, supply-chain management, and other human capital and social justice issues. Finally, the "G" covers the governing of the "E" and the "S" categories, that is, corporate board composition and structure, strategic sustainability oversight and compliance, executive compensation, political contributions and lobbying, and bribery and corruption (Harvard Law School Forum on Corporate Governance, 2020; Li et al., 2021).

ESG, thus, stems from responsible investment and comprises the consideration of ESG aspects (Li et al., 2021) in the pursuit of wealth and profit maximization. Deloitte (2022) reports that ESG seeks to encompass all nonfinancial risks and possibilities that are present in a business's daily operations and that the most complex pillar of ESG is the environmental pillar. This is supported by PwC (2022), which states that ESG encompasses a wider range of factors beyond long-term risk reduction, such as social scores related to gender and diversity, human rights, and labor standards, as well as environmental scores that monitor and limit carbon emissions, pollution, waste, and biodiversity. On the other hand, political lobbying, remuneration, and supervision and accountability are all included in the governance component of ESG (PwC, 2022). According to Harahap et al. (2022), ESG evaluates a business's operations with respect to its governance procedures, social responsibility, and environmental effects, and ESG standards are used by socially conscious investors to evaluate assets and assess the ethical and sustainable implications of their investment decisions. In modern investment practices, ESG-screened investments are seen as wise choices since these investments reduce investor risk and accord preference to businesses with a higher chance of long-term success (Li et al., 2021) and sustainable value creation with altruistic motives instead of opportunism.

The importance of ESG is manifold because it helps companies' investors and other stakeholders to gauge how well a company is managing its operations and ESG-related factors to create value in its journey toward financial growth and long-term sustainability. Giese et al. (2019) state that ESG investing is a very broad field with multiple investment approaches catering to various investment objectives. Today, a company's performance on specific ESG issues is assessed using ESG data. For example, a company's environmental impact can be assessed using carbon emissions per unit of sales, and its labor policies can be assessed using employee turnover rates (IBM, 2024). Giese et al. (2019), therefore, divide ESG investing into three primary areas consisting of, first, ESG integration, which aims to enhance the risk-return characteristics of an investment portfolio. The second area is values-based investing, which involves the investor seeking to align his portfolio with his personal values, norms, and beliefs. Finally, the third area is impact investing in which the investor uses his investment portfolio as a catalyst for environmental/social change such as using agricultural investment in technologies to advance smart farming and produce food in highly safe environments.

The Global Sustainable Investment Alliance defines socially responsible investing (SRI) and its related terms, that is, ethical investment/responsible investing/social investment, as investment that deliberates over ESG aspects in the selection and management of investment portfolios (Martini, 2021). In the same vein, Rizzi et al. (2018) state that ethical investment or SRI comprises investment approaches to finance projects that generate financial returns and produce positive impact on the environment and the society, subsequently leading to sustainable growth. This is also known as "blended value creation," which refers to investing activities that generate a combination of financial returns and optimistic environmental/social outcomes (Emerson, 2003; Nicholls, 2010). Similarly, Sparkes (2002) asserts that SRI and corporate social responsibility (CSR) are mirror images of each other, which essentially means that business should generate wealth for the society but within societal and environmental norms. In this context, CSR is interpreted from the viewpoint of companies, while SRI is viewed from the perspective of the companies' investors/shareholders. In the context of Islamic finance, the exponential rise of Islamic bonds, or *sukuk*, and ASEAN sustainable bonds, as well as the increased emphasis on energy, green buildings, and transportation in investment decisions, along with the expanding issuance of products with sustainability themes, are some of the noteworthy trends in the SRI sector (EY, 2021).

6. Understanding ESG in the Context of Islamic Finance

ESG criteria are increasingly recognized globally as important factors for sustainable and responsible investing. In the context of Islamic finance, ESG principles align closely with the ethical and social values inherent in *Shari'ah* law

(Agustin et al., 2023). ESG considerations can be understood and applied within an Islamic framework elaborated further below:

Environmental (E)

- *Resource use*: Islamic teachings emphasize responsible stewardship of natural resources. Practices that promote conservation, efficiency, and sustainability in resource use are encouraged.
- *Pollution and waste*: Islamic ethics prohibit activities that cause harm to the environment, such as pollution and excessive waste. Investments in industries that adhere to environmentally friendly practices are favored (Helfaya et al., 2018). Green financing and issuance of Sukuk (Islamic Bonds) for the purpose of financing environmentally friendly investments related to efficient use of resources mentioned above are highly encouraged (Piratti & Cattelan, 2018).

Social (S)

- *Fair labor practices*: Islamic finance promotes ethical labor practices that uphold workers' rights and ensure fair wages and working conditions.
- *Community engagement*: Investments should benefit local communities and contribute positively to their development. Islamic finance encourages businesses to engage responsibly with communities, respecting their social and cultural norms (Ahmed et al., 2015).
- *Social justice*: ESG in an Islamic context emphasizes social justice, aiming to reduce inequality and promote inclusive economic growth. Investments should contribute to poverty alleviation and enhance societal well-being.

Governance (G)

- *Ethical business practices*: Islamic finance requires adherence to ethical business practices and transparency in governance structures (Mansour & Bhatti, 2018). Companies are expected to uphold integrity, accountability, and fairness in their business activities and operations.
- *Shari'ah compliance*: Governance practices must align with *Shari'ah* principles, ensuring that business activities and decisions are ethically sound and legally permissible under Islamic law (Agustian et al., 2023).
- *Shareholders' rights*: Islamic finance emphasizes the protection of shareholder rights and encourages governance structures that promote long-term sustainability and ethical behavior.

6.1. Synergies Between ESG, Ethical Investment in Islamic Finance, and Sustainable Growth

The creation of a sustainable future requires substantial investment. The International Energy Agency projects that achieving net-zero emissions by 2030 may require investments of approximately $5 trillion annually and $4.5 trillion annually by 2050, and the amount that would need to be spent on decarbonization in the transportation, agricultural, and other sectors may almost treble (McKinsey & Company, 2021). Hence, the attainment of sustainable growth requires significant insights and contributions from various sectors including Islamic finance. The Islamic transaction (*muamalat*) principle seeks to build a shared sustainable future for employees, clients, shareholders, and the society in accordance with UN Agenda 2030 principles. In a similar vein, the SDGs aim to promote human rights and sound corporate governance while bringing all nations together in the fight against poverty, inequality, and climate change (Bursa Malaysia, 2023). The UN's 17 SDGs and the *maqasid-al-Shari'ah* (objectives of *Shari'ah*) are closely related since they aim to improve community development, global sustainability, resilience, and environmental, economic, and social impacts (Bursa Malaysia, 2023). In the same vein, Alshaleel (2019) states that with its emphasis on asset-backed financing, and the social and moral code that forbids *riba*, Islamic finance presents a viable alternative source of funding for projects and activities related to sustainable development through ethical investment opportunities. Similarly, Ahmed (2017) concurs that Islamic finance is well-suited to attain the UN SDGs' goals of alleviating poverty and achieving sustainable growth due to the Islamic ethical and social principles and focus on asset-backed financing and risk-sharing.

ESG and Islamic finance, thus, share common values and objectives as both areas focus on social development within the business community and society, and the fundamental premise of avoidance of harm in the pursuit of sustainable growth. According to Al Ansari and Alanzarouti (2020), the fundamental tenets of Islamic finance are comparable to those of sustainable finance, including financial stability and economic growth, wealth distribution and poverty alleviation, financial and social inclusion, and environmental preservation. As a result, Islamic finance has been able to take advantage of these parallels and use them to spread the principles of green finance. This is in line with the aspirations of ESG, which aims to measure the environmental and social impact of organizations in the pursuit of sustainable performance and value creation. Similarly, McKinsey & Company (2022) states that investors, customers, and employees are now expecting companies to take a stand on social issues and make sustainable and purposeful decisions. In the same vein, PwC (2022) elucidates that from the perspective of theory, there is a chance for a market convergence that would place Islamic financial products like *sukuk* bonds that adhere to *Shari'ah* law or *waqf* (also known as endowment) funds in the portfolios of ESG-obsessed investors across the globe. This would also give Islamic banking institutions a growing portion of what is probably going to grow to be one of the largest, if not the dominant, investment sector in the future (PwC, 2022).

Al Ansari and Alanzarouti (2020) further affirm that Islamic finance and ESG investing are complimentary methods of raising cash and making investments that share many values, such as being a good steward toward the environment and the society, because both offer products that cater to both Muslim and non-Muslim investors. ESG considerations within Islamic finance, thus, integrate ethical values and principles derived from *Shari'ah* law (Al Ansari & Alanzarouti, 2020). Investments are evaluated not only for financial returns but also for their impact on the environment, society, and governance practices. By aligning with ESG criteria, Islamic finance aims to promote sustainable growth and development, uphold ethical standards, and contribute positively.

Even though ESG and Islamic finance may share a common goal, there exist some glaring distinctions in the adopted investment approaches. For example, the distinction may be seen in the different methods used for screening of investments whereby ESG screening is usually selective and motivated by client mandates, whereas IF screening is often exclusionary based on generally recognized principles (PwC, 2022). In line with this, Bursa Malaysia (2023) affirms that *Shari'ah* investors usually screen investment opportunities based on Islamic religious and ethical guidelines that exclude specific products and sectors. Two layers of screening are usually used to ensure *Shari'ah*-compliant investing comprising financial screening and business activity (sector) screening. Revenues from the selling of alcohol, pork, tobacco, gambling, pornography, traditional financial services, traditional insurance, and the deferred cash basis trade of gold and silver are examples of sector-based *Shari'ah* exclusions (Bursa Malaysia, 2023). ESG investors, in contrast, undertake positive and negative screening to arrive at informed investment decisions. Top-performing companies that lead by example by providing eco-friendly goods and upholding moral business principles are found through positive screening. On the other hand, negative screening is employed to weed out businesses that participate in environmentally or socially detrimental practices (Bursa Malaysia, 2023).

7. Integration of ESG in Islamic Investment Products

Due to the magnitude of SRI on business sustainability, Malaysia and the rest of ASEAN are accelerating their transition to sustainable, responsible investing to achieve positive impact and favorable returns. With 92% of the region's total Islamic assets under management and 23% of all mutual fund assets under management in Malaysia, the country emerged as a leader in *Shari'ah*-compliant assets in 2021. This market has also been driven by the rise of ASEAN sustainable bonds and *sukuk*, the expanding issuance of goods with sustainability themes, and the growing attention that investors are paying to industries like energy, green buildings, and transportation (Bursa Malaysia, 2023). Furthermore, the ASEAN6[1] nations are working collectively to improve or include sustainability into their investment and organizational goals, while simultaneously developing regulations to lessen the effects of climate change (EY, 2021).

As ESG gains notoriety in the local and global business platform, financial institutions within Malaysia are engaging in steps to promote sustainable growth through their banking and financing strategies. The Securities Commission Malaysia introduced the SRI *sukuk* framework in 2014 followed by Khazanah Nasional's *Ihsan Sukuk* in 2015, the world's first green SRI *sukuk* in 2017, and

[1]The ASEAN6 countries are Malaysia, Indonesia, the Philippines, Singapore, Thailand, and Vietnam.

the SRI *Sukuk* Roadmap in 2019 (Euromoney, 2021). In addition, HSBC Malaysia launched the first ESG Islamic Structured Product in the Malaysian market in 2019 as a response to Bank Negara Malaysia's timely call for values-based intermediation. HSBC Amanah's ESG-related Islamic Structured Product, which is linked to the Hang Seng Corporate Sustainability Index (HSCSI), essentially provides customers with investment opportunities in a product that matches their personal values on social and environmental causes (Bursa Malaysia, 2019). The HSCSI monitors the performance of Hong Kong public listed companies that excel in corporate sustainability from various areas such as corporate governance, impact of climate change, human rights, gender equality, efficient use of energy, and business ethics (Bursa Malaysia, 2019).

In addition, AmBank Group has made the principles of values-based intermediation (VBI)[2] part of its sustainability agenda through the adoption of VBI by AmBank Islamic, which is expected to enhanced facilitation of entrepreneurship, community well-being, a sustainable environment, and economic growth, all of which are strongly correlated with shareholders' focus on long-term, sustainable profits (AmBank Group, 2024). To further enhance the market dynamics between ESG and Islamic finance, several indices have been introduced by *Bursa Malaysia* and FTSE Russell in reaction to volatile market movements due to the aftermath of the Covid-19 pandemic. For example, the FTSE4Good *Bursa Malaysia Shari'ah* Index (F4GBMS) was launched in July 2021 to measure *Shari'ah*-compliant F4GBM Index members. The F4GBMS encourages best practice disclosure for a more sustainable and low-carbon economy and supports investors in making ESG investments in Malaysian public listed firms. The other indices are the FTSE *Bursa Malaysia* Top 100 ESG Low Carbon Select *Shari'ah* Index, which consists of all *Shari'ah*-compliant companies in the FTSE *Bursa Malaysia* Top 100 ESG Low Carbon Select Index, the FTSE *Bursa Malaysia* Hijrah *Shari'ah* Index, which consists of companies in the FBM EMAS Index that meet international *Shari'ah* screening requirements, and the FTSE *Bursa Malaysia* EMAS *Shari'ah* Index, which serves as a broad benchmark for investors adhering to *Shari'ah* (Bursa Malaysia, 2023).

8. Conclusion

ESG investing and Islamic finance seem to be approaching convergence to an extent due to their similarities despite the existence of distinct differences. This trend toward the adoption of common approaches and analysis is anticipated to continue because of investors having a stronger awareness of Islamic finance and ESG investment, and the growing significance of social and environmental issues (CFA Institute, 2019). However, even though the ethical and social ideals

---

[2]VBI shares similarities with ESG and ethical finance but exhibits key distinguishing factors consisting of (1) central position of *Shari'ah* in determining the Islamic bank's underlying values, moral compass, and priorities; (2) focus on the real economy; and (3) incorporation of networking and cross-fertilization to benefit the stakeholders of Islamic banks (AmBank Group, 2024).

and principles of Islamic finance are aligned with the concerns raised by ESG, several issues must be addressed to allow the merger between ESG and Islamic finance (Habib, 2023) subsequently resulting in sustainable growth. According to Habib (2023), *shari'ah* compliance must be defined more widely to incorporate the *maqasid* viewpoint, inclusive of ethical, social, and environmental concerns. In addition, there must be an organizational shift from shareholders' perspective to stakeholders' perspective to implement the more comprehensive idea of *shari'ah* compliance taking into consideration the best interest of the community (Habib, 2023). According to research conducted by Maybank Islamic Berhad and IslamicMarkets.com, a top platform that provides access to financial opportunities and expert knowledge, 86% of respondents are of the opinion that ESG and sustainability will play a major role in growing Malaysia's *halal* economy and the Islamic finance sector (Business Today, 2022). Moreover, almost 85% of respondents also believe that the responsible and ethical investing principles of Islamic finance could increase investments among Muslims and non-Muslim investors (Business Today, 2022). It is, therefore, imperative that improved synergy and convergence between ESG and ethical investments under Islamic finance take place to promote sustainable growth and a happier, healthier, and wealthier society.

References

Agustian, K., Hejazziey, D., Zen, A., Sekarini, R. A., & Wiwin, W. (2023). Comparative analysis of ethical and legal principles in the Islamic business management model. *Journal of Contemporary Administration and Management (ADMAN)*, *1*(2), 101–107.

Agustin, F., Muhtadi, R., & Sahal, S. (2023). The importance of implementing environment, social and government (ESG) and maqasid sharia-based Islamic finance in Islamic bank. *Journal of Islamic Economic Laws*, *6*(2), 133–158.

Ahmed, H. (2017). *Contribution of Islamic finance to the 2030 Agenda for sustainable development*. Retrieved July 16, 2024, from https://www.un.org/esa/ffd/wp-content/uploads/sites/4/2017/11/Background-Paper_Islamic-Finance_17-Nov.pdf

Ahmed, H., Mohieldin, M., Verbeek, J., & Aboulmagd, F. (2015). *On the sustainable development goals and the role of Islamic finance*. World Bank Policy Research Working Paper (7266).

Alam, M. M., Akbar, C. S., Shahriar, S. M., & Elahi, M. M. (2017). The Islamic Shariah principles for investment in stock market. *Qualitative Research in Financial Markets*, *9*(2), 132–146.

Al Ansari, R., & Alanzarouti, F. (2020). ESG and Islamic finance: An ethical bridge built on shared values. *Journal of Islamic Financial Studies*, *6*(1), 5–11.

Alshaleel, M. K. (2019). Islamic finance, sustainable development and developing countries: Linkages and potential. In O. Osuji, F. N. Ngwu, & D. Jamali (Eds.), *Corporate social responsibility in developing and emerging markets: Institutions, actors and sustainable development* (pp. 281–305). Cambridge University Press.

AmBank Group. (2024, July 15). *Value based intermediation*. https://www.ambankgroup.com/eng/islamic/IslamicBanking/Pages/ValueBasedIntermediation.aspx

Ash-Shiddiqy, M., Mujtahid, & Khamim (2023). Islamic banking and finance. In Z. Hasan (Ed.). *Islamic banking and finance* (2nd ed.). Routledge. https://doi.org/10.1080/14697688.2023.2270495.

Bursa Malaysia. (2019). *HSBC Malaysia launches ESG Islamic structured product*. Retrieved July 15, 2024, from hsbc-malaysia-launches-esg-islamic-structured-product | Bursa Sustain (bursamalaysia.com)

Bursa Malaysia. (2023). *Exploring the intersection and distinctions: ESG vs. Islamic finance investing*. Retrieved July 16, 2024, from https://bursaacademy.bursamarketplace.com/en/article/ESG/exploring-the-intersection-and-distinctions-esg-vs-islamic-finance-investing

Business Today. (2022). *ESG to boost growth for Islamic finance, study shows*. Retrieved July 16, 2024, from https://www.businesstoday.com.my/2022/03/09/esg-to-boost-growth-for-islamic-finance-study-shows/

CFA Institute. (2019). *ESG integration and Islamic finance: Complementary investment approaches*. Retrieved July 16, 2024, from https://www.unpri.org/download?ac=9578

Deloitte. (2022). *ESG explained: Article series exploring ESG from the very basics*. Retrieved July 9, 2024, from https://www.deloitte.com/ce/en/services/consulting/perspectives/esg-explained-1-what-is-esg.html

Emerson, J. (2003). The blended value proposition: Integrating social and financial returns. *California Management Review*, *45*(4), 35–51.

Euromoney. (2021). *Malaysia brings Islamic finance and ESG together*. Retrieved July 9, 2024, from https://www.euromoney.com/article/297ljl7o060lbd1wh23nk/esg/malaysia-brings-islamic-finance-and-esg-together

EY. (2021). *Trending: Sustainable responsible investment in Malaysia and the region*. Retrieved July 9, 2024, from https://www.bing.com/ck/a?!&&p=bd2246a15d37396-0JmltdHM9MTcyMDM5NjgwMCZpZ3VpZD0xMTU2ZjM5YS05YmE3LTY1ZDQtMjc1NC1lNzliOWFhNjY0NmImaW5zaWQ9NTI5Mg&ptn=3&ver=2&hsh=3&fclid=1156f39a-9ba7-65d4-2754-e79b9aa6646b&psq=exqamples+of+environmental+responsible+investment&u=a1aHR0cHM6Ly9hc3NldHMuZXkuY29tL2NvbnRlbnQvZGFtL2V5LXNpdGVzL2V5LWNvbS9lbl9teS90b3BpY3MvYWNj-ZWxlcmF0aW5nLWdyb3d0aC9leS10cmVuZGluLW1hbGF5c2lhLWFuZC10aGUtcmVnaW9uLnBkZj9kb3dubG9hZA&ntb=1

Giese., G. & Lee, L., Melas, D., Nagy, Z., & Nishikawa, L. (2019). Foundations of ESG investing: How ESG affects equity valuation, risk, and performance. *The Journal of Portfolio Management*, *45*(5), 69–83.

Habib, F. (2023). Islamic finance and sustainability: The need to reframe notions of shariah compliance, purpose, and value. In *Islamic Finance, FinTech, and the Road to Sustainability*. doi: 10.1007/978-3-031-13302-2_2.

Harahap, D., Uula, M. M. & Nasution, A. A. (2022). Environmental, social, governance (ESG) and Islamic finance: A review. *Management and Sustainability*, *1*(1). https://pdfs.semanticscholar.org/e02b/bffe9ce6a7f87acdacc94af280b175e52116.pdf.

Harvard Law School Forum on Corporate Governance. (2020). *Introduction to ESG*. Retrieved July 9, 2024, from https://corpgov.law.harvard.edu/2020/08/01/introduction-to-esg/

Helfaya, A., Kotb, A., & Hanafi, R. (2018). Qur'anic ethics for environmental responsibility: Implications for business practice. *Journal of Business Ethics*, *150*, 1105–1128.

Herianingrum, S., Supriani, I., Sukmana, R., Effendie, E., Widiastuti, T., Fauzi, Q., & Shofawati, A. (2024). Zakat as an instrument of poverty reduction in Indonesia. *Journal of Islamic Accounting and Business Research*, *15*(4), 643–660.

Hussain, M., Shamoradi, A., & Turk, R. (2015). *IMF working paper: An overview of Islamic finance*. https://www.imf.org/external/pubs/ft/wp/2015/wp15120.pdf

IBM. (2024, July 9). *The history of ESG: A journey towards sustainable investing*. https://www.ibm.com/blog/environmental-social-and-governance-history/

Imam, P., & Kpodar, K. (2016). Islamic banking: Good for growth? *Economic Modelling*, *59*, 387–401.

Izzeldin, M., Johnes, J., Ongena, S., Pappas, V., & Tsionas, M. (2021). Efficiency convergence in Islamic and conventional banks. *Journal of International Financial Markets, Institutions and Money*, *70*, 101279. https://doi.org/10.1016/j.intfin.2020.101279

Khalidin, B. (2024). Economic empowerment with Islamic economics-based instruments. *American Journal of Humanities and Social Sciences Research*, *7*(3), 18–27.

Khan, A. K., Al Aboud, O. A., & Faisal, S. M. (2018). Muamma (conundrum) of *riba* (interest and usury) in major religions in general and Islam in particular. *The International Journal of Social Sciences and Humanities Invention*, *5*(2), 4438–4443.

Khan, M. A. (2019). Dilemmas of Islamic economics 1. *Methodology of Islamic Economics* (pp. 52–114). Routledge.

Li, T. T., Wang, K., Sueyoshi, T., & Wang, D. D. (2021). ESG: Research progress and future prospects. *Sustainability*, *13*(21), 11663. https://doi.org/10.1016/j.indic.2022.100218

Mansour, W., & Bhatti, M. I. (2018). The new paradigm of Islamic corporate governance. *Managerial Finance*, *44*(5), 513–523.

Martini, A. (2021). Socially responsible investing: From the ethical origins to the sustainable development framework of the European Union. *Environment, Development and Sustainability*, *23*, 16874–16890. https://doi.org/10.1007/s10668-021-01375-3

McKinsey & Company. (2021). *Our future lives and livelihoods: Sustainable and inclusive and growing*. Retrieved July 16, 2024, from https://www.mckinsey.com/featured-insights/sustainable-inclusive-growth/our-future-lives-and-livelihoods-sustainable-and-inclusive-and-growing

McKinsey & Company. (2022). *The role of ESG and purpose*. Retrieved July 15, 2024, from https://www.mckinsey.com/capabilities/strategy-and-corporate-finance/our-insights/the-role-of-esg-and-purpose

Nicholls, A. (2010). The institutionalization of social investment: The interplay of investment logics and investor rationalities. *Journal of Social Entrepreneurship*, *1*(1), 70–100.

Nik Abdullah, N. A. I. (2022). ESG reporting practices among Islamic banks: A global perspective. *IIUM Law Journal*, *30*(S2), 1–37.

Nordin, N., Aziz, S. A., Ahmad, A. A., & Daud, N. (2014). Contracting with *Gharar* (uncertainty) in forward contract: What does Islam says? *Asian Social Science*, *10*(15), 37.

Piratti, M., & Cattelan, V. (2018). *Islamic green finance: A new path to environmental protection and sustainable development Islamic social finance* (pp. 144–172). Routledge.

PwC. (2022). *Islamic finance & ESG investing: Ready for convergence?* Retrieved July 16, 2024, from https://www.pwc.com/m1/en/publications/documents/islamic-finance-and-esg-investing.pdf

Rahim, A. B. A. (2013). Understanding Islamic ethics and its significance on the character building. *International Journal of Social Science and Humanity*, *3*(6), 508.

Razak, S. H. A. (2020). *Zakat* and *waqf* as instrument of Islamic wealth in poverty alleviation and redistribution: Case of Malaysia. *International Journal of Sociology and Social Policy*, *40*(3/4), 249–266.

Rizzi, F., Pellegrini, C., & Battaglia, M. (2018). The structuring of social finance: Emerging approaches for supporting environmentally and socially impactful projects. *Journal of Cleaner Production*, *170*, 805–817.

Safiullah, M. (2021). Financial stability efficiency of Islamic and conventional banks. *Pacific Basin Finance Journal*, *68*(May), 101587. https://doi.org/10.1016/j.pacfin.2021.101587

Soemitra, A. (2021). The relevance of Islamic economics and finance fundamentals to the contemporary economy: Islamic economist perceptions. *Jurnal Ekonomi dan Kewangan Islam*, *10*(2), 325–352.

Sparkes, R. (2002). *Socially responsible investment: A global revolution*. Wiley.

S&P Global Ratings. (2022). *Islamic finance outlook*. Retrieved July 16, 2024, from https://www.spglobal.com/ratings/en/research/pdf-articles/islamic-finance-outlook-2022-28102022v1.pdf

The Edge Malaysia. (2023). *ESG 101: The origins of ESG*. Retrieved July 9, 2024, from https://theedgemalaysia.com/node/682788

Yasin, M. Z., Noor, M. A., Bibi, A., & Fakhar, A. (2024). The purposeful life: An exploration of life's priorities according to the objectives of Islamic Shariah. *Remittances Review*, *9*(2), 574–593.

Zaker, S. (2019). Islamic banking in Bangladesh: An alluring prospect ahead. *Bangladesh Journal of Political Economy*, *35*(1), 447–502.

Chapter 4

Embedding Social Responsibility in Islamic Banking: Ethical Foundations and Modern Practices

Salman Bashir Memon[a], Sumaiya Syed[b] and Abdul Samad Dahri[a]

[a]*Shaheed Benazir Bhutto University, Pakistan*
[b]*Shah Abdul Latif University, Pakistan*

Abstract

The subject of social responsibility in Islamic banking encompasses the ethical principles that create a link between operations in the financial sphere with reference to Shariah. The purpose of this chapter is to explain historical backdrop of social responsibility together with its remits in Islamic finance. As an aspect of banking in the Islamic world, it is the legal, moral, and religious duties that preserve the banking sector's ethical practices also producing positive outcomes for the society. Islamic banks also provide social welfare activities which include Zakat, Sadaqah, and Qard Hasan that help improve the state of welfare. To understand the history of social responsibility in Islam and Islamic financial systems, one must look all the way back to the early Islamic age, during which the money's distribution is equal, injustice was punished through 'Bay'ah (or pledge), a form of contract that funded community services provided to public commonwealth like education and health, namely through Waqf (or endowment). Islamic financial institutions all over the world can be said to have created a revolution on incorporating ethical attributes in financial systems. This evolution also underlined the questions of ethical investments, the prohibition of unethical or haram, and the support for sustainable development goals. The social responsibility in Islamic banking does not mean the rules and regulation of the particular country but has deep Islamic values embedded in it. Thus, Islamic banks

Islamic Finance and Corporate Governance: Synergies for Sustainable Growth, 57–74

doi:10.1108/978-1-83662-346-520251008

maintain Shariah law, and therefore, their activity positively impacts society and contributes to the development of the economy and stability.

Keywords: Social responsibility; Islamic banking; ethics; Shariah and Shariah law

1. Introduction

Islamic banking, which adheres to the provisions of Shariah law, is an embodiment of a special model of banking that incorporates ethical and social component into its functioning. On the conceptual level, Islamic banking is centered on the notions of justice, non-usury, and the ban on gyrating against society's welfare, making business practice in the Islamic banks conform to the tenets of the Islamic Shariah as well as being good for the society (Habibullah et al., 2023). This chapter aims to analyze the social responsibility in the Islamic banking by defining what it entails, discussion on its boundaries, as well as a brief history. The field of social responsibility under this context involves the companies' practices which include investment ethically, engage in donations, and support of community development (El Melki & Ben Salah Saidi, 2023). All these practices have been sponsored under Islamic economic system that stresses on economic justice, sound economic management, and fair economic relation. Consequently, through the identification of the historical sentiment of social responsibility in Islamic finance, this chapter seeks to establish how modern banking systems remain committed to the principles of simplicity and compassion where helping one's fellow human being remains a valued virtue. It underlines the compliance of financial activities with ethical norms and benefits of society, which demonstrates the ability of Islamic banking to bring positive change in the development of the economies.

1.1. Definition

Corporate and financial responsibility as a concept deals with the proper role of organizations especially business entities and other enterprises to function for the overall positive effect of the society development (El Melki & Ben Salah Saidi, 2023). This concept entails a broad common element for maintaining activities of these entities from causing negativity to society while maximizing on the creation of positive impacts. It is not limited to conformity to the legal expectations; it involves striving to enhance the social, economic, and natural context. Business sustainability as well as social responsiveness incorporates social justice, environmental stewardship, and fiscal stability into an organization's strategies and daily activities (Caulfield & Lynn, 2024). This entails embracing integrity, reporting, and answering for one's decisions and actions by taking into account the repercussions on the society, personnel, clientele, and natural environment.

1.2. Scope

The concept of social responsibility is rather broad and encompasses several aspects rooted on the socioeconomic structure of the first Islamic society. They are corporate governance, which is a system by which organizations check the right management practices as well as the rights of shareholders and other stakeholders. Another priority area is the protection of the environment by reducing the company's impact on natural surroundings through waste management, optimum energy consumption, and the rational utilization of resources. Social responsibility also touches on the involvement of organizations within the society through charitable donations, volunteering, and sponsorship of projects. Also as a part of the social responsibility, the company supports labor relations and the practices of nondiscrimination and child protection, equal remuneration for equal work, workers' freedom association, safe workplaces, and humane working conditions (Kandpal et al., 2024). Another component is financial integrity particularly among banking and financial institutions that require financial credibility, proper credit production, and handling of credit risks while observing legal and ethical benchmarks within the banking and non-banking industries. Last but not the least, consumer protection is the area that is concerned with need satisfaction without exploitation of consumers whenever they purchase goods and services with regard to their safety, quality, reliability, and other aspects.

Altogether, these elements comprise a vast conception of social corporate management, which tries to improve social outcomes on business and achieve greater social impacts while conforming business processes to ethical and moral goals. From this perspective, the calculations means of organizing that lean toward social responsibility should become an element of a strategic outlook, acting as a basis for creating commitment to responsibility and impact by organizations for the benefit of the organization itself and the whole society (Carroll, 2021). In this way, through the instrument of Waqf, people could donate their assets for charity by providing an opportunity for the result from this property to be used for public needs, for students, the sick, or for the construction of necessary buildings, without focusing on material interest, as ill-gotten gains, in regard to all members of society. It provided the basis for poverty eradication which is one of the basic requisites for social justice and welfare and also had the provision of corporate social responsibility built into it as a norm for the financial business dealings among the Islamic population.

While the civilizations of Islamic world spread, the structure and demand for its new systems of financing also increased. There was more developed trade and commercial activities during the classical age of Islamic history, which required more complex tools and structures of financing. Thus, despite the indicated peculiarity of Islamic finance, the adherence to social responsibility is still a key element of it. Institutionalized practices included Zakat which is the mandatory charity in Islam and Sadaqah which is charity that is given willingly to the needy thus making sure that all the poor people were taken care of (Mazurenko & Vorobiova, 2020). Moreover, prohibition of charging and paying interest and of Gharar (uncertainty) in contracts highlighted the Islamic finance and banks' social responsibility to eliminate and refrain from exploiting people. These principles were strictly followed by scholars and jurists who thereby evolved an entire structure of financial ethics to wean this principle of social responsibility into the very fiber of the economy (Nouman et al., 2021).

These historical principles have been maintained and upheld in the contemporary world after mid-20th century when the Islamic finance was revived. Modern Islamic financial institutions aim at maintaining the dual objectives of pecuniary profitability and the quest for Islamicity, which is acting in a way that the institutions' actions are lawful and proper in the eyes of Shariah (Hasan, 2020). This continuous devotion to social justice is one of the key distinctive features that clearly set IF from conventional finance and at the same time solidifies its responsibility toward the upholding of the tenets of economic justice and sustainable development. It is, therefore, clear that the consideration of social responsibility in the development of Islamic finance has a strong historiographical basis; this generally suggests that the historical past continues to be an important point of reference in the modern world.

2. Theoretical Foundations

2.1. Islamic Economic Principles

Islamic banking and finance is guided by the legal bases of the Islamic economics as it seeks to ensure justice in the economy as well as charitable objectives. These principles are rooted in the Quran and the Sunnah where the Islamic code of ethics and business practices prescribes the Islamization of the economy based on the principle of Tawhid, of fairness and justice where the objective of economic activities is to seek the counter values. These include the ban on riba, which people regard as usury involving a charge of interest on loans advanced. Rather it opt for risk and return sharing which is reflected in Mudarabah (i.e., a phase of profit sharing) and Musharakah (i.e., joint partnership) (Eyerci & Eyerci, 2021). Also, Islamic economics does not allow investments in activities and businesses that are considered forbidden such as gambling, alcohol and pork businesses, and many others because Islamic economics has to be moral in its economic undertakings (Laldin et al., 2020). The principles of Zakat also aim to encourage people and companies to give a part of their earnings or property to the poor in the society, thus raising the idea of social justice as people and businesses are united into one community. Therefore, the Islamic banking system endeavors to provide a sound and fair economic order free from usury, whose aim is welfare and not the deepening of inequality.

2.2. Shariah Compliance and Ethical Considerations

The legal structure of Islamic banking is the Shariah law that governs all the activities of the bank with regards to Islamic laws. This entails a strict procedure of screening and supervision by the Shariah boards which is formed by scholars of Islamic jurisprudence. Another of the cornerstones of Shariah is the ethical consideration when it comes to dealing in the market, this ensures that business is done openly, fairly, and with full disclosure (Ayub et al., 2023). This includes "Gharar" (or excessive uncertainty and risk) which are some of the prohibited aspects of Islamic finance. However, the contract must be very specific and leave no room for ambiguity and all the trading partners should know what they are entitled to and what is expected of them. In addition, Shariah compliance is also manifested in the way corporate governance is done which pressure Islamic finance system from engaging in corrupt practices and embezzlement of people's money. This ethical framework makes certain that advanced Islamic banks do not only have legal compliance but are also ethically right in their dealings, thus making them gain the trust of their stakeholders (Alshubrumi, 2018).

2.3. Maqasid al Shariah (Objectives of Islamic Law)

The knowledge of Maqasid al Shariah (or objectives of Islamic law) is central to deciding on the principles and operations of an Islamic bank. These objectives aim to preserve and promote human welfare by protecting five essential values: religion, life, intellect, progeny, and wealth are five values on which humanist's life principles are based on. When applied to Shariah-compliant finance, Maqasid al Shariah seeks to establish the objectives of Shariah, which include the provisions for economic justice, social justice, as well as the fight against poverty (Hassan et al., 2021). This is done through facilities such as zakat which act to redistribute the wealth that is collected and given to the poor or the needy and "Qard Hasan" which is a form of benevolent lending facilities provided to the needy at no interest rates. Also, the call for expansion of risk-sharing as well as ethical investment proposals has also been made due to the pursuit of the common goal of segregation and protection of property as well as proper distribution of wealth (Kunhibava et al., 2024). Hence, it is essential to note that while serving law's letter, Islamic banking also follows its spirit, targeting the formation of a just and prosperous society. Such a combined strategy may be viewed as a distinctive feature of Islamic finance, stressing adherence to the approaches that address social and economic objectives other than, or in addition to, the exploitation of profit opportunities.

2.4. Core Principles of Social Responsibility in Islamic Banking

Shariah laws are the pillars for both the operations and the sustainability of Islamic banking because they outline the legal and moral activities of the banks as well as their corporate social responsibilities. Major precepts of social responsibility in Islam regarding the banking system recognize the goals as balancing on the provision of financial wealth and the quest for equity. In following these principles, Islamic banking system makes it possible to avoid negative impacts of the financial activities on the members of the society and encourage the right business conducts, justice, and franchise. The following are the principles that support social responsibility in Islamic banks.

2.5. Prohibition of Interest (Riba)

It is also important to consider one of the key pillars of Islamic banking and that is the nonacceptance of any amount charged in exchange for a delay in the repayment of a loan commonly referred to as Riba. There is a problem with Riba in the Islamic finance system, which is to charge or to earn an interest on a loan regarded exploitative and unjust since it entails the concentration of wealth in the absence of commensurate risk exposure or work (Benaicha, 2020). The reason for this prohibition is merely the fact that money cannot create money but is used as a medium of exchange and means of production. According to the Islamic economics prohibition of Riba, Islamic bank desire to achieve justice and gains, the risk and reward of financing transactions should be borne by both parties (Khan, 2024). This leads to a higher level of ethical financial practices and reduces activities that in effect promote risky business that destabilize the economy. On the other hand, Islamic banks introduce profit-and-loss sharing modes like "Mudarabah," "Musharakah" which effectively bring together the stakeholders' standings and fairly distribute the risks and rewards (Nouman & Ullah, 2023).

2.6. Risk Sharing (Mudarabah and Musharakah)

Islamic banking is based on risk sharing which is alluded to in the two major concepts of Mudarabah and Musharakah. As applied to Islamic financing, Mudarabah entails one party contributing funds for the business while the other brings in skills and experience. The structure of the profit appropriation is usually a ratio decided in the initial stage of the business, while the losses are for the account of the capital provider unless negligence or breach of contract by the manager was involved. Musharakah, on the other hand, is partnership in business where two or more people contribute capital to be used in carrying out the business and division of profits and losses in accordance to capital invested (Nouman & Ullah, 2023). These risk sharing instruments make all the parties to incur their efforts toward the success of the business making the exercise coordinated and devoid of exploitation. Thus, the concept of Islamic banking helps to restore fairness and responsibility on both sides of the financial pyramid of investors and entrepreneurs. Besides, this approach not only promotes more stability in economic sector but also revives and fosters entrepreneurships and innovations for the development of any economy (Ullah et al., 2024).

2.7. Avoidance of Unethical Investments (Haram Activities)

Islamic banking eradicates business ventures in sectors prohibited under Islamic law or what is referred to as haram. These include sectors in alcohol, gambling, pork, and any other that are regarded as socially irresponsible to the people and society. As to the logic of this prohibition, it lies in the general outlook of Islamic banking systems, which aims at avoiding socially destructive or ethically reprehensible operations (El-Bassiouny et al., 2023). Thus, abstaining from engaging in the haram investments, Islamic banks remain loyal to the norms of social justice and business ethic as the financial systems of the society. This adherence to Islamic legal standards guarantees that the revenues of the Islamic banks are from permitted activities allowing economic and social welfare on the society. Also, it addresses the goals of development in a way that it is not purely a financial gain for an entity ignoring social and moral implications. It also makes Islamic banks prefer the investment on the sectors that are beneficial to the society and the environment for instance; health, education, and other essential projects (Khan et al., 2021).

2.8. Transparency and Fairness in Transactions

Transparency and fairness can be identified as the significant parts of the Islamic banking social responsibilities. The following principles demand that all financial transactions should be truthful and must not involve any practices that are deemed to withdraw information from the other party. This helps the clients and stakeholders to make the right decisions in their undertakings and know the consequences that arise from any decision they make concerning financial products and services. The authorities of Islamic banks are keen to preserving relatively high level of the banks' ethical standards and accountability, which enhances customers' confidence (Cortelezzi & Ferrari, 2022). Reasonable justice in business interactions is also important, which means that the parties cannot be forced to sign unfavorable contracts, for example, they cannot be deceived. Every contract as well as every agreement that is entered should be reasonable and rational and the price to be charged should be one that is reasonable given the value of the particular service to be rendered or the particular good to be sold. Thus, the conforming to these principles makes higher transparency of transactions, relative justice in Shariah-oriented financial systems, builds enduring mutually beneficial relations with the clientele base, and provides stability for the global economy. Such a commitment of the Islamic banking toward disclosure and fairness improves the image of Islamic banking and affirm the virtue of Islamic banking being an ethical form of banking system compared to the conventional banking system (As Sahara & Setiawan, 2022).

3. Mechanisms and Instruments

In fulfilling the disclosed social responsibilities, the Islamic banking institutions use mechanisms and instruments that would complement Islamic banking in accordance with the Islamic Shariah law. Their operation not only is positive for the improvements of social and economic aspects of the community but also supports financial literacy and the concept of sustainable development. Among the key instruments, there are Zakat (or Islamic charitable donations) which are obligatory, Sadaqah (or voluntary charity), Waqf (or Islamic endowment), and "Qard Hasan" (or interest free benevolent loan). All of the mentioned tools have their important functions with regard to social inclusion, aiding of the needy, and the betterment of society's well-being (Aderemi & Ishak, 2023).

3.1. Zakat (Charitable Giving)

Zakat is another form of charity and being compulsory; is one of the five major practices of Muslims known in Arabic as the "Pillars of Islam." This entails

Muslims to contribute a portion of their wealth every year in the form of zakah, which, according to the majority of scholars, is equivalent to 2. The Islamic 2% fund allocates 5% of their savings to the needy ones. Some of such purposes of zakat funds are targeted at poverty reduction, healthcare provision, education, and emergency or disaster management in the setting of Islamic banking institutions. In this way, a religious obligation is performed while promoting the efficiency of sharing the wealth among all the community members. Hence, through planned collection and distribution of zakat, which is a key concept of Islamic banking, the social inequity issues can be solved and the social justice and welfare improved.

3.2. Sadaqah (Voluntary Charity)

Sadaqah, on the other hand, refers to any other charity that is given in addition to the obligatory Islamic alms or Zakat. While Zakat is obligatory and is calculated based on an amount of wealth that is equal to exactly one's Zakat asset, Sadaqah has no specific rate and can be given to anyone at any time for any needful cause (Kunhibava et al., 2024). Sadaqah is made easy through Islamic banks featuring avenues where people can give out their gifts for the needy, construction of structures, and projects for the needy groups in the community. This voluntary charity also equips the community to attend to the basic as well as auxiliary needs with an emphasis on the voluntary generosity. In Sadaqah, the Islamic banking institutions enhance the religious aspect of charity which helps in consistent act of compassion so that the society is built with mutual responsibility (Aderemi & Ishak, 2023).

3.3. Waqf (Endowment)

Waqf, which can be defined as a long-term giving where gifts are contributed to a social cause and the income produced, is for the general good of the community. Earlier, Waqf provided funding for educational institutions, hospitals, and other services that are beneficial for the public. Waqf endowment assets are utilized in Islamic banks where such assets are utilized in funding Islamic compliant business ventures hence creating sustainable income for the purpose of charity (Ashfaq et al., 2022). Waqf helps to establish perpetual endowments which enhance the generations of societies for many generations without interruption in funding social frameworks. In managing the funds of Waqf, Islamic banks play a part in sustaining and developing the most needed and desired resources of the society, in an effort of attaining financial satisfaction and the needs of the society at one and the same time (Biancone & Radwan, 2019).

3.4. Qard Hasan (Benevolent Loan)

Qard hasan meaning loans given to debtors on certain conditions with no interest charges. These are provided with the intention that it will be repaid without any profit intended as the service is, in fact, charity (Aderemi & Ishak, 2023).

Qard hasan is another type of Islamic banks' financing for micro-business, education fees, medical bills, and other necessary exigent situations. These interest-free loans that are provided by Islamic banks stimulate economic flourishing and social stratification especially among the needy more inclined groups or those at the lower end of the ladder. This practice shows that Islamic financial institutions have a primary goal of eradicating poverty in society as it extends its support to every segment of society with the intention of providing a hand acceptable under the religion's ban on interest charges (Kunhibava et al., 2024).

3.5. Governance and Accountability in Islamic Banking

Some of the essential guidelines for Islamic banks include governance and accountability that provides rigidity on the legal frame governing the banking business while making sure the institutions' practices adhere to the highest ethical standards and uphold the ideals of the Islamic principles. It suggests that to promote the governance frameworks and accountability mechanisms are fundamental building blocks in establishing an Islamic banking system's integrity and sustainability. They give support to the key tenets of transparency, sound ethics as well as adequate risk management, thus making its systems of operation in the Islamic bank just, fair, and responsible. This section shall review the components of governance and accountability in Islamic banking organizations including Shariah boards, corporate governance mechanism and transparency and disclosure.

3.6. Role of Shariah Boards

The operation of an Islamic bank is influenced greatly by a Shariah board that is accountable for reviewing all the offered products, services, and operations for conformity to Shariah (Alam et al., 2022). These boards are made up of scholars and the specialty is with Islamic jurisprudence and finance. Some of the key duties are to approve financial products along with the financial reports, perform Shariah periodicity audits and give advice on issues that are complicated in terms of Shariah.

The composition of Shariah boards increases the reliability of Islamic banks. These boards play a role of ensuring that the banking stakeholders conducts their business in compliance with Islamic standards, thus assisting in appealing to those who base their banking choices on ethical and religion aspects (Karbhari et al., 2020). Also, it plays a part in the growth and development of new generation of financial instruments in meeting the modern world markets and, at same time, it brings out the Islamic injunctions.

The other core check and balance is the direct periodic interaction of the Shariah boards with the bank's management to guarantee the incorporation of Shariah compliance checks into the business strategic planning process. It also helps shun risks that are associated with noncompliance and at the same time enhance the governance systems (Hanefah et al., 2020). Therefore, Shariah boards' task goes beyond legal compliance and establishing organizational culture that is beneficial for the society in general as well as Islamic banking institutions in particular.

4. Corporate Governance Frameworks

The auditor reporting arrangements together with other corporate governance frameworks in Islamic banking institutions are developed to give an account and fulfill accountability, transparency, and integrity. These frameworks translate to a set of policies, procedures, and measures that the bank's executive teams must follow and adopt in their business activities (Algabry et al., 2020). Among the elements of these frameworks are organization and composition of the boards, corporation risks management, controls, and the management of stakeholders. Proper corporate governance structure also helps safeguard the shareholders' and other stakeholders' interests such as customers, employees, and the whole society as well. It defines the mandate of the board of directors as well as the roles and responsibilities of the senior management thus enhancing the process of governance and development of strategies. In Islamic banking, corporate governance also entails to the fact that all human and business activities in the organization are performed in a socially appropriate manner in order to satisfy the corporate objectives of Islamic sharia (Mergaliyev et al., 2021). They have ways of evaluating threats and controlling them with a view of protecting the interests of the bank in terms of financial soundness as well as its image. Furthermore, these frameworks encourage ethical actions and corporate social responsibility, which emphasize the principles of Islamic finance and the bank's activities.

4.1. Transparency and Disclosure Requirements

Transparency and disclosure not only facilitate compliance with the regulations but also assist the Islamic banks in the long-term sustainability of their business. First, they ensure that there is openness of the organizational culture and the stakeholders gain confidence in the organization, thus making the organization acquire a social license (Jan et al., 2021). These principles entail that banks come up with precise, accurate, and timely disclosure of their financial performances, their risk management strategies, and their policies on corporate governance. Always and everywhere, one can agree with the statement that transparency strengthens stakeholder trust when they are exposed to accurate information. In the case of Islamic banking, transparency and disclosure even include Shariah compliance (Mergaliyev et al., 2021). Institutions have in the past been subjected to certain benchmarks of the Islamic finance system and they are required to reveal their level of compliance with Shariah especially the views of the Shariah boards. This guarantees that the customers/investors are fully informed about the ethical and religious aspects pertaining the transaction.

Legal structures of Islamic banking systems require disclosures on certain issues, for example; every banking institution is required to prepare and disclose a Shariah compliance report that is updated annually and financial statements. These are conditions that are aimed at increasing responsibility and avoiding the use of improper actions. In other words, the strategy of using high level of transparency as the principle of operation of Islamic banks can be viewed as an effective way to ensure proper nature of the action of the organizations, as well as to build a more favorable image in the market (Jan et al., 2021).

5. Social Responsibility Programs and Initiatives

5.1. Community Development Programs

Considering the above fundamentals of Islamic banks, it is evident that they participate in social causes meant to enhance the living standards of people in the community. These programs usually target areas like education, health, and the physical sectors mainly the construction (Tok & Yesuf, 2022). For instance, Islamic banks carry out the financing of construction of schools, hospitals, and other societal facilities in the developing regions. They also offer scholarships and other monetary facilities to needy and poor students to be able to study in a good college. Furthermore, these banks participate in heath causes by conducting clinics, immunization, and other related projects in the community. Through such types of investments in community development, Islamic banks now seek to improve the standard of people's living and develop a healthy, sustainable economy in their communities.

5.2. Microfinance and Financial Inclusion

The two main core strategies of Islamic banking in fulfillment of its social responsibilities are microfinance and an intermediary role that addresses the issue of financial inclusion. Islamic banks provide microfinance services to endow small businesses and entrepreneurs who do not get to enjoy the normal banking services. They are microfinance products that are developed with compliance to Shariah standards and, therefore no interest charges and instead of profit maximization, there are profit-sharing structures (Tamanni & Haji Besar, 2019). The literature review finds that Islamic banks eradicate poverty by helping those at the bottom level of society by providing microfinance for economic development. Furthermore, through products and services such as financial literacy and Islamic banks include the unbanked in the system making more people have an economy and financial strength to deal with economic shocks.

5.3. Environmental Sustainability Initiatives

The findings of this study reveal that environment sustainability is now emerging as another radical factor that Islamic banks are beginning to practices. They endorse green financing schemes which finance renewable energy, sustainable farming, food production, and environmentally friendly technologies. For instance, the Islamic banks could lend money for purchasing solar power plants and wind mills as well as energy efficient structures. They also apply sustainable policies in their business involving the environment like discouraging the use of paper in banks, encouraging the use of online banking, and seeing to it that their business premises are energy efficient (Rehman et al., 2021). Hence, by following environmental sustainability, the Islamic banks are not only observing the Shariah law but also having a positive impact on the world by striving to solve the issue of climate change and supporting sustainable development.

6. Challenges and Opportunities

Islamic banking and finance based on the values and norms of Islamic Shariah seeks to deliver justice in providing economic services. However, this sector has some of the challenges and opportunities that accompany it in its endeavor to grow and internationalize in the global financial market. These are the challenges of regulation and compliance, the lack of direct link between financial profitability and the objective of contributing to society improvement, and the necessity for creating the appropriate environment for the development of new products that will serve as a solution to social-oriented needs. If these areas are managed well, it will not only enable Islamic banking to expand but also to stick to the core values of the religion and social accountability.

6.1. Regulatory and Compliance Challenges

Islamic banking also has its own set of regulatory and compliance issues because of its operability on the principles of Shariah. Regulatory frameworks also differ from one country to another due to the difference in the regulatory framework. These banks have to overcome many legal issues, regarding their products and services they need to be Shariah compliant and must follow the national financial laws (Ahmad et al., 2023). Furthermore, there is limited legal precedent and general overviews for specific and systematic rules governing the administration of Islamic finance; common, efficient, and specialized frameworks are some of the issues that give rise to operation disruptions and costly crises. Some of the recommended strategies include building and synchronizing the strong regulatory frameworks and capacity building of the Shariah supervisory boards (Panagopoulos, 2022). Challenges exist in capacity building through promotion of interbanking relations to develop a harmonized legal structure that supplements the expansion of the Islamic banking industry with adherence to the Shariah law.

6.2. Balancing Profitability with Social Objectives

Another critical issue of concern to Islamic banking industry is strive to make profits while at the same time serving the society. It should be noted that unlike the conventional banks, the Islamic financial institutions are allowed to engage themselves in business that are of considerable benefit to the society. This is through funding of schemes that ensure the improvement of the social sector, environmental conservation, as well as the on promotion of economic equity. But it may not be economically profitable in comparison to normal and other commercial investments that seek profitability at any cost. The problem relates to designing financial products, which would conform to the rules of Shariahs and, at the same time, would be economically feasible (Nugroho, 2021). Chances are derived from the growing global market for sustainable pension investments. Islamic banks can offer novel and relevant financial products that reflect the clients' needs for both profit and social impacts without compromising the Shariah guidelines to grow and expand in the long term.

6.3. Development of Socially Responsible Financial Products

Sustainability of socially responsible financial products, therefore, forms the topic of this paper and outlines the various opportunities and threats of Islamic banking. Designing new financial instruments that are Shariah complaint, and that address modern social and economic problems, involves a huge amount of research and innovation (Nugroho, 2021). Islamic banks need to continue to innovate to produce product such as green Sukuk, impact funds, and microfinancing products for the underserved communities. The issue is to achieve the financial sustainability of these products and their interest to various clients (Tamanni & Haji Besar, 2019). Prospect can be observed as the global financial market trends toward the implementation of ethics and sustainability in investment. Thus, only Islamic banks that provide unique financial solutions for present-day problems can become pioneers of the ethical finance segment and attract investors concerned with the global future.

7. Future Directions in Social Responsibility for Islamic Banks

Consequently, future prospects for the development of Islamic banking reveal possible ways for strengthening the undertaking of social responsibility. The above evolution is not only as a result of new regulations but also as an incorporation of ethical standards in the financial activities. Several issues, trends, technologies, and strategic recommendation for the future issues of socially responsible finance of Islamic banking are introduced in this scholastic production.

7.1. Emerging Trends in Socially Responsible Finance

New directions in socially responsible finance in Islamic banking are shifting toward the incorporation of sustainable and impact financing approaches. There is now much focus on the funding of the project with elements compatible with Shariah laws, which are also sustainable for the environment and society (Mohd Zain et al., 2024). This it entails, investments in renewable energy, green infrastructure, and other community development investments. Also, there is the increasing concern for more and better disclosure and governance practices that reveal the Islamic banks' service to society and their ethical responsibilities.

7.2. Technological Advancement and Its Impact

Technological advancement has played a new trend in the functioning and services delivery of these Islamic banks. New forms of financial technologies, such as blockchain, and new models of digital banking platforms seem to increase the efficiency and decrease costs while making products more accessible for clientele. For the notion of socially responsible finance, these innovations help to provide specific services such as crowd-funding, for the charitable purposes, a blockchain for the way of collecting Zakat, and mobile applications for covering rural population preliminary needs (Sarea et al., 2021). In addition, technology helps monitor the compliance with ethical measure in real time, thus enabling the financial transactions to be Shariah compliant more ethical.

8. Recommendations

The portfolio of an Islamic bank must be expanded such that they can target the ethical investors and ethical users diversely. This entails creating unique solutions in the forms of financial instruments that incorporate social returns, configuration with SDGs objectives, and the needs of clients who have been left out of the financial mainstream. Moreover, there is a need to increase cooperation with the international organizations, academia, and civil society to improve the knowledge exchange and capacity development in the context of socially responsible finance. Sound internal controls, regular audits, and staff training are equally important measures that need to be applied to ensure that ethical standards are maintained and stakeholders' trust is preserved. Thus, in addition to increasing the competitive positions of Islamic banks on the market, the effective implementation of policies of proactive social responsibility can help stimulate the socioeconomic development of the world economy. Some of the recommendations for enhancing social responsibility in Islamic banking are provided below:

- *Enhanced disclosure and transparency*: Islamic banks should make their disclosures specific and comprehensive on their social responsibilities, disclosure on how they fulfill the Shariah standards in relations to the welfare of the community.
- *Strengthening ethical screening processes*: Include stringent measures of screening to check if the investment and financing activities fall outside the Islamic law and stay away from areas such as alcoholic products, gambling, and cigarettes.
- *Promotion of financial literacy*: Promote and deliver awareness courses on customers and stakeholders for the understanding of financing Islamic economics in an ethical way and also to preach the benefits of Islamic banking on the society.
- *Collaboration with stakeholders*: Develop collaboration with NGOs, community groups, and other government organizations, agencies, and institutions to pool all the resources, knowledge, and effort to solve social problems and obtain sustainable development.
- *Innovation in socially responsible products*: Promote the innovations to create new financial tools that have Shariah compliance and integrated problem solving of social and environmental needs such as; Islamic micro finance for the needy groups and the Islamic green financing for sustainable projects.
- *Capacity building for Shariah scholars*: Ensure that scholarships and training sessions are attended regularly and continue with the modern social issues which need to be addressed and for scholars to be in a position to offer direction on best practices that can be implemented in the business related to socially responsible banking.
- *Regular impact assessments*: It should conduct the impact assessment from time to time to compare the outcome of the campaign or activity carried out

relating to social responsibility with the intended impact, meaning the improvement of the lives of the community and the achievement of the sustainable development goals.

- *Advocacy and awareness campaigns:* Organize advocacy initiatives to target the shareholders and the customers, fellow workers, and the general population to spread the word on social responsibility in Islamic banking and its benefit in society.
- *Regulatory support and incentives*: Engage the relevant governmental regulatory bodies to encourage the promotion of Islamic banks' social responsibility, such as the identification of the best practice rewards and incentives.
- *Global best practices benchmarking*: Use references from benchmarking the best practices in social responsibility and sustainable finance in order to enhance the implementation of policies, processes as well as the results generated in the operations of Islamic banking.

9. Conclusion

The principle of social responsibility that is closely associated with the Islamic banking deals with the practice of Shariah standards and the positive impact created for society. This chapter has identified the following points.

First, social responsibility in Islamic banking includes ethical aspects such as partnership in profit and loss, prohibition of usury, and permissible investment in permissible business fields. It also contains the Zakat and Sadaqah as the mandatory and voluntary contributions to social welfare along with other arranged ways. Second, the historical approach points that the issue of social responsibility in the Islamic finance has centuries-old roots which originate from the early periods of Islamic civilization through the formation of Waqf institutions. These endeavors were established to promote funding to education schemes, healthcare facilities, and community enhancement programs implying a visionary concern for the economic and uplift of the nation socially.

In addition, the path for the enhancement of Islamic banking in the future is to fully incorporate these basis into the global economy. The path taken is to improve transparency and governance and other related structures in an Islamic financial institutions. Technological developments and increase of financial elaboration to take action on the similar line is also important regarding expansion of socially responsible measures. Furthermore, sustainable development can be attained through the active participation of Islamic banks that should give priority to funding projects that are friendly to his environment and should encourage good ethical standards in business. The international social responsibility committee and their cooperatives will strive for enhancing the capacity of regulatory bodies, educational institutions, and civil society organizations, thus enhancing the capacity of implementing social responsibility initiatives. The case of Islamic banking is an example where the challenge of growth does affect the centrality of social responsibility but can never eliminate it. Thus, by following these regulations, Islamic banks not only perform their religious duties but also bring a positive message to the world community regarding its initiatives in the struggle for global justice and equity and the achievement of lasting development. Therefore, social responsibility can be said not as an option but a necessity for the future of the Islamic banking. The concept of social responsibility in Islamic banking revolves around adhering to Shariah principles while actively contributing to societal welfare.

References

Aderemi, A. M. R., & Ishak, M. S. I. (2023). Qard Hasan as a feasible Islamic financial instrument for crowdfunding: Its potential and possible application for financing micro-enterprises in Malaysia. *Qualitative Research in Financial Markets*, *15*(1), 58–76.

Ahmad, Z., Muneeza, A., Rahman, M. M., & Mahomed, Z. (2023). A comparative analysis of Shariah governance framework of Islamic bank in Malaysia and Pakistan. *Talaa: Journal of Islamic Finance*, *3*(1), 01–17.

Alam, M. K., Rahman, M. M., Runy, M. K., Adedeji, B. S., & Hassan, M. F. (2022). The influences of Shariah governance mechanisms on Islamic banks performance and Shariah compliance quality. *Asian Journal of Accounting Research*, *7*(1), 2–16.

Algabry, L., Alhabshi, S. M., Soualhi, Y., & Alaeddin, O. (2020). Conceptual framework of internal Sharīʿah audit effectiveness factors in Islamic banks. *ISRA International Journal of Islamic Finance*, *12*(2), 171–193.

Alshubrumi, M. A. (2018). *Corporate social responsibility (CSR) in Islamic Banks in the light of Sharia: A comparative study of Islamic and Western perspectives in Saudi Arabia.*

Ashfaq, M., Abdelwahab, H. R., Aziz, S., & Sharif, S. (2022). Wealth creation and management in Islam. In T. Azid, M. Mukhlisin, O. Altwijry (Eds.), *Wealth management and investment in Islamic settings: Opportunities and challenges* (pp. 73–89). Springer Nature Singapore.

As Sahara, M., & Setiawan, D. (2022). The effect of ethical values on Islamic banking performance. *Corporate and Business Strategy Review*, *3*(2), 34–42.

Ayub, M., Hassan, M. K., & Saba, I. (2023). Revisiting the paradigm of Sharīʿah governance of Islamic financial institutions. *Journal of Islamic Accounting and Business Research*, *15*(8), 1245–1265. https://doi.org/10.1108/JIABR-04-2022-0110

Benaicha, M. (2020). An analysis of the normative parameters of reward and risk in Islamic finance. *ISRA International Journal of Islamic Finance*, *12*(3), 303–323.

Biancone, P., & Radwan, M. (2019). Social finance and financing social enterprises: An Islamic finance prospective. *European Journal of Islamic Finance*, (Special Issue), 1–7.

Carroll, A. B. (2021). Corporate social responsibility: Perspectives on the CSR construct's development and future. *Business & Society*, *60*(6), 1258–1278.

Caulfield, M., & Lynn, A. (2024). Federated corporate social responsibility: Constraining the responsible corporation. *Academy of Management Review*, *49*(1), 32–55.

Cortelezzi, F., & Ferrari, A. (Eds.). (2022). *Contemporary issues in Islamic law, economics and finance: A multidisciplinary approach.* Taylor & Francis.

El-Bassiouny, D., Kotb, A., Elbardan, H., & El-Bassiouny, N. (2023). To blow or not to blow the whistle? An Islamic framework. *Journal of Business Ethics*, *187*(2), 385–404.

El Melki, A., & Ben Salah Saidi, H. (2023). Ethical and socially responsible investments in the Islamic banking firms: Heart, mind, and money: Religious believes and financial decision-making in the participatory financing contracts: Charitable donation announcement effect on agents' level of effort and commitment. In N. Naifar & A. Elsayed (Eds.), *Green finance instruments, FinTech, and investment strategies: Sustainable portfolio management in the post-COVID era* (pp. 81–123). Springer International Publishing.

Eyerci, C., & Eyerci, C. (2021). Basics of Islamic economics and the prohibition of Riba. *The causes and consequences of interest theory: Analyzing interest through conventional and Islamic economics* (pp. 87–130).

Habibullah, M., Al Faruque, A., Faruque, M. O., & Atiullah, M. (2023). Islamic economic framework for the exercise of Islamic financial activities: Its conformity with Maqasid Shariah. *AL-BURHĀN: Journal of Qur'ān and Sunnah Studies*, *7*(1), 81–92.

Hanefah, M. M., Kamaruddin, M. I. H., Salleh, S., Shafii, Z., & Zakaria, N. (2020). Internal control, risk and Sharī'ah non-compliant income in Islamic financial institutions. *ISRA International Journal of Islamic Finance*, *12*(3), 401–417.

Hasan, Z. (2020). *Leading issues in Islamic economics and finance*. Springer Singapore.

Hassan, M. K., Muneeza, A., & Saraç, M. (2021). Need to redefine Islamic finance in the light of Maqasid al-Shariah. *Islamic finance and sustainable development: A sustainable economic framework for Muslim and non-Muslim countries* (pp. 11–34).

Jan, A. A., Lai, F. W., & Tahir, M. (2021). Developing an Islamic corporate governance framework to examine sustainability performance in Islamic banks and financial institutions. *Journal of Cleaner Production*, *315*, 128099.

Kandpal, V., Jaswal, A., Santibanez Gonzalez, E. D., & Agarwal, N. (Eds.) (2024). Corporate social responsibility (CSR) and ESG reporting: Redefining business in the twenty-first century. In *Sustainable energy transition: Circular economy and sustainable financing for environmental, social and governance (ESG) practices* (pp. 239–272). Springer Nature Switzerland.

Karbhari, Y., Alam, M. K., & Rahman, M. M. (2020). Relevance of the application of institutional theory in Shariah governance of Islamic banks. *PSU Research Review*, *5*(1), 1–15.

Khan, M. A. (Ed.) (2024). Justice in finance: Prohibition of riba. In *Islamic economics and human well-being* (pp. 109–132). Edward Elgar Publishing.

Khan, S. A. R., Yu, Z., Panait, M., Janjua, L. R., & Shah, A. (Eds.). (2021). *Global corporate social responsibility initiatives for reluctant businesses*. IGI Global.

Kunhibava, S., Muneeza, A., Khalid, M. B., Mustapha, Z., & Sen, T. M. (Eds.) (2024). Sadaqah, Zakat and Qard Hassan: Legal framework. In *Islamic social finance: Law and practice in Malaysia* (pp. 23–43). Springer Nature Singapore.

Laldin, M. A., Mirakho, A., Iqbal, Z., & Sadr, S. K. (2020). Ethics in the light of Maqasid Al-Shari'ah: A case study of Islamic economics and finance. *Handbook of Ethics of Islamic Economics and Finance* (pp. 21–47).

Mazurenko, V., & Vorobiova, A. (2020). New trends in Islamic finance during the transformation of the world economy. *MIND Journal*, *10*, 1–11.

Mergaliyev, A., Asutay, M., Avdukic, A., & Karbhari, Y. (2021). Higher ethical objective (Maqasid al-Shari'ah) augmented framework for Islamic banks: Assessing ethical performance and exploring its determinants. *Journal of Business Ethics*, *170*(4), 797–834.

Mohd Zain, F. A., Muhamad, S. F., Abdullah, H., Sheikh Ahmad Tajuddin, S. A. F., & Wan Abdullah, W. A. (2024). Integrating environmental, social and governance (ESG) principles with Maqasid al-Shariah: A blueprint for sustainable takaful operations. *International Journal of Islamic and Middle Eastern Finance and Management*, *17*(3), 461–484. https://doi.org/10.1108/IMEFM-11-2023-0422

Nouman, M., Siddiqi, M. F., Ullah, K., & Jan, S. (2021). Nexus between higher ethical objectives (Maqasid Al Shari'ah) and participatory finance. *Qualitative Research in Financial Markets*, *13*(2), 226–251.

Nouman, M., & Ullah, K. (Eds.) (2023). Introduction to participatory finance. In *Participatory Islamic finance: Ideals, contemporary practices, and innovations* (pp. 3–28). Springer Nature Singapore.

Nugroho, E. R. (2021). Implementation of sharia-compliance in Islamic bank product innovations. *Prophetic Law Review*, *3*(2), 173–197.

Panagopoulos, A. (2022). The establishment of a global authority and a single framework for the financial products: Labour policies and economic challenges. *International Journal of Business Administration*, *13*(2), 49–66.

Rehman, A., Ullah, I., Afridi, F. E. A., Ullah, Z., Zeeshan, M., Hussain, A., & Rahman, H. U. (2021). Adoption of green banking practices and environmental performance in Pakistan: A demonstration of structural equation modelling. *Environment, Development and Sustainability*, *23*(10), 13200–13220. https://doi.org/10.1007/s10668-020-01206-x

Sarea, A. M., Bin-Nashwan, S. A., & Elsayed, A. H. (2021). *Artificial intelligence and Islamic finance*. Routledge.

Tamanni, L., & Haji Besar, M. H. A. (2019). Profitability vs poverty alleviation: Has banking logic influences Islamic microfinance institutions?. *Asian Journal of Accounting Research*, *4*(2), 260–279.

Tok, E., & Yesuf, A. J. (2022). Embedding value-based principles in the culture of Islamic banks to enhance their sustainability, resilience, and social impact. *Sustainability*, *14*(2), 916.

Ullah, R., Ullah, S., & Saba, I. (2024). An exploratory study on the issues in weightages-based profit distribution mechanism in Islamic banking institutions: The case of Pakistan. *Journal of Islamic Marketing*, *15*(11), 2937–2958. https://doi.org/10.1108/JIMA-10-2023-0311

Chapter 5

Essentials of Corporate Governance for Islamic Banks: A Viewpoint

Hanudin Amin

Universiti Malaysia Sabah, Malaysia

Abstract

This chapter titled "Essentials of Corporate Governance for Islamic Banks: A Viewpoint" delves into the critical elements of corporate governance tailored specifically for Islamic banks. In light of the unique operational frameworks and ethical foundations that differentiate Islamic financial institutions (IFIs) from their conventional counterparts, this paper emphasizes the necessity of robust governance structures to ensure compliance with Shariah principles and global financial standards. The topics included in this chapter are sound corporate governance, differences between Islamic corporate governance and its conventional peers, the importance of sound corporate governance, and key elements enhancing corporate governance for IFIs. Besides, explanations for four fundamental pillars of corporate governance for Islamic banks are also prioritized. One may also be exposed to the Fraud Triangle Theory by Cressey (1953), which provides three interesting reasons for bribery, which are explained in this chapter. The detailed subtopics are provided in this chapter.

Keywords: *Shariah* governance; *Tawheed*; Caliph; Islamic banks; Malaysia

Islamic Finance and Corporate Governance: Synergies for Sustainable Growth, 75–93

Published under exclusive licence by Emerald Publishing Limited
doi:10.1108/978-1-83662-346-520251010

Introduction

The term corporate governance is sourced from two words, namely, corporate which means corporation, drawn from the Latin *corporate* means to establish, while governance refers to the direction of the company, learned from the Greek *gubernare* which means to steer. In its simplest form, corporate governance is a dedicated system and rules which are established to ensure the company can generate benefits for both shareholders and stakeholders, wisdom and justice in avoiding any misleading activities and illegal manners. In Islamic banks, corporate governance has a direct connection to the oneness of Allah, which is called *tawheed*, essential in every routine activity of individuals, and serves as a servant and caliph. An interesting work by Furqani and Echchabi (2022) provides an important relationship between *ibadah* and caliph based on quadrants. *Ibadah* means serving Allah by implementing his orders, allowing good actions to lead, and allowing bad actions to dim. Caliph, on the other hand, is implementing Allah Subhanahu Wa Ta'ala (SWT) commandment accordingly and seriously (Haneef, 1997). Following Furqani and Echchabi (2022), quadrants I, II, and II are considered not sufficient to balance *ibadah* and caliph, but quadrant IV is good and brilliant. At this point, one balances action and perfectly carries out the duties of *ibadah* and caliph.

According to Hassan (2014), the meaning of corporate governance is holistic, linking the goal of why the company has existed, similar to Islamic banks and how the management can bring forward the company to please the interest of shareholders and stakeholders, mainly depositors in the case of Islamic banks. In other words, corporate governance is a fiduciary role performed by the managers of Islamic banks to gain the trust of shareholders via the board of directors. As for depositors, managers gain trust by safeguarding the deposited funds and investing in secured, profitable, and safe outlets, which, in turn, can be fruitful. In turn, depositors can earn *hiba* should *the qard* contract be used and profit should *the tawarruq* contract be used. It takes into account the principle of checks and balances that needs to be practiced and adopted by these authorities to do so within the company to reduce the abuse of power and promote fair treatment between stakeholders. This chapter provides key knowledge about corporate governance with Malaysia as a point of departure. In essence, banks have developed a cogent approach to inculcate sound corporate governance for enhanced reputation at a reduced conflict of interest. The details are provided.

Quran and Corporate Governance

Verses in the *Quran* mandate corporate governance (Al-Quran, 1997). "O you who believe, stand up as a witness for Allah in all fairness, and do not let the hatred of people deviate you from justice ('adl)," for example, is explained in *Surah al-Maidah* (5:8). The closest thing to piety is to be just. This Surah gives rise to five moral tales. (1) The significance of having a fear of God; (2) the significance of justice; (3) *Al-amr bil maruf wan ahi an almunkar*; (4) equity; (5) golden rule, or regard for one another.

Regarding a Hadith, Abdullah Ibn Umar's account of the following *Hadith* best explains the necessity of corporate governance. Abdullah Ibn Umar is the son of the second Caliph Umar Ibn Khattab (RA): "Everyone of you is a shepherd and is responsible for his flock" declares the Prophet Muhammad (p.b.u.h). The people's leader is in charge of his citizens and acts as a guardian. A man is accountable to and the guardian of his family. A woman is accountable for her husband's children and his house; she is their guardian. A man's servant is accountable for and acts as a guardian of his master's belongings. Without a doubt, each of you looks after his sheep and serves as a shepherd (Sahih al-Bukhari 6719, 2024; Sahih Muslim 1829, 2024).

This *Hadith* grants us some interesting lessons, which are explained as follows:

1. Everyone is considered to be a good leader and taking care of his members to achieve Allah SWT's commandment;
2. Everyone needs to hear and follow the lead person who is responsible for his sustenance and livelihood;
3. Everyone who is a lead person should know about his accountability, and he must perform it accordingly for the benefit of all (Amin, 2018);
4. Everyone is accountable and responsible for all of his duties, which are viewed as *ibadah*, like the work by a banker at an Islamic bank, if performed Islamically, spiritual rewards will be found, and a blessing in his heart in this world and guaranteed of rewards in the hereafter (Amin, 2018);
5. Everyone who is a lead person should educate persons who are under his circle, teach them, and empower them accordingly (Amin, 2018); and
6. Everyone, a leader, and a follower should work together to ensure all actions must be good, intent must be good, where the blessings in this world can be found and final success can be found in the hereafter.

Differentiators: Islamic Corporate Governance and Its Peer

As displayed in Fig. 5.1, it is worth noting some differences that can be learned from Islamic corporate governance and its conventional peer. The details are provided as follows:

- *Worldview* – Islamic banks are established to be aligned with the Islamic worldview, which is focused on this world and the hereafter. Conventional banks, however, have been secular, where the concentration on this world is greater at the expense of the hereafter;
- *Concept* – By definition, generally, corporate governance is the relationship between the management and shareholders through improved profitability. Specifically, the concept of corporate governance for Islamic banks remains unchanged, which is static regardless of the culture and geography. In contrast, however, the concept of corporate governance for conventional banks can be changed according to the culture and geography just like in the case of HSBC Bank, a world local bank that offered Islamic banking products in Malaysia but not in the Philippines;
- *Objective* – Corporate governance for Islamic banks is based on duality, first to protect shareholders' and stakeholders' interests and second *Shariah*

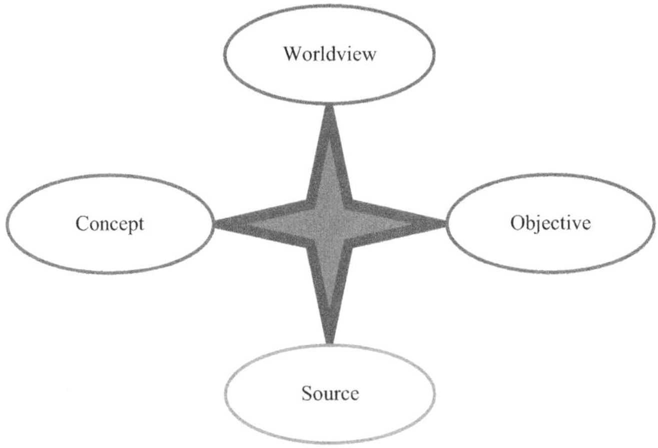

Fig. 5.1. Differentiators for Corporate Governance Between Islamic Banks and Their Conventional Peers. *Source*: Figure by author.

compliance in affairs of the corporation. In contrast, conventional banks place the protection of the rights of the shareholders and stakeholders as the objective. Unlike Islamic banks, conventional banks have no interest in *Shariah* compliance; and

- *Source* – Islamic banks place a greater interest in the primary sources when operating the banks. These include the Quran, Hadith, Ijma, and Qiyas. Human intellect is guided by these sources to govern Islamic banks. In contrast, however, conventional banks have been man-made and human intellect is not stable and can be changed whenever is needed for improvement.

The Governance Structure of Islamic Banks in Malaysia

In Malaysia, *Shariah* governance plays a greater role than corporate governance, which is important to uphold the *Shariah* compliance culture by Islamic banks in Malaysia. According to Islamic Financial Services Board (IFSB) (2009), the definition of *Shariah* governance is provided as follows:

Shariah governance refers to the set of institutional and organizational arrangements through which an IIFS ensures that there is effective independent oversight of *Shariah* compliance over each of the following structures and processes:

- Issuing pertinent *Shariah* rulings and declarations – "*Shariah* pronouncements/resolutions" are legal opinions issued by the duly mandated *Shariah* board on any topic relating to *Shariah* in Islamic finance. The national *Shariah* board or Fatwa Council, for example, are examples of central authorities that have the authority to issue such pronouncements and resolutions. As a result, the *Shariah* board at the IIFS typically focuses solely on making sure the IIFS complies with the pronouncements and resolutions issued by the central authority;

- Providing information on these *Shariah* pronouncements and resolutions to the IIFS operational staff, who keep an eye on the *Shariah* pronouncements and resolutions' daily compliance concerning all operational levels and transactions. Normally, a dedicated "internal *Shariah* compliance unit/department (ISCU)" or, at the very least, a *Shariah* compliance officer who is a member of the IIFS's compliance team, would handle such a responsibility. The IIFS will provide the ISCU with the necessary *Shariah* knowledge and compliance-monitoring abilities, for instance, by putting together a staff team with the two distinct skill sets. The ISCU's independence and separation from the departments and business units should also be guaranteed by the IIFS;
- An internal audit or review of *Shariah* compliance to confirm that *Shariah* compliance has been met; any noncompliance occurrence shall be noted, documented, and, to the extent feasible, addressed and corrected during this process. IFSB-3 states that adherence to the *Shariah* boards' declarations and resolutions must be rigorous. As a result, the internal *Shariah* review would be given to a person who has received sufficient training in *Shariah* compliance review and audit, enabling them to competently handle the procedure. The internal *Shariah* review/audit unit/department (ISRU) may be established to operate similar to the IIFS internal audit team even though the ISCU is a member of the compliance team of the organization; and
- An annual *Shariah* compliance review or audit to confirm that the internal *Shariah* compliance review or audit was properly conducted and that the *Shariah* board duly noted its findings. With feedback and reports from the ISRU, the *Shariah* board that issued the *Shariah* pronouncements/resolutions can now oversee this process. As an alternative, this work could be given to an outside *Shariah* business or auditor who is suitably qualified. The reports from the *Shariah* board or *Shariah* consulting company conducting the *Shariah* compliance review/audit must state whether the IIFS complied with *Shariah* regulations during the entire fiscal year.

Fig. 5.2 depicts the position of *Shariah* governance, which is needed to ensure Islamic banks can comply with *Shariah* principles in an effort to promote public confidence and image accordingly.

Why Do We Emphasize Shariah Governance?

- Maintaining full *Shariah*-compliant – one should learn that Islamic banks exist due to Shariah, which becomes a skeleton for the establishment of the banks;
- Strengthening stakeholders' and shareholders confidence that Islamic financial institutions (IFIs) comply with *Shariah* at all times; and
- Uphold financial stability – the existence of non-*Shariah* compliant elements would not just affect the confidence of the public in Islamic banking and finance but might also expose Islamic financial institutions to risks like fiduciary and reputational risks.

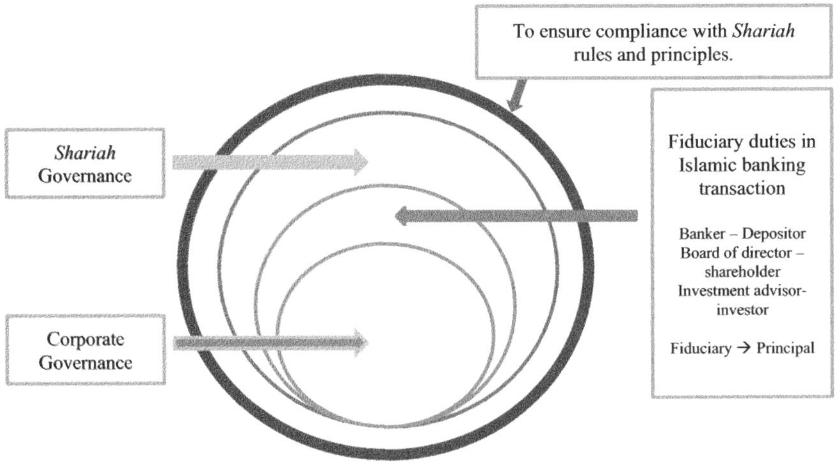

Fig. 5.2. Corporate and *Shariah* Governance. *Source*: Figure by author.

Table 5.1. Two Dominant Models of *Shariah* Governance.

Differentiator	**Centralized**	**Laissez Faire/ Self-regulation Model**
Central bank	Centralized *Shariah* advisory body	Nil
Islamic financial institutions	*Shariah* committee members	*Shariah* committee members
Example	Malaysia, Pakistan, and Indonesia	Kingdom of Saudi Arabia, Kuwait, and Bangladesh

Source: Table by author.

Following Hasan and Sabirzyanov (2015), there are two dominant models of *Shariah* governance existing in the world currently, and some descriptions of these models are found in Table 5.1.

As supported by Fig. 5.3, Malaysia has been significant in promoting *Shariah* governance seriously to the Islamic banking and finance industry. This is done to ensure that the overall Islamic financial system in Malaysia can be operated in tandem with *Shariah* principles. According to the *Shariah* Governance Framework (2010), *Shariah* principles are the foundation for the practice of Islamic finance through the observance of the tenets, conditions, and principles espoused by *Shariah*. Comprehensive compliance with *Shariah* principles would bring confidence to the general public and the financial markets in the credibility of Islamic finance operations. Unlike other Islamic banks in Muslim-majority countries, *Shariah* governance is viewed to be comprehensive and exemplary examples (Muneeza, 2013).

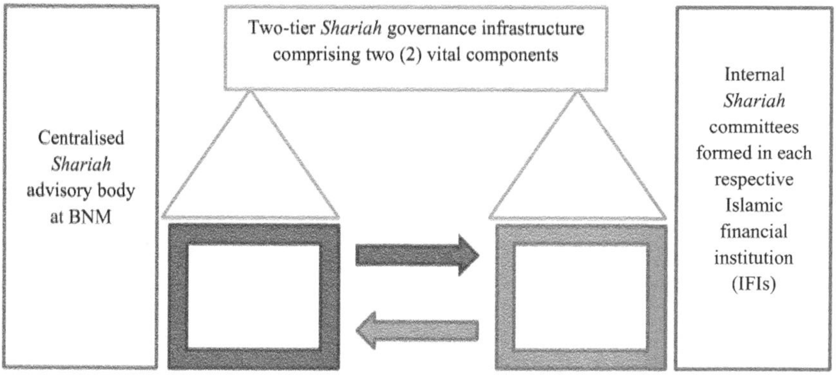

Fig. 5.3. Two-tier *Shariah* Governance. *Source*: Figure by author.

Some reasons explained but are not confined to:

- *All-inclusive regulatory framework* – Bank Negara Malaysia (BNM), the central bank, oversees Islamic financial institutions, ensuring uniformity and consistency in *Shariah* compliance. Besides, *the Shariah* Advisory Council (SAC) which was established under BNM, the SAC provides authoritative rulings on *Shariah* matters, which are binding on Islamic financial institutions in Malaysia;
- *Robust institutional supports* – There exists dedicated *Shariah* committees in which each Islamic financial institution is required to have its own *Shariah* committee to oversee compliance with Islamic principles. There is also support from specialized bodies like the IFSB and the International *Shariah* Research Academy (ISRA) for Islamic Finance provide research, guidelines, and standards for the industry;
- *Legal and regulatory clarity* – Earlier *Shariah* Governance Framework (2010) and later *Shariah* Governance Policy Document (2019): As for the latter, this framework outlines the roles and responsibilities of various stakeholders, including the board of directors, *Shariah* committee, management, and *Shariah* compliance officers. Besides *Shariah* Governance Policy Document (2019), the Islamic Financial Services Act 2013 provides a legal basis for *Shariah* compliance and governance in the financial sector;
- *Talent education* – Malaysia offers various educational programs and certifications in Islamic finance, ensuring a knowledgeable workforce. Institutions like ISRA and universities with dedicated Islamic finance programs contribute to continuous development and innovation;
- *International recognition* – Malaysia hosts numerous international conferences and seminars, positioning itself as a global hub for Islamic finance. Yet, Malaysia actively participates in AAOIFI in accounting and auditing for Islamic financial institutions in the world and IFSB; and
- *Product innovations* – Malaysian Islamic financial institutions offer a wide range of products, catering to different market needs while adhering to *Shariah*

principles along with the applications of *FinTech* in the Islamic banking and finance industry.

These factors collectively contribute to Malaysia's reputation for having one of the best *Shariah* governance frameworks in the world.

Concerning with *Shariah* Governance Framework (2010) and *Shariah* Governance Policy Document (2019), some differences are offered in this chapter for teaching and learning purposes. Table 5.2 details the differentiators.

To understand better, Table 5.3 displays some differences between corporate and *Shariah* governances.

Benefits of Sound Corporate Governance

Sound corporate governance is typically essential for Islamic banks to resolve conflicts of interest among management, the board of directors, shareholders, and other stakeholders. As displayed in Fig. 5.4, particularly, sound corporate governance offers FOUR distinct benefits:

Table 5.2. Five Differences Between Shariah Governance Framework (2010) and Shariah Governance Policy Documents (2019).

Differentiator	**The SGF**	**The SGPD**
Tenure of *Shariah* committee members	No limit	9 years
The final authority	SGF allows the IFIs to adopt their rulings than the published ruling by the NSAC	SGP allows the doing BUT JUSTIFICATIONS are needed for the doing beyond the NSAC rulings
Politically exposed person	Qualified to be a *Shariah* committee member	Not qualified to be a *Shariah* committee member
Effective communication	Marginal – lack of "engagement"	The optimum in which the SGPD mandates the board to establish effective communication with their *Shariah* committee – "engagement" is the KEY
Shariah review function	A qualified *Shariah* officer is in charge	The removal is taken place as part of the overall compliance responsibility under the "Control Function"

Source: *Shariah* Governance Framework (2010) and *Shariah* Governance Policy Document (2019).

Table 5.3. Corporate Governance Versus *Shariah* Governance.

Functions	**Common Corporate Governance**	**Additional for IFI**	**Governance**
Board of directors	*Shariah* committee	Control	Internal audit division, external auditor
Internal *Shariah* review, *Shariah* review by Shariah committee, *Shariah* audit	Compliance	Regulatory and financial compliance division	Internal *Shariah* compliance (research)
Risk management	Risk management division (credit, market, and operational risk)	*Shariah* compliance risk management	

Source: Table by author.

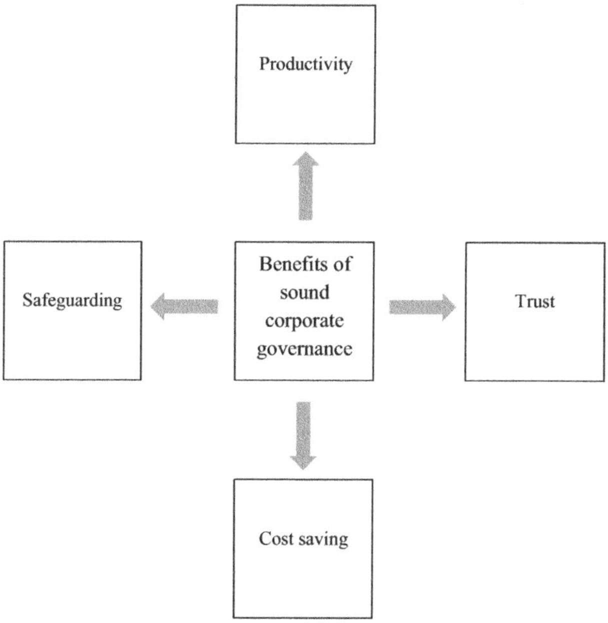

Fig. 5.4. Sound Corporate Governance Benefits. *Source*: Figure by author.

- *Safeguarding* – By implementing higher standards of openness and accountability, an Islamic bank may safeguard its investors. In addition to boosting investor confidence and safeguarding shareholders against dishonest behavior and fraud, sound corporate governance also guarantees that managers and directors are held more accountable to shareholders, ensuring the production of wealth for them;
- *Productivity* – The bank and all stakeholders will gain from the manager and the bank's goal congruence, which will increase profits and accelerate growth. Operating performance, return on equity, and share price performance are all enhanced by good corporate governance;
- *Trust* – An Islamic bank can acquire the confidence of investors, clients, and the community at large by implementing sound corporate governance procedures; and
- *Cost saving* – A bank with good corporate governance is consistently associated with a lower cost of debt capital and cost of equity capital due to extensive disclosure practices, good management quality, and a strong regulatory framework. Additionally, improved stakeholder confidence, *Shariah* compliance, full disclosure, and board oversight all contribute to better public image, enhanced investor acceptance, and improved access to capital.

Key Elements for Sound Corporate Governance

As found in Fig. 5.5, there are FOUR key elements if they are established properly; a financial institution's goal to breed profitable business tends to be greater.

- To start, Islamic banks need to make sure that the contributions made by their staff come first. To avoid favoritism, their performance and contribution must be evaluated fairly;
- Second, responsibility disclosures must be made carefully so that staff members have a channel for concerns and are counseled appropriately;
- Furthermore, a robust internal control system is in place to lessen immoral situations. The internal control system in Islamic banks is the responsibility of the board of directors, senior management, and other individuals. For example, Bank Islam has seven members who serve as leaders to satisfy the bank's business goals and objectives and achieve overall success. The term "control system" refers to a method used by banks to keep an atmosphere that promotes integrity and discourages dishonest behavior on the part of management and staff; and
- Lastly, the significance of having enough business value. For example, the fundamental principles of Bank Islam are to be a reliable organization and consistently pursue the highest standards of integrity, honesty, and responsibility – these being the cornerstones of Islamic beliefs – applied to all aspects of the bank's activities.

In summary, a crucial safeguard against outrageous behavior that damages Islamic banks' reputations and public perceptions is effective corporate governance. It is an improved level of protection for stakeholders and shareholders, who,

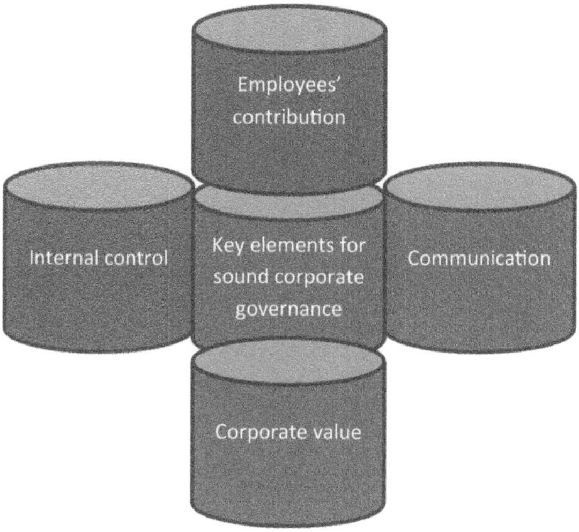

Fig. 5.5. Key Elements for Sound Corporate Governance. *Source*: Figure by author.

to preserve their social responsibilities and profit, respectively, want the bank to give them full consideration. For banks to succeed, they must, at the very least, apply improved ethical decision-making to their daily operations, where dedication and careful consideration are translated into action with fewer mistakes and fraud.

Corporate Governance Pillars

This section intends to examine four fundamental pillars of corporate governance from the context of Islamic banking. Typically, the pillars of effective corporate governance are broken down into FOUR, viz., responsibility, accountability, fairness, and transparency (see Fig. 5.6). The acronym of RAFAT meets the combination of these pillars.

Responsibility

Explained in more detail, the term responsibility is described as one's duty or obligation to deal with. This term emanates from the Latin *responsus* which means *to respond.* In the context of Islamic banking, the term is defined as a form of trustworthiness, in which one is entrusted to do something and must conduct it ethically according to Allah's will for his blessings. It is prescribed in the *Quran*. *Surah al-Anfal* (8:27) mentions "O ye who believe! betray not the trust of Allah and the Messenger, nor misappropriate knowingly things entrusted to you." The implication of this verse to Islamic banking corporate governance is that one should extend the ethical conduct in their professional duties to bridge their position, first as a servant of Allah (*abd*) and only then a role as a caliph of Allah follows.

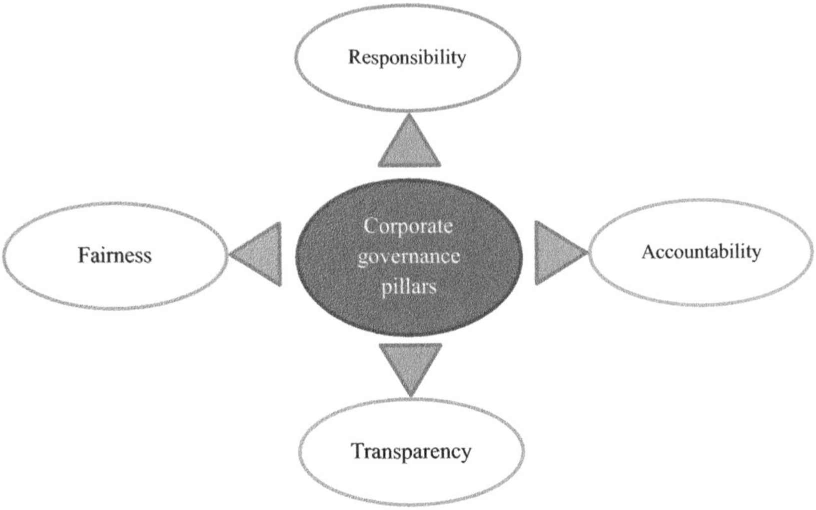

Fig. 5.6. Corporate Governance Pillars. *Source*: Figure by author.

In the case of Islamic banks, generally, the board of directors, for instance, has a great responsibility to act responsively for the benefit of all shareholders.

Accountability

In terms of accountability, by definition, it is defined as an individual who makes both decision and action on a specific financial transaction is held accountable for both of them (i.e., the decision and action). *Surah Ali Imran* (3:30) prescribes that "On the day when every soul will be confronted with all the good it has done, and all the evil it has done, it will wish there were a great distance between it and its evil. But Allah cautions you (to remember) Himself, and Allah is full of kindness to those that serve Him." This verse implies Islamic banking corporate governance. As such, one is required to be accountable for what he is doing in the banking transaction and the hereafter. In the context of Alliance Islamic, for instance, five members of the board of directors are accountable to shareholders. Some banks, however, have appointed one member from their *Shariah* committee as a member of the board of directors in the case of Alliance Islamic. Hong Leong Islamic, on the other hand, does not.

Responsibility and accountability are usually intersected. The former is overtly seen in one's behavior of doing something, while the latter is difficult to observe. In my view, responsibility is "being the owner of an obligation/task" and can be occurred before and after a task while accountability only occurs after a task is finished. For instance, one who is assigned to sell Islamic financing products to a client is "the owner of the task to sell the products alone" not others. Responsibility is pondered both times, be it before or after a transaction has taken place. Accountability, instead, occurs after the responsibility is accomplished and brings consequences, whether good or bad. For instance, one is answerable for the mistake of selling the product to an unqualified customer which leads to acute losses to the bank. In other words, he takes the consequences in full. On balance, the two are interrelated although there exists a discrepancy.

Fairness

To practice effective corporate governance, Islamic banks are urged to promote fairness in their dealings. Fairness is defined as being impartial and just behavior without "favouritism" and "discrimination." In the Islamic banking context, however, the rights of various stakeholders are protected, recognized, and valued. For example, minority shareholder interests must obtain identical deliberation to those of the dominant shareholders. Bank Muamalat, for example, has shareholders that consist of DRB-HICOM, which holds 70% of shares in the Bank, while Khazanah Nasional Berhad holds the remaining shares. This means, somewhat, that the former is the dominant shareholder, while the latter is a minority shareholder. The importance of this pillar is told in the *Quran*. *Surah An-Nisa* (4:58) mentions that "Allah doth command you to render back your trusts to those to whom they are due; and when ye judge between man and man, that ye judge with justice: Verily how excellent is the teaching which He giveth you! For Allah is He Who heareth and seeth all things."

Transparency

The last pillar is transparency which is related to information disclosure. The higher the extent of information disclosure, the better the bank's corporate image is. It is also defined as a degree of how decent the bank is at constructing important information accessible to outsiders not only in terms of audited data but also unaudited data. The *Quran* provides evidence of the importance of this pillar. This is related to *Surah al-Baqarah* (2:282) in which we can summarize at least two important lessons, namely, (1) the significance of recording and recognition of any transactions between different parties for security and future references and (2) recording any transaction for future disclosure is taught by Allah SWT for improved justice between the transacting parties relevant. As such, the bank is urged to disclose information concerning its business policy, activities, and the protection of the environment where integrity acts as a key for enhanced disclosures.

Taken as a set, these fundamental pillars are a key ingredient for the successful corporate governance practice of Islamic banks in Malaysia. The said pillars are of utmost importance to put together into practice by management and board of directors of Islamic banks for the well-being and sustainability of the banks where enhanced performance comes into play.

Weak Corporate Governance Can Lead to Graft?

The graft is one of the unethical practices that occur universally. By definition, unethical practices are actions that fall outside of what is considered morally right among individuals in both the public and private sectors. According to the Malaysian anticorruption commission, graft is a reward for some individuals who are performing illegal behaviors beyond routine and formal duties. Individuals may earn bribes in the form of financial incentives like bonuses and nonfinancial incentives like votes and women. For example, Ali presents a watch to a banker of XYZ Bank for approving the financing to a company owned by Ali. There are a total of 1,137 cases occurred pertinent to corruption cases in 2023, Malaysia (Suruhanjaya Pencegahan Rasuah Malaysia, 2024). These cases are recurring issues in nature that flow down from one generation to another at the expense of public confidence and trust. Indeed, owing to its subjectivity, it is somehow difficult to detect how and why bribery occur. It is only explicitly learned when a third party makes a report to the authority. Likewise, I consider graft in the banking industry.

To be specific, corruption presented in Fig. 5.7 refers to bribery. One must acknowledge that bribery or *risywah* is *haram* by rulings and cannot exist in our society, as the implication that it can bring forward is nothing but negative. When one party has a favor for something, he tends to give a bribe to get the goal in although we believe and see it is wrong and not acceptable. However, there are exemptions when one faces uncertainties due to the inability to get a compromise from responsible parties associated with certain duties. Giving a bribe should be no other means to obtain your rights or ward off the very acute and growing harm from yourself. In this case, however, it is *haram* for the one who takes it but not the giver. For instance, a father bribes an evildoer so that he could take her daughter back from being harmed or raped provided it is the only way out. In other words, it is *darurah*. As such, the evildoer earns the sin, not the father. The giver is not sinful, but the taker will be (it is because the taker steals the giver's right).

The interdiction for bribery in Islam is enunciated by the *Quran* as prescribed in the *Surah al-Baqarah* verse 188 in that it states "…and do not consume one another's wealth unjustly or send it (in bribery) to the rulers so that (they might aid)

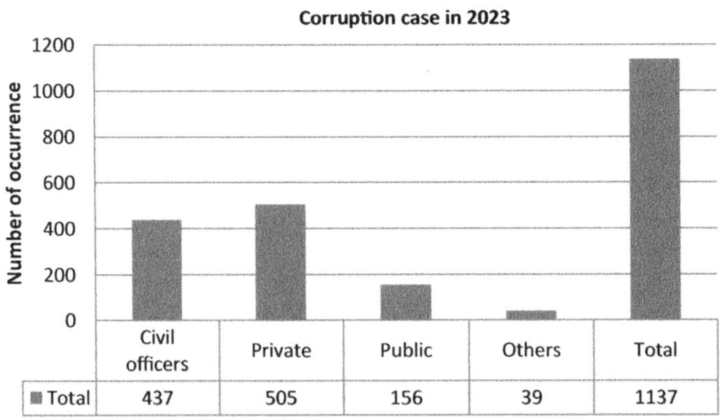

Fig. 5.7. Corruption Cases in 2023. *Source*: Suruhanjaya Pencegahan Rasuah Malaysia (2024).

you to consume a portion of the wealth of the people in sin, while you know it is unlawful." Surely, three lessons found but are not limited to:

- First, the act of compliance toward Islamic principles is of the essence in the appearance of any form of business transactions, where mutual consent matters;
- Second, bribery is a method that ingests others' wealth unfairly upsurges the likelihood of hostility at the expense of brotherhood; and
- Third, bribery introduces vagueness in which one in any way performs certain behaviors should a financial incentive be given than that of the accomplishment of a trust.

In our contemporary society, however, bribery is a recurring issue. The reasons are at least threefold. First, the lack of just enforcement to scrutinize and indict corrupt officials. Second, the discrimination and favoritism that exist among quarters involved. Third, there exists a lack of integrity and faith among employees in both public and private sectors.

Theoretically, Cressey (1953) introduced three reasons leading one individual to commit fraud/corruption, namely pressure, opportunity, and rationalization (see Fig. 5.8). In terms of pressure, one may have pressure in terms of financial or heavy workloads. In the case of financial stress, one faces a high amount of indebtedness due to a lavish lifestyle and also due to heavy financial commitments out of a huge number of children and wives. Individuals who commit bribery are due to low paid salary when compared to the workloads that they must do everyone. In terms of opportunity, when there is weakest internal control, bureaucracy, no monitoring, no job isolation, and the use of wide discretion can lead to bribery. For instance, due to a huge amount of red tape, one dealing tends to be slower and this opens a new door for customers who need speedy approval to offer bribery. The same thing occurs when the procedures are multiple, leading the officials to provide "assistance" in return for a kickback. Besides, rationalization is also the reason. One who makes the bribe will not see himself as a criminal.

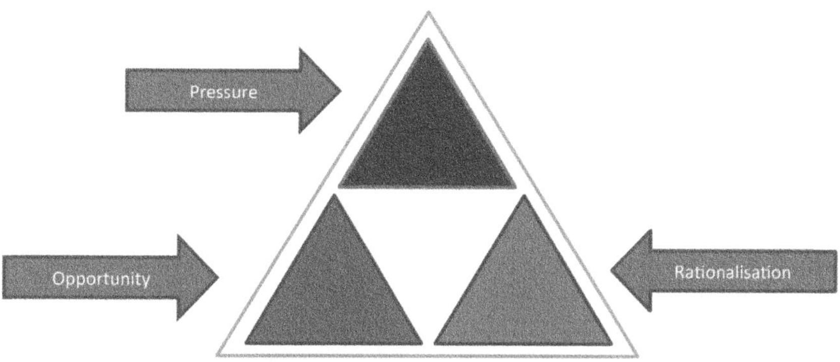

Fig. 5.8. The Fraud Triangle (Causes for Bribery: Pressure, Opportunity, and Rationalization). *Source*: Cressey (1953).

He views himself as honest and is trapped by a false situation, making bribery occur. This is also related to subjective norms. For instance, my boss took a bribe, and so did me. I need to help those in need by taking a sum of bribery, from the giver.

There can be no bribery should individuals be truthful, impartial, and dedicated in all fairness of their works or duties by upholding the golden rule for improved camaraderie and mutual respect. In a country like Malaysia, bribery is of two sides should it happen. One is known as a bribe-giver, and second is known as a bribe-taker. Both are equally responsible for bribery and are cursed in Islam. A *hadith* as narrated by Abdullah ibn Amr, "the Prophet Muhammad (p.b.u.h) cursed the one who offers (bribe-giver) bribe and the one who accepts it (bribe-taker)," concur it. Whenever possible, the act of bribery should be evaded.

Bribery is pervasive and deceptive. There are some problems sprung from bribery that could disrupt officials' responsibility and accountability from both sectors.

- First, bribery leads to a double standard wherein undeserving persons are given chances while deserving ones are not;
- Second, bribery leads to the increasing spirit of gluttony pervades society in place of the spirit of accountability. One only works when connected to a bribe but not when it is disconnected;
- Third, bribery spoils incentives among contractors to compete on quality work and business acumen to obtain a contract from the government; and
- Fourth, the investment potential is debilitated and the loss of confidence among investors due to their expectation that bribery creates an extra cost to make their investment fail and inefficient.

Consider, too, should bribery is a norm and everyone engages in it, what will happen to our country? What happens to those who are upholding ethical behaviors in business or at university? Without any corrective measure, bribery makes a clean person weaker and a corrupt person stronger. At its worst, the corrupt person becomes a leader, while the clean one becomes a follower. When this happens, people can completely separate themselves from the spirit of brotherhood. All in all, education with a soul is the key in confronting bribery to promote certainty in doing ethical practices at reduced uncertainties derived from it in every aspect of work done.

One should acknowledge that taking other wealth bribery is considered to be a lustful act and defined to be wrong in any form. A person who has a position like a judge, who controls other faiths through bribery, can harm the harmony of society and civilization. Our assertion here is in tandem with Al-Qaraḍāwī (1984) who argued taking a bribe is *haram* and there is no place for bribery in our society. It is clearly understood that bribe-taking is condemned by the Almighty as prescribed in the *Quran*. Allah SWT reminded us pertinent to the right way to acquire wealth where no stealing of other wealth like in the case of bribery which is considered to be *haram*. See *Surah al-Baqarah* (2:188). This verse suggests that a proliferation of graft in a society leads to corruption and oppression, where the value of brotherhood is eroded. It is worth noting that accepting and taking a bribe can tarnish the employees' morale and productivity. Doing such immoral behavior makes them the lowest of the lowest – disturbing the reputation and performance of the company they work for. The Prophet Muhammad (S.A.W.) reminds us about the negative sources of bribery. The Almighty curse parties involved in graft and the behavior have no good in Allah SWT and so do we. Small or big, bribery is not only a source of income for good people but also for bad ones.

To uphold the prohibition of graft, six Islamic remedies provided but are not limited to:

- Upholding *taqwa* mechanism – the term *taqwa* means Allah-fearing. This mechanism is more powerful than the government regulatory framework. The reason is twofold. First, a person's realization that Allah knows the manifest and the hidden and will hold all accountable for their deeds. Second, an improved sense of brotherhood where one helps another in good things as prescribed in the *Quran* (5:2);
- Creating an Islamic working environment – Islamic banks should develop an Islamic working environment to mollify the multiplicity of needs of various stakeholders. This may include the importance of work as an *ibadah* for better relationships with fellow *Muslims* and Allah – the former is *habluminannas* and the latter is *habluminallah*. Everybody should be treated equally with dignity no matter what their circumstances, ethnicity, and color, inter alia. It captures the true notion of treating individuals with respect according to Islam protects them from discrimination and racism;
- Friday gathering – In a bank, it thinks that perhaps at least one assembly is conducted to gather all employees, whereas a *tazkirah is* conducted by the top management that allows a better flow of ethics to all layers of employees for better practice on Islamic ethics. This gathering creates a sense of belonging to employees for enhanced ethical attitudes among them;
- Engaging all in decision-making – It is important to put *musyawarah* first as an important means to get approval from all staff regarding a particular issue that needs a succinct decision. Everyone is allowed to speak freely within a controlled parameter to gain access to one's opinion of a particular issue for an improved resolution;
- Establishing cogent Islamic ethical principles – The underlying philosophy of doing this is to eliminate any chance of corruption through the closure of any weakest point found in a company or a person by making Islamic ethical culture a priority. This principle focuses on changing the game rule by directing one's behavior to follow *Shariah* and avoiding misconduct. Collaboration and cooperation by employees, top management, and stakeholders related to performing their roles along with Islamic ethical principles are then essential; and
- Instituting Islamic talent program – Employees of Islamic banks are having discrepancies in terms of knowledge, ability, and acumen. Some officers perform well, while some are not. The imbalance is likely to create five soul diseases (i.e., self-admiration, anger, prejudice, envy, and pretending virtuousness) among the parties involved. To address this issue, knowledge transfer through

a know-how approach should be established to promote prosocial behavior. Well-performed individuals tend to extend their hand to improve others' performance. Thus, the giver and the taker build a valuable mutual respect that produces a well and harmonious culture in an organization.

Importantly, graft is a serious challenge for banks since it lessens business credibility and profits when bankers abuse their positions for personal gain. Public confidence will be tarnished out of customers lose respect, requiring banks to spend time and resources to regain the confidence to reassure customers the bank is still doable. In all, the Islamic remedies introduced should be extended to both parties – Islamic banks and their customers. With a proper plan, the remedies offer an effective directive to discourage corrupt behavior for better and more secure banking dealings, at least.

Conclusion

To sum up, the fundamentals of corporate governance for Islamic banks are key to guaranteeing that these financial establishments follow *Shariah* while upholding accountability, ethics, and openness. Islamic finance's distinct framework demands a customized governance approach that not only satisfies legal requirements but also adheres to Islamic moral and ethical principles. Robust *Shariah* governance, comprising a *Shariah* board specifically designated for that purpose, extensive *Shariah* compliance systems, and ongoing monitoring and auditing procedures, is necessary for Islamic banks to have effective corporate governance. By ensuring that all financial operations strictly adhere to Islamic law, these components promote trust among interested parties and the larger Muslim community.

Furthermore, to preserve the values of justice, equity, and social responsibility that are fundamental to Islamic banking, Islamic banks must place a high priority on stakeholder participation and moral decision-making. Islamic banks can set themselves apart from conventional banks and further the socioeconomic advancement of the communities they serve by incorporating these concepts into their corporate governance systems. In all, Islamic banks' ability to develop and survive as well as play a part in advancing ethical banking and economic justice all depend on their adoption and application of strong corporate governance procedures. To handle new possibilities and problems in the global financial landscape as the industry develops, governance standards and processes must be continuously improved.

References

Al-Qaraḍāwī, Y. (1984). *The lawful and the prohibited in Islam: Al-Halal Wal-haram Fil Islam*. International Islamic Federation of Student Organizations.

Al-Quran. (1997). *English translation of the meaning of al-Quran, translated from Arabic by Muhammad Farooq-i-Azam Malik Houston*. The Institute of Islamic Knowledge.

Amin, H. (2018). *Islamic approach in leadership*. Retrieved July 20, 2024, from https://www.nst.com.my/opinion/letters/2018/03/343534/islamic-approach-leadership

Cressey, D. R. (1953). *Other people's money: A study in the social psychology of embezzlement*. The Free Press.

Furqani, H., & Echchabi, A. (2022). Who is homo Islamicus? A Qur'ānic perspective on the economic agent in Islamic economics. *ISRA International Journal of Islamic Finance*, *14*(2), 206–220.

Haneef, M. A. M. (1997). Islam, the Islamic worldview, and Islamic economics. *IIUM Journal of Economics and Management*, *5*(1), 39–65.

Hasan, A., & Sabirzyanov, R. (2015). Optimal *Shari'ah* governance model in Islamic finance regulation. *International Journal of Education and Research*, *3*(4), 243–258.

Hassan, R. (2014). *Corporate governance practice in Islamic financial institutions*. IBFIM.

Islamic Financial Services Board. (2009). *Guiding principles on Shariah governance systems for institutions offering Islamic financial services*. Kuala Lumpur.

Muneeza, A. (2013). *Corporate governance of Islamic Banks in Malaysia*. A.S. Noordeen.

Sahih al-Bukhari 6719. (2024, July 1) https://sunnah.com/bukhari:6719

Sahih Muslim 1829. (2024, July 1). https://sunnah.com/muslim:1829a

Shariah Governance Framework. (2010). *Shariah governance framework*. Bank Negara Malaysia.

Shariah Governance Policy Document. (2019). *Shariah governance policy document*. Bank Negara Malaysia.

Suruhanjaya Pencegahan Rasuah Malaysia. (2024, July 20). *Corruption cases in 2023*. https://www.sprm.gov.my/index.php?id=21&page_id=120&year=2023

Chapter 6

Corporate Governance in Islamic Banks: Concepts and Cases from the Islamic Banking Industry of Pakistan

Imam Uddin[a], *Muhammad Faisal Sultan*[b] *and Muhammad Asim Rafiq*[c]

[a]*Institute of Business Management, Pakistan*
[b]*Khadim Ali Shah Bukhari Institute of Technology (KASBIT), Pakistan*
[c]*National University of Modern Languages (NUML), Pakistan*

Abstract

This chapter is specifically developed to make readers understand the corporate governance practices in Islamic Banks. Studies indicated that there is no difference in the purpose of corporate governance for Islamic and Conventional Banks. However, there is a substantial difference in the corporate governance structure for Islamic Banks compared to their counterparts. However, a lack of research and understanding of corporate governance practices in the Islamic banking industry is evident. Hence, there is a need for more studies and a thorough focus on research to develop better mechanisms required for corporate governance for Islamic Banks. Therefore, this chapter is written specifically regarding the elements of corporate governance of Islamic Banks. Moreover, the prime focus is to relate the elements of corporate governance with the banking industry of Asia and the Islamic banking industry of Pakistan. Thus, the overall significance of this study has multiple folds associated with better understanding and comprehensive research work but also for better policy-making for the governance mechanisms of Islamic Banks.

Keywords: Corporate governance; Islamic Banks; Islamic banking; structure of corporate governance, Asia & Pakistan

Islamic Finance and Corporate Governance: Synergies for Sustainable Growth, 95–105

doi:10.1108/978-1-83662-346-520251012

1. Introduction

The major difference between Islamic and Commercial Banks is Fiqah al-Muamalat, that is, commonly known as Sharia. Hence, the basic principle of Islamic banking is the sharing of profit and loss along with the prohibition of interest. However, a bank that is involved in Islamic banking must obey all the regulations that are imposed on Conventional Banks as well as those that are about Islamic Banks. Hence, Islamic Bank can only offer those products and services that fall under the principles of Islam and the rules of the Sharia Board. Hence, every Islamic Bank has its own Sharia Board to assess the products and services and transactions that they are conducting for business activities. Therefore, an efficient mechanism of corporate governance is required in Islamic Banks to ensure the quality of voluntary disclosure and to increase performance (Ghayad, 2008). On the other hand, in initial studies by Ahmed and Chapra (2002), Corporate Governance is defined as the set of relationships between the company, its management, board, shareholders, and stakeholders. The major objective of Corporate Governance is to assure equality for all stakeholders by assuring a high level of accountability and transparency. Therefore, it is legitimate to mark Corporate Governance as the structure that relates the board of directors with an entire list of stakeholders including shareholders, managers, employees, suppliers, and customers. Hence, corporate governance has a massive tendency to improve the financial performance of the banks. Agency theory is the most reliable theory that explains the entrepreneurial efforts of the firm and its association with the financial performance of the bank (Aslam & Haron, 2020). On the other hand, companies operating in different countries are required to follow different codes of corporate governance, for example, companies operating in the UK follow a combined code of corporate governance, and companies working in the USA need to follow the Sarban Oxley Act. In fact, in Pakistan, companies are required to follow the code of corporate governance formulated by the Security Exchange Commission of Pakistan (Qureshi & Qurashi, 2013).

1.1. Theoretical Framework

The use of agency theory is best for explaining the relationship between structures of corporate governance in banks. Theory entails the development of an efficient structure of corporate governance that not only enforces entrepreneurial behavior within the firm but also controls conflicts and diminishes agency costs (Aslam & Haron, 2020).

1.2. Research Gap

Tremendous growth in Islamic banking in comparison to their counterparts is the prime reason for the interest and concern of researchers in issues and threats prevailing in the sector (Safiullah & Shamsuddin, 2018). However, Islamic Banks are found to be in legitimate need of effective corporate governance mechanisms. This need is not only to protect stakeholders but also to make people realize that Islam is the best-suited religion. The point is valid as if the performance of Islamic Banks drops people may feel that religion cannot be associated with the modern world requirements, etc. Therefore, the structure of corporate governance in Islamic Banks is not the same as the other forms of organizations (Ahmed, 2017). However, there is much to explore in Islamic banking and also about the mechanism of corporate governance associated with Islamic banking. Hence, it is imperative to understand the mechanism of corporate governance in Islamic banking in which some of the elements, for example, Sharia Boards, are not been discussed nicely (Abdullah Saif Alnasser & Muhammed, 2012). Some of the studies also mentioned that the practices of corporate governance are found to be on the lower side in Islamic Banks. Responsibility for lacking in the quality of corporate governance of Islamic Banks lies in inexperienced boards, political interventions, anomalies in information, and inadequate disclosure (Ahmed, 2017). Research emphasized on the analysis of factors that are responsible for the increased financial performance of Islamic Banks. Similar is true for Islamic and Asian countries (Tarmizi et al., 2023). Studies further claimed that Islamic Banks are also required to disclose their characteristics of corporate governance to stakeholders. Therefore, the purpose of this study is to describe in detail the components and structure of Islamic Banks operating in Islamic countries (Srairi, 2015). Thus, this study not only is beneficial for academicians and students but also has significance for customers, researchers, and analysts to understand the importance of every element associated with the corporate governance of Islamic Banks.

2. Literature Review

Islamic banking is the top financial sector of the global financial industry, prevailing at almost 12.5% annually. Moreover, past years also proved that the Islamic banking industry is efficient, maintains a strong and better quality of assets, and optimizes its reputation, which causes lower loan default rates. However, the overall mechanism of governance for Islamic and Conventional Banks is similar which is implemented to protect shareholders (Aslam & Haron, 2020). Although we must not take the overall structure of conventional and Islamic Banks as the same the number of stakeholders involved with Islamic Banks is much higher as compared to the misunderstanding of their counterparts (Grassa & Matoussi, 2014). In short, Islamic corporate governance follows all the elements of good corporate governance along with compliance of moral and social values highlighted by sharia law (Tarmizi et al., 2023).

Studies reflected that five major areas create more threats for Islamic Banks and make the mechanism of governance differentiated as compared to their counterparts. These areas include compliance with Sharia law for every activity, the existence of investment accounts, and lesser transparency and weaker market forces supplemented with chances of government misunderstanding (Grassa & Matoussi, 2014). Sharia law is the major point of governance in Islamic Banks as Sharia is not only used to check transactional structure but also the presence of elements that may damage or harm the nature of earning. Hence, sharia is also associated with the form of businesses (Ahmed, 2017). Hence, the investigation has been made to understand the effective structure and components of corporate governance. Analysis revealed some of the necessary elements that must be included in the structure of corporate governance to ensure accountability, efficiency, and a firm's performance. These elements include board size, nonexecutive directors, CEO duality, Sharia committee, and audit committee (Aslam & Haron, 2020). The upcoming literature will discuss in detail all the elements that are required to be used in the effective structure of corporate governance.

2.1. Board Size

The board of directors is required to provide strategic direction to the institutions and assess the institution's progress toward its strategic objectives (Haris et al., 2019). Board size is one of the major components of corporate governance. In developing countries, the large size of the board is beneficial for protecting the rights of shareholders. This point is especially important to protect the rights of minority shareholders, and it is also vividly associated with the resource dependency theory which highlights the importance of firm resources in maintaining transparency, accountability, and fostering a firm's performance (Haider et al., 2015). Studies also claim that an increase in the size of the board is a valuable addition to the structure of corporate governance. The postulate is effective as the addition of board members might also bring broader knowledge which ultimately helps the bank in attaining strategic objectives (Haris et al., 2019). Previous studies have also found to be in favor of larger boards as the increase in the size of the board is directly proportional to the voluntary disclosure of information in the annual reports. Similar is valid for Islamic Corporate Governance where the probability of quality in disclosure might be increased with the increase in board members. The reason behind the postulate is the diversity in knowledge and expertise of board members which may result in better disclosure of information in the annual reports (Grassa et al., 2018). However, some studies pointed otherwise, for example, Yermack (1996), which highlighted that a smaller size of the board has a more significant impact on the firm's performance.

Moreover, some of the studies, for example, Holthausen and Larcker (1996), highlighted a lack of evidence to believe any firm association between board sizes and firm's performance. Studies on board size on bank performance, that is, Haris et al. (2019), also highlighted that some of the studies, for example, Titova (2016) and Yeung (2018), indicated a nonlinear relationship between board size and the performance of the bank. Thus, it is optimal to highlight that the addition of too many directors to the board might result in the decline of the bank's performance. This may happen due to the problems associated with communication and coordination which affect the decision-making negatively (Haris et al., 2019). Although relating the board size, concerning the corporate governance of Islamic Banks studies, for example, Hassan et al. (2017), indicated that there is a negative association between the board size of Islamic Banks in Pakistan and banks financial performance. Therefore, the study recommended that the board size must be adequate and the board must include members with higher knowledge and expertise in the relevant field. Studies also provide reasons for the negative association between board size and firm performance and indicate that an increase in board size creates a negative impact on the firm performance. Especially, studies conducted in countries like Pakistan may find negative associations due to the cost of larger boards. However, board size doesn't need to always have a negative association with the financial indicators of firm performance for Islamic Banks (Haider et al., 2015). Although the analysis indicated that the size of the board is negatively correlated with the performance of Islamic Banks, Mansoor et al. (2019) also indicated that an increase in the size of board members is negatively associated with the long-term credit ranking of Islamic Banks from Pakistan.

2.2. Sharia Board

Islamic Banks are also required to follow the instructions and requirements of the Sharia Board. Hence, compliance with the Sharia Board is one of the major components of Islamic Banks. The report of the Sharia Board reflects the compliance rate of Islamic Banks with the laws and principles of the Sharia. Hence, a larger size of Sharia Boards is required to show conformance with the standards (Grassa et al., 2018). A similar is found true for Islamic Banks from Pakistan where the Sharia Board is found to be positively correlated with the financial performance of Islamic Banks. The study further indicated that the performance of the bank relies on the advice and recommendations of the Sharia committee (Hassan et al., 2017). Similarly, the presence of a Sharia Board as well as the skills, abilities, and knowledge of Sharia Board members is found to be positively correlated with the long-term credit ranking of Islamic Banks from Pakistan. Studies further revealed the presence of Sharia Board members in different countries also has a positive impact on vigilance. Thus, ultimately affects the long-term credit ranking of Islamic Banks positively (Mansoor et al., 2019).

2.3. CEO Duality

CEO duality is one of the important components associated with the governance of Islamic Banks (Grassa et al., 2018). Studies indicated that there is no bounding that the CEO of the company cannot serve as the chairman of the board (ur Rehmans & Mangla, 2010). The duality of the CEO tends to increase the board's knowledge about the operations and activities of Islamic Bank which may cause improved disclosure of information in annual reports. A similar has been highlighted by the stakeholder-agency theory that CEO duality leads the CEO toward a better understanding of the information required by stakeholders. Therefore, it is legitimate to predict that CEO duality is an effective tool to reduce asymmetrical information and increase voluntary disclosure of product and service information (Grassa et al., 2018). However, dual roles of the CEO may cause an increase in agency cost as CEO duality as the chairman of the board may cause a conflict of interest which ultimately decreases the quality of disclosure. However, it is still not clear and inconclusive through the evidence from past literature as the similarity of decision management and decision control may reduce board effectiveness in controlling the top management (ur Rehman & Mangla, 2010).

2.4. CEO Tenure

The duality of the CEO is found to have positively correlated with the voluntary disclosure of information by Islamic Banks. However, studies claim the increase in the tenure of the CEO causes an entrenchment effect. The postulate is legitimate as CEO tenure leads to lower quality of information disclosure in the annual reports. Therefore, prior studies also claim that an increase in the length of a CEO's tenure decreases the quality of voluntary disclosure of information. Hence, CEO with longer tenure tends to restrict voluntary disclosure of information in annual reports. This restriction is to make condensed information specifically available to the prime stakeholders of the Islamic Bank. Hence, it is legitimate to believe that there is a negative association between CEO duality and voluntary disclosure of information (Grassa et al., 2018).

2.5. Nonexecutive Directors

Every board includes different types of directors to ensure the quality of disclosure and transparency. Studies conducted in different parts of the world highlighted that the presence of nonexecutive directors affects financial performance (Ahmed, 2017) by improving the return of assets (RoA) and return on equity (RoE) (Awan, 2012). A similar is also found true for the firms in India that corporate governance is beneficial for a firm's performance (Jackling & Johl, 2009). However, a study conducted by Haris et al. (2019) about corporate governance in banks from Pakistan indicated that the relationship between the inclusion of nonexecutive directors and bank performance is not clear yet. The study indicated that there are multiple studies, for example, Bukair and Rahman (2015) and Ofoeda (2017), which highlighted the negative association between the presence of nonexecutive directors on the board of the bank and its performance. Similarly, Mayur and Saravanan (2017) and Nawaz (2017) found no association between the presence of nonexecutive directors on the board of the bank and its performance. Last but not least, studies, for example, De Andres and Vallelado (2008), found a U-shaped nonlinear relationship between the nonexecutive directors and the bank's performance.

2.6. Independent Directors

Several studies have been conducted to understand the relationship between the inclusion of independent directors and the performance of the firm (O'connell & Cramer, 2010). The inclusion of independent directors is effective for optimized monitoring which, in turn, affects the bank's performance and profitability positively (Haris et al., 2019). Evidence indicated that there is a significant and direct association between the independence of the board and firm performance (O'connell & Cramer, 2010). Some of the studies also mentioned that board independence is based on the inclusion of outside directors. The presence of outside directors is critically important for emerging markets which are subjected to external shocks. Hence, the board must use the expertise of outside directors to leverage the firm with effective decision-making during crises (Choi & Wong, 2007). However, some of the studies also mentioned that independent directors are found to be involved in the long-term growth of the institution. Hence, the behavior is quite different as compared to the executive members who are willing to improve the company's performance in short-run. Similar has also been reflected through stewardship theory that independent directors are willing to attain their benefits which affect firm performance positively in the long run. Similar has also been reflected through agency theory that the inclusion of more executive directors leads to an increase in concentrated decision-making. Thus, produces significant over the firm performance (Musleh Alsartawi, 2019). Liang et al. (2013) also voted in the favor of inclusion of independent directors. The study mentioned the inclusion of independent directors as the prime theme of corporate governance. However, some of the studies like Hermalin and Weisbach (1991) do not highlight any significant relationship between the board's independence and the performance of the firm. Similarly, Rosenstein and Wyatt (1990) reflected that there is no relationship and Agarwal and Knoeber (1996) predict negative association.

2.7. Board Ownership

Agency theory indicates that the board must include foreign directors to foster creativity and diversity. Thus, creates a positive impact on the financial performance of the bank. However, the literature also indicated some of the points associated with board ownership that may overshadow the importance and need of foreign directors. The literature claims that it is very difficult for foreign directors to attend the board meetings which creates negative impact over decision-making and reduces the performance of the bank (Haris et al., 2019). Similar indications were found from the performance of Chinese Banks where the inclusion of foreign directors reduces the RoA and RoE (Liang et al., 2013).

2.8. Board Meetings

Board meetings are also termed as an important tool for increasing monitoring and sustainability. Studies termed this tool as the prime factor for reducing agency costs and for increasing the effectiveness of corporate governance. Agency theory also supports the increase in the conduction of board meetings for the optimization of supervision, control, and effective corporate governance (Haris et al., 2019). Most of the studies indicated a positive relationship between board meetings and firm performance, for example, Haß et al. (2016). Increase in board meetings also found to be positively correlated with the performance of banks in Pakistan. However, there is still lot to be explored with reference to the board meetings and impact of corporate governance on bank's performance in Pakistan (Haris et al., 2019). However, Musleh Alsartawi (2019) highlighted that inclusion of independent directors may also cause delays in decision-making. The postulate looks optimal that carrying more and more independent directors will waste time in protocols and understanding of matters about the firm. Hence, most of the meetings will not cause any benefits to the firm. Therefore, there are some studies concerning other parts of the world, for example, Farag et al. (2018) and Liang et al. (2013), which highlighted negative impact of increase in board meetings on the firm's performance. Relating the impact of Islamic Corporate Governance Practices with the scenario of Pakistan it has been revealed by Haider et al. (2015) increase in a number of meetings in Islamic Banks of Pakistan produced a negative impact over the financial indicators of banks performance.

3. Methodology

The purpose of writing this study is descriptive in nature as this study is developed to make readers analyze the elements that are critical for the optimization of corporate governance practices of Islamic Banks. Hence in line with Sekaran and Bougie (2016), it is one of the descriptive studies that have been done in cross-sectional time horizon with minimal researcher's interference. However, the philosophy of the research is epistemology as the study is developed to increase and foster level of knowledge through providing details of all the elements of corporate governance that are essential for enhancing the bank performance. Therefore, according to Saunders et al. (2007) and Saunders et al. (2015), epistemology is the philosophy of research, and deductive is the research approach; mono-method is the choice and archival is the research strategy.

4. Implications from Pakistan

4.1. Origin of Islamic Banking in Pakistan

Past indicated that banking sector in Pakistan has gone through phenomenal changes. However, most of the market share belongs to state-owned banks. The postulate is valid as in 1972 most of the commercial banks except foreign banks were nationalized. Although due to continuous decline in the performance of banking sector of Pakistan stat Bank of Pakistan came into action.

Hence, in 1990, state bank rate revolutionized action and allowed 10 new private banks to enter into Pakistan's banking industry. At the same time, the privatization of Habib Bank Limited, Allied Bank Limited, and Muslim Commercial Bank Limited also took place which ultimately changed the market structure and holding of market share. In addition to this, state-owned banks from Pakistan have also gone through structural changes, and due to restructuring and downsizing in the year 1997, the structure of Corporate Governances of Pakistan has been revolutionized with mergers and acquisitions. A new policy from the State Bank of Pakistan also supported mergers and acquisitions of small and struggling banks with stronger entities and foreign banks. Hence during the span of five years from 2000 to 2005, the scale of mergers and acquisitions was found to be much higher as 12 banks were found to be merged and 9 of the foreign banks were taken by private banks. During this period, Islamic banking was also launched by local and foreign banks. Islamic banking gained mass popularity in Pakistan and within a brief slice of time the industry attains growth of 6.1% and holds around 411 billion. Hence, investors are also found to be inclined toward Islamic Banks rather than the conventional banking industry. This phenomenal growth also required effective governance and Pakistan initially implemented a three-tier Sharia compliance structure for extensive supervision and Sharia compliance working of Islamic banking (ur Rehman & Mangla, 2010).

4.2. Fundamental Difference in the Governance Structure of Corporate Governance

Pakistan is a Muslim country having both forms of banking systems. However, despite of similarities in the governance of Islamic and Commercial Banks, the distinctiveness in the governance of Islamic Banks is based on Sharia which has two major elements ethics and Tawheed. Hence to assure effective corporate governance in Islamic Banks, it is required that the Sharia supervisory board, top-level management, and lower-level management must understand the model of Islamic corporate governance. However, studies in Pakistan highlighted that a lower understanding of the model of Islamic corporate governance by lower-level management is one of the premier issues faced by Islamic Financial Institutions in Pakistan. Hence, there is a legitimate need of staff training according to the protocols and recommendations of IFSB & AAOIFI (Noreen et al., 2016).

4.3. Importance of Sharia Board in the Governance Mechanism of Islamic Banks from Pakistan

Hassan et al. (2017) indicated that there is a positive association between the Sharia committee and the financial performance of the Islamic Banks in Pakistan. The Sharia committee is the most important for influencing the performance of Islamic Banks as the Sharia committee tends to diminish the negative association between increased board size and firm performance. Similarly, Mansoor et al. (2019) also added to the importance of the Sharia Board that the members of the Sharia Board have the desired knowledge, skills, and competencies to observe the practices of corporate governance which is an essence of Islamic Corporate Governance. A similar has been found true through the study that the Sharia Board also optimizes the long-term credit ranking of the Islamic Banks from Pakistan eventually optimizing the bank's performance.

5. Conclusion and Significance

This chapter presented the structure and composition of Islamic Corporate Governance in detail concerning the Islamic banking industry in Pakistan. Hence, the study includes all the relevant points, elements, implications, and examples to make readers understand the concept effectively and efficiently concerning Pakistan. This study blends and condenses the available information to provide a better understanding to the readers. Therefore, this study can be used by academicians, researchers, scholars, and policy-makers to increase knowledge, understanding, and research activities to benefit a wider set of stakeholders. Therefore, it is legitimate to declare this study as a pervasive study. The claim is legitimate as this study is based upon theoretical research gap, and all the pertaining literature, examples, and implications are related to the gaps and lack found in the literature.

References

Abdullah Saif Alnasser, S., & Muhammed, J. (2012). Introduction to corporate governance from Islamic perspective. *Humanomics*, *28*(3), 220–231.

Agarwal, A., & Knoeber, C. R. (1996). Firm performance and mechanisms to control agency problems between managers and shareholders. *Journal of Financial and Quantitative Analysis*, *31*(3), 377–397.

Ahmed, H., & Chapra, M. U. (2002). *Corporate Governance in Islamic Financial Institution (Occasional Paper)* (No. 93). The Islamic Research and Teaching Institute (IRTI).

Ahmed, I. E. (2017). The impact of corporate governance on Islamic banking performance: The case of UAE Islamic banks. *Journal of Banking & Finance*, *9*(9), 1–10.

Aslam, E., & Haron, R. (2020). Does corporate governance affect the performance of Islamic banks? New insight into Islamic countries. *Corporate Governance: The International Journal of Business in Society*, *20*(6), 1073–1090.

Awan, S. H. (2012). Effect on board composition on firm performance: A case of Pakistan listed companies; interdisciplinary. *Journal of Contemporary Research in Business*, *3*(10).

Bukair, A. A., & Rahman, A. A. (2015). Bank performance and board of directors attributes by Islamic banks. *International Journal of Islamic and Middle Eastern Finance and Management*, *8*(3), 291–309.

Choi, J. H., & Wong, T. J. (2007). Auditors' governance functions and legal environments: An international investigation. *Contemporary Accounting Research*, *24*(1), 13–46.

De Andres, P., & Vallelado, E. (2008). Corporate governance in banking: The role of the board of directors. *Journal of Banking & Finance*, *32*(12), 2570–2580.

Farag, H., Mallin, C., & Ow-Yong, K. (2018). Corporate governance in Islamic banks: New insights for dual board structure and agency relationships. *Journal of International Financial Markets, Institutions and Money*, *54*, 59–77.

Ghayad, R. (2008). Corporate governance and the global performance of Islamic banks. *Humanomics*, *24*(3), 207–216.

Grassa, R., Chakroun, R., & Hussainey, K. (2018). Corporate governance and Islamic banks' products and services disclosure. *Accounting Research Journal*, *31*(1), 75–89.

Grassa, R., & Matoussi, H. (2014). Corporate governance of Islamic banks: A comparative study between GCC and Southeast Asia countries. *International Journal of Islamic and Middle Eastern Finance and Management*, *7*(3), 346–362.

Haß, L. H., Johan, S., & Schweizer, D. (2016). Is corporate governance in China related to performance persistence?. *Journal of Business Ethics*, *134*, 575–592.

Haider, N., Khan, N., & Iqbal, N. (2015). Impact of corporate governance on firm financial performance in Islamic financial institution. *International Letters of Social and Humanistic Sciences*, *51*, 106–110.

Haris, M., Yao, H., Tariq, G., Javaid, H. M., & Ain, Q. U. (2019). Corporate governance, political connections, and bank performance. *International Journal of Financial Studies*, *7*(4), 62.

Hassan, M., Rizwan, M., & Sohail, H. (2017). Corporate governance, Shariah advisory boards and Islamic banks' performance. *Pakistan Journal of Islamic Research*, *18*(1), 173–184.

Hermalin, B. E., & Weisbach, M. S. (1991). The effects of board composition and direct incentives on firm performance. *Financial Management*, *20*, 101–112.

Holthausen, R. W., & Larcker, D. F. (1996). The financial performance of reverse leveraged buyouts. *Journal of Financial Economics*, *42*(3), 293–332.

Jackling, B., & Johl, S. (2009). Board structure and firm performance: Evidence from India's top companies. *Corporate Governance: An International Review*, *17*(4), 492–509.

Liang, Q., Xu, P., & Jiraporn, P. (2013). Board characteristics and Chinese bank performance. *Journal of Banking & Finance*, *37*(8), 2953–2968.

Mansoor, M., Ellahi, N., & Malik, Q. A. (2019). Corporate governance and credit rating: Evidence of Shariah governance from Pakistan Islamic banks. *International Transaction Journal of Engineering, Management, & Applied Sciences & Technologies*, *10*, 10A18G.

Mayur, M., & Saravanan, P. (2017). Performance implications of board size, composition and activity: Empirical evidence from the Indian banking sector. *Corporate Governance: The international Journal of Business in Society*, *17*(3), 466–489.

Musleh Alsartawi, A. (2019). Board independence, frequency of meetings and performance. *Journal of Islamic Marketing*, *10*(1), 290–303.

Nawaz, T. (2017). Momentum investment strategies, corporate governance and firm performance: An analysis of Islamic banks. *Corporate Governance: The International Journal of Business in Society*, *17*(2), 192–211.

Nawaz, T. (2019). Exploring the nexus between human capital, corporate governance and performance: Evidence from Islamic banks. *Journal of Business Ethics*, *157*, 567–587.

Noreen, S., Tariq Majeed, M., & Zainab, A. (2016). Corporate governance at Islamic financial institution in Pakistan. *International Journal of Economics and Empirical Research. International Journal of Economics and Empirical Research*, *4*(411), 582–589.

O'connell, V., & Cramer, N. (2010). The relationship between firm performance and board characteristics in Ireland. *European Management Journal*, *28*(5), 387–399.

Ofoeda, I. (2017). Corporate governance and non-bank financial institutions profitability. *International Journal of Law and Management*, *59*(6), 854–875.

Qureshi, A., & Qurashi, M. (2013). Islamic corporate governance practices in Pakistan. *Journal of Research in Business and Management*, *1*(3), 01–15.

Rosenstein, S., & Wyatt, J. G. (1990). Outside directors, board independence, and shareholder wealth. *Journal of Financial Economics*, *26*(2), 175–191.

Safiullah, M., & Shamsuddin, A. (2018). Risk in Islamic banking and corporate governance. *Pacific-Basin Finance Journal*, *47*, 129–149.

Saunders, M., Lewis, P., & Thornhill, A. (2007). *Research methods*. Business Students 4th Edition Pearson Education Limited.

Saunders, M. N. K., Lewis, P., Thornhill, A., & Bristow, A. (2015). *Understanding research philosophies and approaches: Research methods for business students*. Pearson.

Sekaran, U., & Bougie, R. (2016). *Research methods for business: A skill building approach*. John Wiley & Sons.

Srairi, S. (2015). Corporate governance disclosure practices and performance of Islamic banks in GCC countries. *Journal of Islamic Finance*, *4*(2), 115.

Tarmizi, R., Nasaruddin, I. Y., & Hidayah, N. (2023). Analysis of the influence of corporate governance on the financial performance of Islamic banks in Indonesia 2016–2021. *APTISI Transactions on Management*, *7*(2), 179–190.

Titova, Y. (2016). Are board characteristics relevant for banking efficiency? Evidence from the US. *Corporate Governance*, *16*(4), 655–679.

ur Rehmans, R., & Mangla, I. U. (2010). Corporate governance and performance of financial institutions in Pakistan: A comparison between conventional and Islamic banks in Pakistan. *The Pakistan Development Review*, *49*(4), 461–475.

Yermack, D. (1996). Higher market valuation of companies with a small board of directors. *Journal of financial economics*, *40*(2), 185–211.

Yeung, J. C. (2018). Nonlinear effect of board size on corporate performance: Impact of the cultural backgrounds of directors in Hong Kong. *Asia-Pacific Journal of Financial Studies*, *47*(1), 107–131.

Chapter 7

Enhancing the Framework of Islamic Corporate Governance

Muhammad Faisal Sultan[a], *Amir Firoz Shamsi*[b] *and Jahangir Tanveer*[a]

[a]*Khadim Ali Shah Bukhari Institute of Technology (KASBIT), Pakistan*
[b]*Bahria University, Pakistan*

Abstract

This chapter aims to make readers understand the elements that must be included in the Islamic Corporate Governance (ICG) model to make it more rigorous and adaptive. The addition may make the model applicable to other countries, especially those following Islam. Thus, this study is beneficial for academia as well as industry as this study may open the domain of thoughtfulness by researchers, academicians, and other stakeholders regarding the improvement in the model of ICG. Ample literature about the practices, impact, and hurdles associated with corporate governance. However, with the growth of the Islamic financial industry, there is a need for a better understanding of Islamic corporate governance which still has some issues. Therefore, a thorough understanding of issues, complexities, limitations, and lack is required to make the model of Islamic corporate governance rigorous enough that it can be implemented in other countries. This study has been derived from prior studies that were conducted to explore differences in conventional and Islamic corporate governance. However, to leverage the formulation support has been taken from studies that were based on issues, problems, and lacking Islamic corporate governance. However, the work and model are mainly based on the thorough analysis of previous work, gaps, and literature. Therefore, this study has been developed by using archival strategy to address the issues in the model of ICG. Hence, this study will

Islamic Finance and Corporate Governance: Synergies for Sustainable Growth, 107–115

doi:10.1108/978-1-83662-346-520251015

leverage researchers, academicians, and stakeholders to think out of the box and conduct more studies to explore, understand, and improve the issues that are hindering in the way of Islamic corporate governance.

Keywords: Corporate governance; Islamic corporate governance; model of Islamic corporate governance; improving the model of Islamic corporate governance & mechanism of corporate governance

1. Introduction

Governance is defined as the association that the government holds with its constituents. Therefore, corporate governance is the structure through which a corporation holds an association with its constituents. In literature, corporate governance has been defined as a structure developed to address the conflicts between management and shareholders of the firm. The topic of "Corporate Governance" has been in the limelight for more than 20 years. Therefore, an ample amount of literature is now available on issues and problems of corporate governance concerning the developed sides of the world. Similarly, studying literature in depth also revealed that now we also have a considerable amount of literature associated with developing sides of the world. Hence, legitimate to indicate that corporate governance is termed as the key element for the success, growth, and development of an organization which is associated with maximization of value, decreasing the cost of capital pushing capital formulation, etc. (Bhatti & Bhatti, 2010). However, research emphasized the point that corporate governance practices in any particular country are based upon the country's culture, history, and religion. Hence, it is proved that organizational activities in different parts of the world are based on religion, education traditions, etc. Hence, research also indicates significant differences in business policies, styles of leadership, and practices of corporate governance. Therefore, most of the time, practices of corporate governance followed and practiced in one country cannot be exactly copied and adopted by the others. Hence, resolutions of issues on corporate governance require principles rather than rules and regulations. Therefore, there is always a discussion and debate over the resolution of issues and problems in corporate governance practices and procedures (Bindabel et al., 2017).

1.1. Definition of Corporate Governance

The first Definition of Corporate Governance that explains the gist of the concept is given by Cadbury (1992) which highlights that corporate governance is the system by which companies are directed and controlled. Later on, the concept was revolutionized as the association between the company's management, board of directors, and stakeholders. The concept is more vividly explained by Bindabel et al. (2017) by using parameters of OECD (2004) that corporate governance is an association among a company's management, board, and stakeholders.

Therefore, corporate governance is perceived to be a tool that is not only used for the betterment of a company's economic and growth potential which will also improve investor's trust (Kocmanová et al., 2011). There are multiple ways in which conventional corporate governance and Islamic corporate governance look similar. However, Islamic corporate governance aims to direct the governance mechanism on the base of Shariah rules and practices. Hence, all of the corporate, business, and economic activities must be conducted ethoreligious paradigm which may provide holistic benefits (Bhatti & Bhatti, 2010).

1.2. Corporate Governance and Islamic Financial Organization

Studies indicated that regardless of the differences between conventional methods of corporate governance and Islamic corporate governance we cannot differentiate both of these models based on Islamic financial law. Thus, the model is also required to be implemented in the Islamic Banks and other forms of Islamic financial organizations. Researchers posited legitimate questions about whether the model can effectively be implemented in Islamic countries?, especially those that are ranked high in the corruption index (Bhatti & Bhatti, 2010). These questions are somehow highlighted by Bindabel et al. (2017) that corporate governance in Islamic financial organizations is based on Shariah principles. Hence, the mechanism of corporate governance is much different in conventional and Islamic Financial organizations. Studies about the Middle East and South-Asian regions also highlighted this difference when the data were gathered from Gulf and Western countries. Hence, the study claimed cultural differences as the major reason for the difference in the code of corporate governance in conventional and Islamic financial institutions.

1.3. Structure of Islamic Corporate Governance

Ethics are perceived as the main point of conflict between conventional practices of corporate governance and Islamic corporate governance. Studies indicated that ethics included in the Anglo-Saxon model of corporate governance is based on "Secular Humanist" values instead of religious authority. Hence, the major points that are creating differences in ethics in conventional and Islamic corporate governance are the focus on self-interest instead of the wider needs of the society and the need for stronger accountability which may be assured through religious authority and presence of god-fearing participants in the company (Bhatti & Bhatti, 2010). Adding to this, one of the reasons for differentiation is the theory that provided the base of corporate governance as Islamic financial organizations tend to use "Stewardship Theory" instead of "Agency Theory" for governing corporate and related issues and problems (Bhatti & Bhatti, 2010). Hence, Islamic financial organizations do not allow the control of self-interest and opportunistic people as the agent of shareholders. However, some of the other studies, for example, Iqbal and Mirakhor (2004), emphasized the point that the structure of corporate governance for Islamic Financial Organizations resembles studies like Ahmed and Chapra (2002) and Hasan et al. (2015) also support the stakeholders' view of corporate governance through holding the concerns of stakeholders rather than only those who have the equity holdings in the firm. Studies further emphasized the point that the stakeholder model of corporate governance tends to maximize the interest of all the stakeholders which is also allowed through Shariah principles and contractual framework to attain social order (Bhatti & Bhatti, 2010).

2. Theoretical Underpinning

Agency theory is the prime theory that has been used in most of the studies associated with corporate governance. The authors also postulated this theory as the theory of ownership structure of the firm. The gist of this theory has aligned principle with the concept of corporate governance as this theory highlights the role of directors that they have to play on the behalf of shareholders. This includes overseeing top management and commanding staff to achieve organizational goals. However, executives might be focusing on short-term goals, for example, job security, reputation, and personal resources, but shareholders are always required to support the company's long-term objectives which ultimately results in conflict between managers and shareholders. Hence, a more diverse board is required to handle a diverse range of issues more effectively. Similarly, use of a Shariah Board is the practice of assessing internal policies and governance tools used to optimize firm performance. The Shariah Board is also helpful in disseminating early and publicly available information. Thus, the representation of a diverse Shariah Board illustrates greater sustainability performance. Therefore, it is not possible to ignore agency theory as the theory has a definite association between the use of Islamic corporate governance and sustainable organizational performance (Jan et al., 2021).

Moreover, studies related to Islamic Financial Institutions also mentioned that stakeholder theory is also an important theory for the effective administration and governance of Islamic Banks. The theory has a definite association with the practices of the board as well as the Shariah supervisory board (SSB) (Al-Nasser Mohammed & Muhammed, 2017). The New Institutional Sociology Perspective is also associated with Islamic corporate governance as organizations are also required to meet the social aspirations of their external stakeholders. Meeting these social aspirations is a need of the operating organization to validate its reputation in the market. This is one of the prevailing issues in the market as organizations are facing tremendous pressure from their stakeholders to operate in an eco-friendly manner. To deal effectively with these issues, institutional ownership is the key as through majority holdings institutional shareholders may play a dominant role in devising and providing better strategies for the sustainability of the firm (Jan et al., 2021).

Baydoun et al. (2013) investigated the role of cultural and religious practices on practices of corporate governance. Analysis indicated that religion and cultural practices have a dominant impact on the practices of corporate governance. Similar is the case of Islamic values and beliefs that have a significant impact on corporate governance practices. Studies further claimed that following Shariah principles is the major difference between conventional corporate governance and Islamic governance and has a major impact on the governing protocols in the Islamic world (Bindabel et al., 2017). However, very few studies, for example, Mansour and Bhatti (2018), indicated some of the areas that need improvement in the structure of Islamic corporate governance.

2.1. Literature Review

In recent times, growth of Islamic investment and Islamic corporations fostered the need for an effective governance mechanism that is not only Shariah-compliant but also matches with international standards of corporate governance (Bhatti & Bhatti, 2010).

However, weak corporate governance is not the only factor that creates issues associated with the performance of the firm. Other factors like environmental, social, and human damages are also included in the prevalent reasons for the decline in financial performance and the decline in the level of sustainability (Bindabel et al., 2017). However, continuous research and betterment in the processes of Islamic corporate governance are increasing the impact of Islamic corporate governance day after another. Recently, some new features have also been added to the list of activities and advantages that may be achieved through following Islamic corporate governance, for example, improving the competitiveness of the global Islamic industry and serving a larger spectrum. However, a review of the literature also indicated that some of the governance elements are still missing from the governance mechanism of Islamic organizations (Mansour & Bhatti, 2018).

Similar arguments were given by Bhatti and Bhatti (2010) that it is a debatable point that the model of Islamic Corporate Governance (ICG) can be implemented effectively in all of the Muslim countries as most of the countries that are trying to develop the structure of ICG are third-world countries rated on higher sides of corruption index. Therefore, there is a need for powerful strategies that may improve the mode of ICG and make this model stable enough that can be implemented in the larger segments. This point was not previously included in the model of ICG which makes the model rigid and less flexible. The inclusion of these parameters makes the model of ICG applicable to other areas, especially to the region of the Muslim community, and may provide holistic benefits that were not on the priority list previously. Some of the points that may be included in the model of ICG to lure the model with adaptability and tendency to be implemented in other countries are as under (Mansour & Bhatti, 2018).

a. *Regulatory guidelines*: According to studies, the model of ICG lacks detailed guidelines and methods of recovery. Studies supported this claim by pointing out elements like asset sales as Islamic financial institutions cannot sell distressed assets to recover their capital (Mansour & Bhatti, 2018).

   Hence, debt-base Islamic products have seemed to be covering the major portfolio of services offered by Islamic Financial Institutions. Hence, there is a need for tools, methods, or guidelines regarding the Shariah-compliant recovery method (Mansour & Bhatti, 2018).

b. *Fiqh-related issues*: ICG must address fiqh-related issues as in case of recovery from customers using products like Murabaha and Tawarruq especially SMEs bear a high risk of bankruptcy. Therefore, ICG required addressing the comparison of legal versus Shariah reference. However, if the conventional legislation can enforce a more successful recovery strategy, at the cost of Shariah requirements, then what should be done to maximize the benefit of stakeholders? Hence, the motive of ICG in this case is to compare the conventional and Shariah-compliant methods of recovery along with the potential violations of Shariah requirements if the traditional recovery seems to be more successful (Mansour & Bhatti, 2018).
c. *Dissociation between Shariah board and recovery bodies*: In the codes of Islamic corporate governance, there is also no prominent differentiation between Shariah board and authorities for recovery and supervision. This lack may cause problems in implementing recovery tools. This point may become especially critical during the extreme events of bankruptcy (Mansour & Bhatti, 2018).
d. *Resolution of potential conflicts in hybrid banking system*: Islamic banking structure is a bit complex compared to conventional banking. Therefore, to deal with the technological parameters of recent times, there is a need to develop Islamic banking products (IBPs) in a manner that the formulation of these products does not contradict the explicit source (Mihajat, 2014). According to studies, standards developed by international Shariah bodies, for example, AAOIFI, also restrict the use of hybrid contracts for the formulation of IBPs. In fact, following the standard of Shariah, these hybrid products might fall into the domain of riba and gharar (Mihajat, 2014). Therefore, the potential conflicts related to hybrid banking can harm the goodwill of Islamic financial institutions. Studies indicate that leveraging the regulatory mandate of the central bank may resolve these issues and protect stakeholders (Mansour & Bhatti, 2018).
e. *Risk of investment account holders*: Shariah requirements cause an increase in the risk of investment account holders. The statement is valid due to the absence of commercial and conventional laws from the procedures of IFIs and ICG. Hence, investment account holders are likely to lose their investments (Mansour & Bhatti, 2018).
f. *Concentrated share holding*: Studies are required to check and understand the ownership in Islamic Banks. Studies observed that Islamic Banks with SSB have more concentrated shareholding (Almutairi & Quttainah, 2017). However, concentrated shareholding leads to a lack of financial performance in the company (Maniruzzaman et al., 2024).

On the contrary, there are some studies, for example, Yasser and Mamun (2017), indicated that for emerging countries like Pakistan concentrated shareholding may improve the firm's performance. However, findings of the latest study by Maniruzzaman et al. (2024) might be considered more valuable to improve the overall performance of Islamic financial enterprise. This is also consistent with Yasser and Mamun (2017) who indicated that less concentrated shareholding will lead to better market monitoring and discipline of managers. Overall, Fig. 7.1 illustrated the proposed model that suggests improvement in corporate governance in Islamic finance.

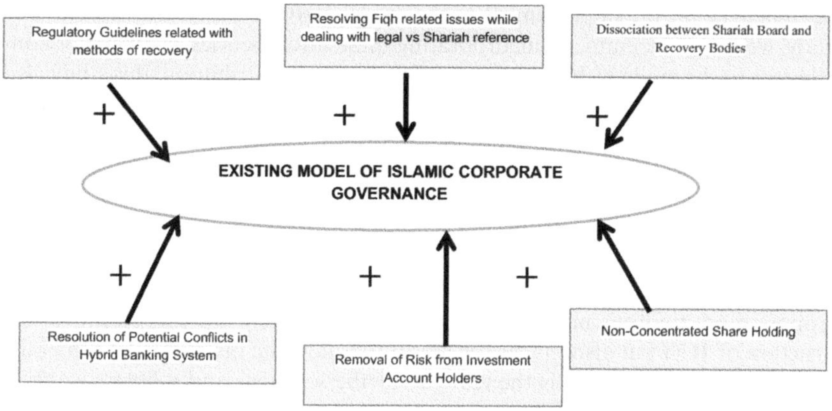

Fig. 7.1. Improving the Islamic Model of Corporate Governance. *Source*: Researcher's own work.

3. Methodology

The purpose of writing this chapter is to make readers understand the improvements that must be made to the model of ICG to make it rigorous enough to be implemented in other parts of the world. Hence, the literature has been surfed in detail and through combining elements from related studies an area has been selected which may not only attract readers but may also foster research work and optimize the practices of ICG. However, the study has been developed to highlight the points that need to be improved in ICG.

Therefore, in line with Sekaran and Bougie (2016), the purpose of the research is descriptive and the researcher's interference in the study is minimal. However, the gist of the study is to optimize the knowledge of readers by pointing out the points that need to be improved in the model of ICG. Hence, in line with Saunders et al. (2007), the philosophy of this study is epistemology which is the philosophy of knowledge, the unit of analysis is cross-sectional. However, as indicated earlier, the study has been formulated through selecting points from prior studies. Thus, the philosophical stance for this study is post-positivism and the research strategy is archival (Saunders et al., 2015).

4. Discussion

This study is developed through theoretical triangulation of agency theory, stakeholder's theory, and new institutional sociology perspective. Hence, through combining these three theories, six major elements are highlighted that can be enforced in the model of ICG to make the model of ICG rigorous enough to be implemented in larger portions of the world. The theoretical triangulation for the study is effective as elements that are proposed to be included in the model of ICG are for the betterment of the society as indicated by the new institutional sociology perspective, but these points can never be adapted without the consent of the board members and SSBs. Hence, agency theory and stakeholder theory all come true for the improvement in the model of ICG. Therefore, through this study, we would recommend incorporating these three theories as the major contributors to the mode of ICG. Other than theoretical contribution, this study also proposed the addition of six elements in the model of ICG which may increase the adaptability of the model.

However, there are chances that Shariah scholars, researchers, and academicians may raise some objections, criticism, and points against the inclusion of these elements in the model of ICG. However, these objections and criticism will pave the way for the improvement in the model of ICG as through incorporating these objections and criticism other researchers and academicians may propose more rigorous models for ICG which ultimately not only improves the structure of ICG but also makes the world to follow the model of ICG than the conventional model which is the real gist of the scientists and scholars working the domain of ICG.

5. Conclusion

This study is one of the unique studies on ICG as it does not emphasize on importance or significance of ICG. The major purpose of this study is to highlight the points and areas that need to be improved to make the model of ICG subtle, so it can be implemented effectively at diversified locations. However, elements that make this study differentiated as compared to the rest in this vein are the plot and its relationship with the literature to give readers the required understanding of the issues and problems that need to be encountered to make the model of ICG more effective. Other than this point, this chapter is written to highlight points that may be incorporated in ICG to make it rigorous enough to be implemented in the other parts of the world. Therefore, the significance of this study has many folds as it is not only beneficial for academic purposes but also beneficial for a better understanding of intrapreneurs to optimize the procedures and methods associated with ICG and its applications.

References

Ahmed, H., & Chapra, M. U. (2002). *Corporate Governance in Islamic Financial Institution (Occasional Paper)* (No. 93). The Islamic Research and Teaching Institute (IRTI).

Almutairi, A. R., & Quttainah, M. A. (2017). Corporate governance: Evidence from Islamic banks. *Social Responsibility Journal*, *13*(3), 601–624.

Al-Nasser Mohammed, S. A. S., & Muhammed, J. (2017). The relationship between agency theory, stakeholder theory and Shariah supervisory board in Islamic banking: An attempt towards discussion. *Humanomics*, *33*(1), 75–83.

Baydoun, N., Maguire, W., Ryan, N., & Willett, R. (2013). Corporate governance in five Arabian Gulf countries. *Managerial Auditing Journal*, *28*(1), 7–22.

Bhatti, M., & Bhatti, M. I. (2010). Toward understanding Islamic corporate governance issues in Islamic finance. *Asian Politics & Policy*, *2*(1), 25–38.

Bindabel, W., Patel, A., & Yekini, C. O. (2017). The challenges faced by integrating Islamic corporate governance in companies of Gulf countries with non-Islamic companies across border through merger and acquisition. *Australasian Journal of Islamic Finance and Business*, *3*(1), 29–38.

Cadbury, A. (1992). *Report of the committee on the financial aspects of corporate governance* (Vol. 1). Gee.

Hasan, T., Kadapakkam, P.-R., & Kumar, P. C. (2015, June 26). Firm investments and corporate governance in Asian emerging markets. *Multinational Finance Journal*, *12*(1/2), 21–44. https://ssrn.com/abstract=2623426

Iqbal, Z., & Mirakhor, A. (2004). Stakeholders model of governance in Islamic economic system. *Islamic Economic Studies*, *11*(2), 44–63.

Jan, A. A., Lai, F. W., & Tahir, M. (2021). Developing an Islamic Corporate Governance framework to examine sustainability performance in Islamic Banks and Financial Institutions. *Journal of Cleaner Production*, *315*, 128099.

Kocmanová, A., Hřebíček, J., & Dočekalová, M. (2011). Corporate governance and sustainability. *Economics & Management*, *16*, 126.

Maniruzzaman, M., Hossain, S. Z., & Sayaduzzaman, M. (2024). Ownership concentration and corporate financial performance: A study on listed manufacturing companies in Bangladesh. *The Cost and Management*, *51*(06), 12–22.

Mansour, W., & Bhatti, M. I. (2018). The new paradigm of Islamic corporate governance. *Managerial Finance*, *44*(5), 513–523.

Mihajat, M. I. S. (2014). Hybrid contract in Islamic banking and finance: A proposed Shariah principles and parameters for product development. *Special Issue: Islamic Management and Business*, *2*(2), 89–99.

OECD (2004). The OECD principles of corporate governance. *Contaduría y Administración*, (216).

Saunders, M., Lewis, P., & Thornhill, A. (2007). *Research methods*. Business Students 4th Edition Pearson Education Limited.

Saunders, M. N. K., Lewis, P., Thornhill, A., & Bristow, A. (2015). *Understanding research philosophies and approaches: Research methods for business students*. Pearson.

Sekaran, U., & Bougie, R. (2016). *Research methods for business: A skill building approach*. John Wiley & Sons.

Yasser, Q. R., & Mamun, A. A. (2017). The impact of ownership concentration on firm performance: Evidence from an emerging market. *Emerging Economy Studies*, *3*(1), 34–53.

Chapter 8

Corporate Governance in Islamic Microfinance Institutions: Evaluating Current Mechanisms and Opportunities for Improvement

Muhammad Faisal Sultan[a], *Muhammad Ali*[b], *Muhammad Asim*[c] *and Muhammad Asim Rafiq*[d]

[a]*Khadim Ali Shah Bukhari Institute of Technology (KASBIT), Pakistan*
[b]*School of Accounting & Finance, Taylor's University, Malaysia*
[c]*Karachi University Business School, University of Karachi, Pakistan*
[d]*National University of Modern Languages (NUML), Pakistan*

Abstract

This chapter is written to understand the mechanism of corporate governance for Islamic microfinance institutions. However, there is a lack of studies that are focused on governance mechanism of Islamic microfinance institutions. Therefore, this study is developed by combining various parameters and elements associated with corporate governance from Asian and Western markets. However, the lack of literature associated with the governance of Islamic microfinance institutes is one of the barriers to the conduct of rigorous and thorough research. This study also utilized some parameters, significance, and criteria that seem homogenous for traditional and Islamic microfinance institutes. The purpose of deep understanding and analysis is to provide a better and conceptual model for the increase of effectiveness of corporate governance in Islamic microfinance institutes. However, this is one of the initial studies on this domain and further studies are also required to

Islamic Finance and Corporate Governance: Synergies for Sustainable Growth, 117–126

Published under exclusive licence by Emerald Publishing Limited
doi:10.1108/978-1-83662-346-520251017

test, validate, and optimize the model provided for corporate governance of Islamic microfinance institutes.

Keywords: Microfinance; Islamic microfinance; Islamic microfinance institutes; corporate governance; corporate governance mechanism

1. Introduction

In recent times, corporate governance is defined as structure used for relating company, its board, shareholders, management, and other stakeholders. This definition is aligned with the definition of corporate governance given by the organization for economic cooperation and development in 2015. Hence, in recent times, the purpose of corporate governance is not to assure the interest of the shareholders, but the structure is to benefit all the stakeholders of the firm (Ajili & Bouri, 2018). Therefore, recently, the focus and concern toward governance is attaining consistent growth for complying with requirements of efficiency and accountability of institutes. Hence, it is almost mandatory to have effective structure of corporate governance in microfinancial institution (MFIs) in order to address concern of diverse stakeholders and to assure sustainability. Moreover, research highlights a significant surge in the importance, requirements, and scope of the MFIs. Therefore, governance and structure of corporate governance of MFIs is also considered important tool for their financial and social growth. Previous studies are highlighting that issues of governance are one of the most critical reason for the failure of MFIs. However, due to lack of concern, severe impact has been observed which causes organization for economic cooperation and development to recommend MFIs to implement effective corporate governance measures. These measures must be effective enough to avoid any issues and mishaps in the working of MFIs. However, the Islamic microfinance institute needs some extra elements, for example, Sharia compliance based on Islamic laws is deemed necessary for the growth of Islamic MFIs (Kassim et al., 2018).

However, the presence of IMFIs is on lower side; even in Islamic countries like Pakistan, the number of authentic IMFIs is under 10. However, the importance of these MFIs cannot be underestimated as the institutions are offering asset-based financing to avoid Riba. Moreover, IMFIs also provide financial and nonfinancial services aligned with Islamic values that will create justice for all types of consumers. On the other side, IMFIs are also perceived as the most important tool for poverty elevation as they aim to serve the poor as well as extremely poor people who can even reach to MFIs (Aman & Ullah, 2016). Studies with reference to Asian countries compare traditional MFI with IMFIs and indicated that IMFIs are performing better than their traditional counterparts and also have sufficient charm to grow. However, there are some major issues as well, for example, lack of funds that are creating issues for IMFIs. Still, studies observe probability of significant growth for IMFIs from Pakistan (Mahmood et al., 2014).

1.1. Research Gap

Most of the studies, in recent times, are based upon the differentiation between the practices of corporate governance in the Western and Islamic world. Studies also pointed that regardless of similarities the governance in Islam is more complex than the traditional mode of corporate governance (Ajili & Bouri, 2018). However, one of the most important outcomes and benefits of corporate governance is sustainability. Therefore, effective corporate governance is required by Islamic MFIs to optimize their sustainability through managing issues of fund mobilization and reducing administration costs. However, studies reflected that every variable associated with corporate governance does not have a significant impact on the performance of IMFI. Hence, there is a need to understand the effective structure that may optimize the performance of IMFIs (Kassim et al., 2018).

2. Literature Review

The purpose of the existence of IMFIs is more holistic as comparison with their conventional counterparts. Therefore, profitability is not perceived as the major indicator of optimized performance as the prime aim for the existence of IMFIs is to ensure social well-being in the country. Hence, the measure to check the performance of IMFIs is to provide facilities that may motivate communities to prefer Riba-Free services (Akbar & Siti-Nabiha, 2022). Higher transaction costs also burden Islamic microfinancial institutions (IMFIs) due to the adaptation of the profit and loss sharing model. The adoption of the profit and loss model has not only increased products and services but also imposed additional costs of monitoring, research, and enforcement. The reason behind the increased cost is information asymmetry from rural markets. Moreover, smaller loans are also expensive due to higher overhead costs and a larger proportion of fixed costs. Therefore, there is a legitimate need to understand the elements that have a considerable impact on the performance of IMFIs (Kassim et al., 2018).

2.1. Ownership Structure

The literature highlighted three major types of ownership structures for IMFIs, that is, cooperatives, nongovernmental organizations, and shareholder-owned firms. Nongovernmental organizations are the most common form of MFIs, and most of the MFIs around the globe are associated with or operated by nongovernmental organizations. Hence, several studies investigated the impact of ownership structure on the performance of MFIs. The findings indicated that shareholder-owned firms are the most suited structure for MFIs in comparison to other forms of structures. Studies also indicated that NGO is the least preferred structure for the MFI and through using this structure MFIs may be struggling to have adequate funding and equity. Therefore, MFIs with NGO ownership cannot offer high-quality services. In this regard, studies preferred ownership structure as MFIs using this form of structure do not rely mostly on external funding and also can reach a mass audience with innovative services. Therefore, it is adequate to believe that ownership structure is the potent variable that may influence the performance of MFIs (Kassim et al., 2018). However, there are very limited studies that are conducted on the ownership structure of MFIs. MFIs working as NGOs have board members who do not have any financial stakes in the organization and may also lack in expertise and abilities to control the operations and risks associated with the process of corporate governance (Rasel & Win, 2020). Moreover, investors may also be reluctant to finance IMFIs that are based on NGO structure (Seibel, 2008).

2.2. *Composition of Board*

The importance of board size is deemed to be highly important for effective management of internal matters and transparency. Involvement of the board of directors is perceived as a sign of effective control and monitoring. Therefore, board composition must be evaluated in terms of required skills, competencies, characteristics of board members, and commitment toward the company's mission as well as allocated responsibilities (Kassim et al., 2018). Initially, studies, for example, Hartarska and Mersland (2012) indicated that there is no association between the composition of the board and MFIs performance. Although some of the latter studies, for example, Bakker et al. (2014), found contrary results. Past studies also highlighted that clients may also be a part of the board of MFIs. This statement has also been supported by findings that the inclusion of employees and clients on the board of directors will optimize the performance of MFIs. Moreover, the board that is comprised of local rather than members from other countries has more tendencies to improve the performance of MFIs. Similar is found for the inclusion of female board members as well as the use of female CEOs rather than males as female board members may also reduce asymmetry of information through better analysis of female customers (Kassim et al., 2018).

2.3. *Internal Audit and Control*

The internal audit and control function of the firm is required to boost operational efficiency, optimize financial reporting, safeguard assets, and also provide observations for the improvement of policies and practices of the firm. Hence, proper upgradation and settings is required for sustainability and growth in the long run. Companies that do not set their internal controls have to bear significant expenses in the long run. In MFI, internal controls are required to comply with the requirements of quality, integrity, and transparency of transactions and operations. Moreover, internal control and audit are also required to ensure that the institution is marching in the right direction and aligning with its mission. However, some of the MFIs are unable to establish internal control and audit mechanisms due to a lack of human capital and financial resources. Studies also mentioned that MFIs are found to be on the lower side in evaluating the quality of the board and hence seem to be on the lower side in internal quality and control measures (Kassim et al., 2018). However, the scope of internal audit for MFIs seems very broad as through effective internal audit MFIs may be able to improve financial and social performance. Hence, it is recommended that in MFIs internal audit must directly report to the board of directors. Therefore, some of the MFIs have their internal audit departments, but most of the growing MFIs are not leveraged with internal audit departments. Therefore, there is a need to hire external auditors who are required to play their role in formulating transparent financial reporting practices (Kassim et al., 2018).

2.4. Regulations

Recent developments in the MFI industry have initiated a call for external governance in the sense that MFIs must be able to bear and sustain external shocks. However, there is a difference in opinion of researchers for MFI that use the facility of external audit as compared to those who do not use facility external audit. Studies indicated that MFIs that focus more on balancing regulatory affairs may diverge from their actual mission of reducing poverty. Adding to this point studies also reflected that regulated MFIs may also not have a larger customer base as compared to the nonregulated MFIs and lastly regulated MFIs may also have lower return on assets as compared to their counterparts. However, regulated MFIs may also be found to be more attractive for microfinance investment vehicles as regulated MFIs are the better option for microfinance investment vehicles to channel their funding. Lastly, regulated MFIs may also have a higher level of self-efficiency as compared to nonregulated MFIs (Kassim et al., 2018). The study indicated that government-owned MFIs are the most preferred type of MFIs as they are highly regulated due to governmental ownership (Rasel & Win, 2020).

2.5. Rating System

The rating system is one of the important external governance mechanisms for the effective corporate governance of MFIs. However, the number of studies on this mechanism is very rare, but there is no doubt on the importance of a rating system in the structure of corporate governance. According to studies, the investor uses the insights from the rating system to assess the stock price (Kassim et al., 2018). Moreover, a change in the credit ranking indicated the creditworthiness of the firm over a longer period (Kassim et al., 2018). Rasel and Win (2020) also highlighted the importance of a rating system and marked it as one of the major indicators for setting governance attributes. Studies also claim that ownership type, board expertise, board committee, board activity quality of internal audit, CEO's duality, and presence of foreign directors are the main factors that optimize the rating of MFI. However, if the rating agencies do not incorporate revisions in the previous ranking, then it would result in a substantial increase of asymmetrical information associated with the firm and market (Hung et al., 2017).

2.6. Sharia Governance

Sharia compliance is one of the most significant parts of any Islamic entity. The inclusion of Sharia governance in the governance structure of any Islamic entity forces the requirement of a new code of governance to comply with Sharia

Principles (Kassim et al., 2018). Sharia compliant finance might be defined as financial activities that are aligned with Islamic rules and regulations. That means the company will only be involved in those financial activities that are Riba-Free & also not associated with prohibited products or businesses. Hence, Sharia compliant is the activity that differentiates between Islamic and conventional finance. However, Islamic microfinance must not only be accompanied by Sharia principles but also must be approved by Muslim Clientele. Studies mentioned three major elements related to Sharia governance is Sharia supervisory board whose role is not only limited to Sharia-compliant procedures but also to manage elements like Bai contract issues and divergence in client perception (Mansori et al., 2015).

a. *Sharia supervisory board (SSB)*: These boards are composed of renowned experts and scholars of fiqh. The purpose of these groups of scholars is to maintain a check over all the operations of IMFIs (Mansori et al., 2015). SSBs must also be allowed to work freely and independently as the SSBs are hired by the board of directors and their job is to ensure Sharia compliant for all the services of the bank (Jan et al., 2021). Hence, all the operations must be accompanied by Sharia rules. The presence of SSB is to gain the trust of all the stakeholders of Islamic microfinance and to make them inclined toward IMFIs and their services. However, surveys from IMFIs operating in Islamic countries indicated that none of the IMFIs has an SSB board due to the cost of setting up the SSB. However, it is one of the greatest challenges for IMFIs as the importance of SSB is massive and having an alternative to SSB is a significant challenge (Mansori et al., 2015).
b. *Bai contract issues*: Disagreement and divergence in Sharia scholars is also some of the most critical challenges for IMFIs. Most of the time the debate between Shari scholars is based on work practices of MFIs that allow variation in the standardized set and also with of ways of the contract are associated with penalties imposed for delays and delinquencies (Mansori et al., 2015).
c. *Variation of client perception*: The client has differentiated opinions about the different products of Islamic banking like Mudarabah and Murabhah. However, clients may also perceive quard-al-Hassan due to its benevolent nature (Mansori et al., 2015).

3. Structure of Corporate Governance and Performance of IMFIs

Seibel (2008) mentioned the reasons for the pathetic performance of Islamic microfinance institutions (IMFIs) operating in Indonesia. The study mentioned that governance and managerial problems seem to be the major forces behind the lack of performance. Among the measures of corporate governance research highlighted internal control, external audit, and effective supervision are the major factors that cause harm to the IMFIs. Studies with relevance to IMFIs of Middle-East and North American region by Karim (2012) also indicated that investors and commercial banks hesitate to be willing to finance those IMFIs that have structure. Similarly, a study about the IMFIs of Indonesia reflected that

IMFIs were actually in trouble due to the lack of governance guidelines as no regularized body is handling the issues of the IMFIs. On the other hand study of Alshebami and Khandare (2015) highlighted the importance of a Sharia advisor as the non-presence of a Shria Advisor in Yemen is hindering the performance of IMFIs.

4. Implications and Modeling

Based on the literature review, it has been believed that IMFIs are in different and difficult conditions as compared to traditional MFIs. These problems are based on structure, management, and corporate governance. Therefore, there is a need for an effective model that may guide IMFI, policy-makers, and researchers to conceptualize, understand, and improve the structure and mechanism of corporate governance. Fig. 8.1 presents the conceptual model for the improvement

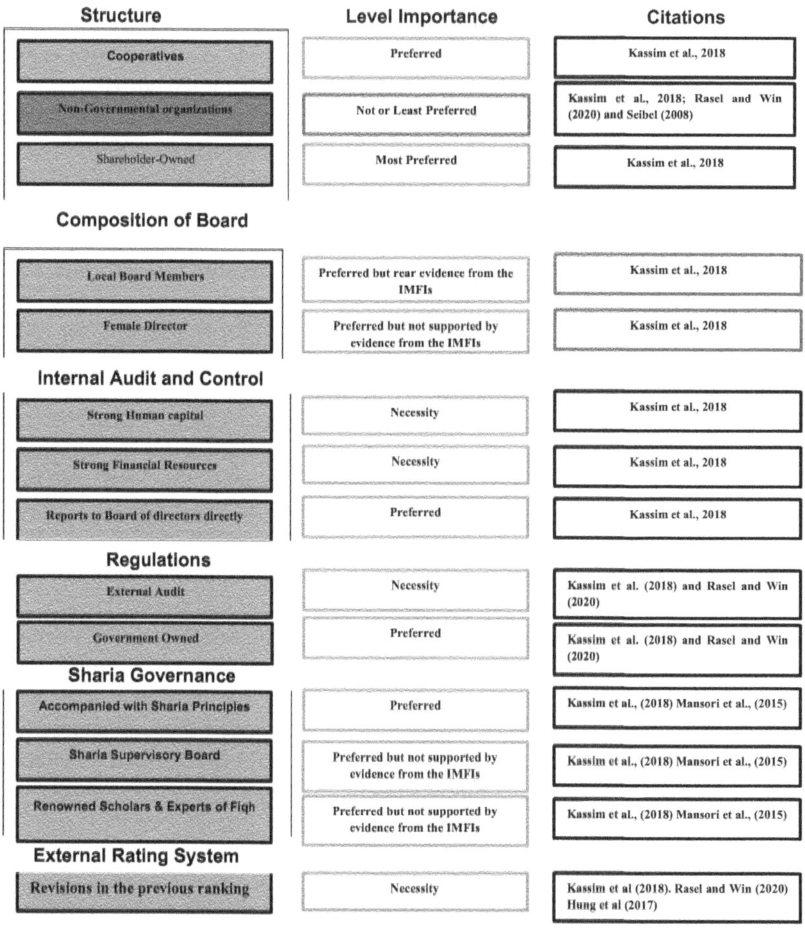

Fig. 8.1. Conceptual Model for the Improvement in Practices of Corporate Governance in IMFI. *Source*: Researcher's own creativity.

in practices of corporate governance in IMFIs. The first column belongs to the futuristic mechanism of corporate governance and its elements for IMFIs. The red color is the indication of the least preferred element, and the green color indicates the preferred or required element for effective practices of corporate governance The second column belongs to the importance of every element that is associated with the mechanism of corporate governance while the last column is reflecting pieces of evidence which are in the form of citations from prior research work. The use of red color in the outline of the second column only means that the structure is not preferred for growth as well as effective corporate governance, and the use of red color in the third column indicates that the reference is in line only with traditional MFIs.

5. Methodology

There is significant increase in concern toward Islamic banking and governance of Islamic banking. Evidence can be traced from scholarly publications on the topic of "*Islamic Banking*" and "*Governance of Islamic Banking*" with reputed research publishers. Concern has also been increased from Asian Islamic countries even from Pakistan. However, publications stream from Pakistan is still on lower-side as compared to the Malaysia and United Kingdom (Zuhroh, 2022). On the other side, research work associated with corporate governance of IMFI is a rear topic of research. Very few studies discussed this point one of the studies that discuss the structure of corporate governance of IMFIs is conducted by Mohd Kassim et al. (2022) from Malaysia. Hence, this study tries to link points mentioned by Mohd Kassim et al. (2022) with Islamic banking and MFI literature from Pakistan, for example, Mahmood et al. (2014) and Zuhroh (2022). Therefore, the major aim of this study tries to provide comprehensive understanding of corporate governance structure which helps growth of IMFIs from other Asian Muslim countries. Thus, the philosophy associated with this study is epistemology which is treated as the philosophy of knowledge as indicated by Saunders et al. (2007) and supported and legitimized by Hashim et al. (2018) and Hadiwijaya et al. (2016) with reference to MFIs and Islamic Banks. However, this chapter is focused toward the structure of corporate governance in IMFI. Hence, it is not suited to use positivism that was highlighted by Saunders et al. (2015) and used by Hashim et al. (2018) as the philosophical stance. However, the purpose of this study is to understand and devise matter mechanism of corporate governance; therefore, this study uses post-positivism as the philosophical stance. However, due to relaying over available secondary data associated with MFIs, IMFIs, and banking industry, this study has been compiled through using monomethod, archival research strategy and cross-sectional time horizon as indicated by Saunders et al. (2007) and Saunders et al. (2015).

6. Implications and Significance

IMFIs have higher costs of transactions and operations. Hence, the preference is to associate innovation with the process of transaction. Therefore, the importance of efficient model and application of corporate governance is a legitimate need of IMFIs to attract and motivate investors that will ultimately help IMFIs in managing cost of information and issues of sustainability (Kassim et al., 2018). Therefore, through using prior studies, we have developed a rigorous and practical model that can be used for the improvement in mechanism of corporate governance by IMFIs. The model is based on thorough literature review and, therefore, has the capacity to serve entrepreneurs, social entrepreneurs, government bodies, researchers, and academicians to improve their understanding, research work, and policy-making with respect to the corporate governance mechanism in IMFIs. Hence, this study is one of the pervasive studies that has the tendency to create holistic impact over academia, economy, and society.

References

Ajili, H., & Bouri, A. (2018). Corporate governance quality of Islamic banks: measurement and effect on financial performance. *International Journal of Islamic and Middle Eastern Finance and Management*, *11*(3), 470–487.

Akbar, T., & Siti-Nabiha, A. K. (2022). Objectives and measures of performance of Islamic microfinance banks in Indonesia: the stakeholders' perspectives. *ISRA International Journal of Islamic Finance*, *14*(2), 124–140.

Alshebami, A. S., & Khandare, D. M. (2015). Islamic microfinance industry inYemen: Challenges and opportunities. *International Journal of Societal Work*, *2*(2), 1–9. https://doi.org/10.5296/ijsw.v2i2.7937

Aman, N., & Ullah, K. (2016). Challenges faced by the Islamic microfinance institutions in Pakistan. *Asian Journal of Islamic Finance*, *1*(1), 1–13.

Bakker, A., Schaveling, J., & Nijhof, A. (2014). Governance and microfinance institutions. *Corporate Governance*, *14*(5), 637–652.

Hadiwijaya, T., Lahindah, L. & Pratiwi, I. R., (2016). Effect of capital structure and corporate governance on firm value Study of listed banking companies in Indonesia Stock Exchange. *Journal Of Accounting And Business Studies*, *1*(1), 39–58.

Hartarska, V., & Mersland, R. (2012). Which governance mechanisms promote efficiency in reaching poor clients? Evidence from rated microfinance institutions. *European Financial Management*, *18*(2), 218–239.

Hashim, M. J., Adeyemi, A. A., & Alhabshi, S. M. (2018). *Effects of intellectual capital on microfinance institutions' performance*. Proceedings of the 2nd advances in business research international conference: ABRIC2016 (pp. 187–196). Springer Singapore.

Hung, C. H. D., Banerjee, A., & Meng, Q. (2017). Corporate financing and anticipated credit rating changes. *Review of Quantitative Finance and Accounting*, *48*, 893–915.

Jan, A. A., Lai, F. W., & Tahir, M. (2021). Developing an Islamic Corporate Governance framework to examine sustainability performance in Islamic Banks and Financial Institutions. *Journal of Cleaner Production*, *315*, 128099.

Karim, A. (2012). *Global Islamic microfinance landscape.* Global Islamic finance report. http://gifr.net/gifr2012/ch_25.pd

Kassim, S., Hassan, R., & Kassim, S. N. (2018). Good governance and sustainability in Islamic microfinance institutions. *Journal of Islamic Finance*, *7*(2), 021–028.

Mahmood, H. Z., Khan, R., Mehmood, B., & Khan, K. (2014). Efficiency analysis of conventional vs. Islamic microfinance: An appraisal for sustainability in Pakistan. *International Journal of Empirical Finance*, *3*(4), 192–201.

Mansori, S., Chin, S. K., & Safari, M. (2015). A shariah perspective review on Islamic microfinance. *Asian Social Science, 11*(9), 273–280.

Mohd Kassim, A. W. B., Noordin, R. B., Jaidi, J., & Tahajuddin, S. B. (2022). Ownership Structure and the Quality of Corporate Social Responsibilities Disclosures in Malaysian Companies. In *The Implementation of Smart Technologies for Business Success and Sustainability: During COVID-19 Crises in Developing Countries* (pp. 747–754). Springer International Publishing.

Rasel, M. A., & Win, S. (2020). Microfinance governance: A systematic review and future research directions. *Journal of Economic Studies, 47*(7), 1811–1847.

Saunders, M., Lewis, P., & Thornhill, A. (2007). *Research methods*. Business Students 4th Edition Pearson Education Limited.

Saunders, M. N., Lewis, P., Thornhill, A., & Bristow, A. (2015). *Understanding research philosophy and approaches to theory development.*

Seibel, H. D. (2008). Islamic microfinance in Indonesia: The challenge of institutional diversify, regulation, and supervision. *SOJOURN: Journal of Social Issues in Southeast Asia, 23*(1), 86–103.

Zuhroh, I. (2022). Mapping Islamic Bank Governance studies: a systematic literature review. Cogent Business & Management, *9*(1), 2072566.

Chapter 9

Governance and Ecosystem in Islamic Fintech: Frameworks, Opportunities, and Challenges

Aisha Naz[a], *Muhammad Ali*[b] *and Muhammad Ashfaq*[c]

[a]*Iqra University, Pakistan*
[b]*School of Accounting & Finance, Taylor's University, Malaysia*
[c]*IU International university of applied sciences, Germany*

Abstract

This chapter delves into the governance of Islamic fintech, examining how modern technology and traditional Islamic finance principles interact. It provides an overview of how Islamic fintech has evolved, highlighting the differences between Islamic and conventional fintech and discussing the roles of key players such as startups, financial institutions, and regulators. The chapter underscores the significance of Shariah compliance in ensuring that fintech innovations align with Islamic laws and ethics. It explores emerging trends and innovations in the sector, while addressing the challenges and opportunities that arise from integrating cutting-edge technology with traditional financial practices. Key recommendations include strengthening governance frameworks, supporting research and development, fostering collaboration, and implementing policies that promote innovation and growth. Real-world examples, such as successful Islamic fintech companies and effective regulatory frameworks, are used to illustrate how thoughtful governance and supportive policies can drive sustainable development in Islamic fintech.

Keywords: Islamic fintech; governance; Shariah compliance; financial technology; financial institutions

Islamic Finance and Corporate Governance: Synergies for Sustainable Growth, 127–146

doi:10.1108/978-1-83662-346-520251020

1. Introduction

In the dynamic realm of finance, Islamic fintech represents an exciting convergence of tradition and innovation. Rooted in the principles of Islamic finance, which emphasize justice, transparency, and risk-sharing, Islamic fintech leverages modern technology to offer financial solutions that align with Shariah law (El-Gamal, 2006). Unlike conventional finance, which often relies on interest-based transactions, Islamic fintech platforms adhere to principles such as profit-sharing (Mudarabah) and asset-backed financing (Murabaha). These principles ensure that investments are ethical and support real economic activities. Islamic fintech encompasses a wide range of services, from digital banking to blockchain solutions, each designed to meet the needs of a growing Muslim demographic that seeks Shariah-compliant financial products. For instance, mobile banking apps enable users to perform transactions and manage investments in ways that adhere to Islamic principles, while blockchain technology is being explored for its potential to enhance transparency and traceability in financial transactions (Khan & Bhatti, 2008). This technological advancement is reshaping how Islamic finance is perceived and practiced, making it more accessible and efficient. Islamic fintech with in corporate governance importance that involves ensuring that financial practices not only comply with Shariah law but also uphold ethical standards and accountability. Effective governance structures are critical in maintaining the integrity of Islamic fintech platforms and fostering trust among users (Dusuki & Abozaid, 2007). By adhering to these governance principles, Islamic fintech can provide financial solutions that are both innovative and aligned with ethical values.

1.1. Importance and Relevance in Modern Finance

Islamic finance is not just a niche market; it's becoming increasingly important in today's global financial world. It offers a unique approach that emphasizes fairness and ethical behavior, which is gaining attention as more people look for financial options that align with their values. For instance, instead of traditional loans with interest, Islamic finance uses methods like profit-sharing, which can be more equitable for everyone involved (El-Gamal, 2006).

In modern finance, where issues like fairness and transparency are crucial, Islamic finance provides valuable lessons. Its rules require that investments be backed by real assets and that profits and risks be shared. This approach can lead to more stable and responsible financial practices (Khan & Bhatti, 2008). Corporate governance in Islamic finance also highlights the importance of good practices in business. By ensuring that companies operate ethically and follow strict guidelines, Islamic finance helps build trust and ensures that financial activities are transparent and just (Dusuki & Abozaid, 2007). As global finance continues to evolve, the principles of Islamic finance offer new perspectives on creating a more ethical and stable financial system.

1.2. Objectives of the Chapter

This chapter aims to uncover the essential aspects of Islamic finance and its impact on modern financial practices. First, we will explore what makes Islamic finance unique, focusing on its core principles like fairness and transparency. These principles differ from traditional finance, which often relies on interest. By understanding these differences, readers can appreciate how Islamic finance provides alternative solutions that align with ethical values (El-Gamal, 2006). It examines how Islamic finance integrates with new technologies, such as fintech. This will show how modern tools can support Islamic finance principles and make these practices more accessible to people today (Khan & Bhatti, 2008).

The chapter will discuss the role of corporate governance in Islamic finance. Good governance ensures that financial institutions operate with integrity and follow ethical guidelines. By highlighting the importance of strong governance, this chapter aims to demonstrate how it contributes to the overall effectiveness and trustworthiness of Islamic financial practices (Dusuki & Abozaid, 2007). Through these objectives, readers will gain a clear understanding of how Islamic finance functions and why it is relevant in the contemporary financial landscape.

2. Literature Review

2.1. Historical Evolution of Fintech

The story of fintech, or financial technology, is like a thrilling adventure through the progress of financial tools and systems. It all began with simple innovations such as the mechanical cash register and early calculators, which made handling money a bit easier for businesses and consumers. Moving into the mid-20th century, computers started making their mark, introducing electronic banking and stock trading platforms that revolutionized how people managed their finances (Narayanan, 2005). As we entered the digital age, the 1990s and 2000s brought about a wave of new fintech developments. The internet allowed for online banking and e-commerce, drastically changing how people conducted transactions and managed their money from home. Services like digital wallets and online payment systems became popular, making financial transactions more convenient and accessible (Gomber et al., 2018).

The 2010s saw even more dramatic changes with the rise of mobile technology and innovations like block-chain. Mobile apps provided on-the-go banking solutions, while block-chain technology offered a new way to securely record transactions. Additionally, artificial intelligence (AI) started playing a role in analyzing financial data and automating services, further transforming the industry (Catalini & Gans, 2016). This evolution of fintech globally shows how technological advancements have continuously shaped and reshaped the financial world, making it more efficient, accessible, and secure.

2.2. Islamic Fintech Versus Conventional Fintech

When comparing Islamic fintech with its conventional counterpart, it's essential to recognize their distinct origins and guiding principles. Islamic fintech is deeply rooted in the principles of Islamic finance, which trace back to the 7th century. Islamic finance operates on principles of fairness, risk-sharing, and the prohibition of interest, reflecting the teachings of the Quran and Hadith. This means that Islamic financial products, such as profit-sharing investments (Mudarabah) or cost-plus financing (Murabaha), are structured to avoid interest and ensure that transactions are ethical and transparent (El-Gamal, 2006). In contrast, conventional fintech emerged from the financial practices developed over centuries in the Western world. Its history can be traced to the early 20th century with the advent of electronic banking and trading. Conventional finance relies heavily on interest-based transactions and various financial instruments such as loans and bonds, which are central to its operations (Narayanan, 2005).

Both Islamic and conventional fintech have embraced modern technology, but they apply these tools differently. Islamic fintech uses technology to offer financial services that comply with Shariah law, such as apps for Shariah-compliant investments and blockchain systems for transparent financial transactions (Khan & Bhatti, 2008). On the other hand, conventional fintech focuses on improving efficiency and accessibility of traditional financial services, like digital payments and robo-advisors (Gomber et al., 2018). While both types of fintech strive to modernize and enhance financial services, Islamic fintech remains committed to adhering to ethical and religious guidelines, offering an alternative to the interest-based models prevalent in conventional finance.

2.3. Previous Studies on Fintech Governance

Governance in fintech has been the subject of increasing academic and practical interest, as the sector rapidly evolves. Previous studies highlight the unique challenges and opportunities faced by both conventional and Islamic fintech in managing and regulating their operations. In conventional fintech, research has focused on the balance between innovation and regulation. For example, the introduction of the General Data Protection Regulation in the European Union in 2018 set new standards for data privacy and security, impacting fintech companies across the continent (Kaal, 2019).

Studies have shown that effective governance in conventional fintech involves not only compliance with regulatory frameworks but also the implementation of robust internal controls and risk management practices (Gomber et al., 2018). Islamic fintech, on the other hand, navigates a distinct regulatory landscape shaped by Shariah law. Research indicates that Islamic fintech companies must ensure their financial products and operations comply with Islamic principles, which include prohibitions on interest and speculative transactions (El-Gamal, 2006). For instance, the Accounting and Auditing Organization for Islamic Financial Institutions (AAOIFI) provides guidelines for Shariah compliance and governance, which are critical for maintaining trust and credibility in Islamic financial services (Dusuki & Abozaid, 2007).

Historically, Islamic finance has had a structured approach to governance that dates back to early Islamic banking practices. The first known Islamic banks were established in the 1960s and 1970s, with institutions like the Dubai Islamic Bank, founded in 1975, setting standards for Shariah-compliant financial practices

(Iqbal & Mirakhor, 2011). These early models focused on integrating Islamic principles with banking practices, setting a precedent for contemporary Islamic fintech governance. The study of governance in fintech reveals that while conventional and Islamic fintech both face significant regulatory challenges, their approaches to governance are shaped by their respective financial principles and regulatory environments. Effective governance remains crucial for ensuring transparency, accountability, and ethical conduct in both sides.

2.4. Role of Technology in Islamic Finance

The role of technology in Islamic finance has evolved significantly, reflecting broader trends in the financial industry. Historically, Islamic finance began with a focus on principles such as risk-sharing and asset-backed transactions based on the teachings of the Quran and Hadith. The first modern Islamic bank, Dubai Islamic Bank, was established in 1975, marking the beginning of institutionalized Shariah-compliant finance (Iqbal & Mirakhor, 2011). In these early days, Islamic finance relied on traditional banking systems and manual processes.

With the advent of the digital age, technology has profoundly transformed Islamic finance. Early technological innovations, such as computerized accounting systems and electronic funds transfer, facilitated more efficient and accurate financial operations. As technology advanced, Islamic financial institutions began adopting digital banking platforms, allowing them to offer services like online account management and electronic transactions. For instance, the introduction of Islamic mobile banking apps has made it possible for customers to perform transactions and manage their investments from their smartphones, aligning with Shariah principles while enhancing convenience (El-Gamal, 2006).

The latest technological advancements, such as blockchain and AI, are also making their mark on Islamic finance. Blockchain technology offers a secure and transparent way to record transactions, which is particularly valuable for Islamic finance's asset-backed and contract-based transactions. For example, the use of blockchain can ensure that contracts, like those for Murabaha (cost-plus financing) or Ijarah (leasing), are executed and recorded accurately and transparently (Catalini & Gans, 2016).

AI is another game-changer, enabling Islamic financial institutions to better analyze data and provide personalized financial solutions that adhere to Shariah laws. AI can assist in automating compliance checks and risk assessments, ensuring that financial products and services meet regulatory and ethical standards (Gomber et al., 2018).

The integration of technology in Islamic finance not only enhances operational efficiency but also expands the reach of Shariah-compliant financial products. For instance, fintech innovations have made it possible for Islamic finance to penetrate new markets and serve a broader range of customers. As technology continues to evolve, it is expected to further transform Islamic finance, making it more accessible and aligned with modern financial practices while preserving its core principles.

3. Islamic Fintech Ecosystem

3.1. Key Components of the Ecosystem: Startups, Financial Institutions, Regulators

The Islamic finance ecosystem is a vibrant network where startups, financial institutions, and regulators each play a vital role in shaping the industry. This dynamic interplay drives the growth and evolution of Shariah-compliant financial services, integrating traditional principles with modern technology to meet contemporary needs.

i. *Startups*:
Startups are at the forefront of innovation in Islamic finance, utilizing technology to offer new and accessible Shariah-compliant financial solutions. Companies like Wahed Invest and Ethis Crowd exemplify how modern fintech startups are revolutionizing ethical investing and crowdfunding while adhering to Islamic finance principles (El-Gamal, 2006). These ventures help bridge the gap between traditional financial services and the digital age, bringing Islamic finance to a broader audience.

ii. *Financial institutions*:
Established financial institutions form the backbone of the Islamic finance sector. Pioneers such as Dubai Islamic Bank, founded in 1975, and Al Baraka Bank, which began in the 1980s, have set the standard for Shariah-compliant banking (Iqbal & Mirakhor, 2011). These institutions offer a wide array of financial products and services that comply with Islamic law, ensuring that transactions are conducted in a fair and ethical manner. Their long-standing presence and expertise are crucial in maintaining the sector's integrity and trustworthiness (Dusuki & Abozaid, 2007).

iii. *Regulators*:
Regulators are essential in ensuring that the Islamic finance industry adheres to both Islamic and global financial standards. Bodies like the AAOIFI, established in 1991, provide comprehensive guidelines for Shariah compliance and governance (El-Gamal, 2006). These regulations help ensure that financial practices are transparent and aligned with Islamic principles, fostering confidence and stability in the industry.

The synergy between startups, financial institutions, and regulators is fundamental to the ongoing development of Islamic finance. While startups drive technological advancements, financial institutions offer traditional and innovative Shariah-compliant products, and regulators provide the necessary oversight to ensure compliance. Together, these components create a robust and evolving ecosystem that addresses both current and future financial needs.

3.2. Emerging Trends and Innovations

As Islamic finance continues to evolve, several emerging trends and innovations are reshaping the landscape and enhancing its reach. These developments reflect both technological advancements and a growing demand for Shariah-compliant financial solutions.

i. *Digital transformation*:
One of the most significant trends in Islamic finance is digital transformation. The rise of digital banking has revolutionized how Islamic financial services are delivered. Institutions like Dubai Islamic Bank have been at the forefront of adopting online and mobile banking platforms, allowing customers to manage their finances and conduct transactions with ease (Iqbal & Mirakhor, 2011). These digital tools not only enhance convenience but also broaden access to Islamic financial products, catering to a tech-savvy generation seeking ethical and accessible financial solutions.

ii. *Block-chain and smart contracts*:
Block-chain technology is making waves in Islamic finance by offering secure and transparent ways to conduct transactions. This technology ensures that financial contracts, such as Murabaha (cost-plus financing) and Ijarah (leasing), are executed with full transparency and accuracy. For example, some Islamic fintech startups are exploring block-chain to create immutable records of transactions and agreements, reducing the risk of fraud and enhancing trust (Catalini & Gans, 2016). Smart contracts, powered by block-chain, can automate the execution of Shariah-compliant agreements, streamlining processes and improving efficiency.

iii. *Green and sustainable finance*:
Another emerging trend is the focus on green and sustainable finance. Islamic financial institutions are increasingly incorporating environmental, social, and governance criteria into their investment strategies. The issuance of green Sukuk (Islamic bonds) is a notable example, providing funding for projects that promote environmental sustainability. In 2019, Malaysia became a leader in this area by launching its first green Sukuk, aimed at financing eco-friendly projects while adhering to Shariah principles (Khan & Bhatti, 2008). This trend reflects a growing commitment to integrating ethical investment practices with environmental responsibility.

iv. *AI and data analytics*:
AI and data analytics are also transforming the Islamic finance sector. AI-driven tools are used for customer service, risk management, and compliance checks, offering more personalized and efficient financial services. For instance, AI can analyze customer data to provide tailored investment advice that complies with Islamic principles. The use of AI in automating Shariah compliance checks ensures that financial products adhere to Islamic laws while improving operational efficiency (Gomber et al., 2018).

These emerging trends and innovations highlight the dynamic nature of Islamic finance and its capacity to adapt to modern challenges while staying true to its core principles. As technology continues to advance, Islamic finance will likely see further innovations that enhance its reach and impact, ensuring that it remains relevant in a rapidly changing financial world.

4. Challenges and Opportunities

4.1. Challenges in Islamic Finance

Shariah compliance variability: Ensuring consistent Shariah compliance is a significant challenge in Islamic finance. Diverse interpretations of Islamic law across different institutions and regions lead to variability in financial products and practices. While some institutions adhere to guidelines set by the AAOIFI, others follow different Shariah boards, creating inconsistencies that can confuse consumers and hinder growth (El-Gamal, 2006).

Shortage of qualified shariah experts: The Islamic finance sector faces a shortage of qualified Shariah scholars. The demand for expertise in Shariah compliance often exceeds the supply of knowledgeable professionals, leading to increased costs and delays in the development of new products and services. As the industry expands globally, there is a critical need for more scholars who are proficient in both Islamic jurisprudence and contemporary financial practices (Iqbal & Mirakhor, 2011).

Regulatory and legal challenges: Navigating the regulatory and legal landscape is another challenge. Islamic finance operates under both Shariah law and national financial regulations, which can sometimes conflict. For instance, regulatory requirements in some jurisdictions may not fully accommodate Shariah-compliant practices, creating legal and operational hurdles for Islamic financial institutions (Dusuki & Abozaid, 2007). This regulatory complexity can impede the growth and innovation of Islamic finance.

Limited product diversification: Despite significant growth, the range of Shariah-compliant financial products remains relatively narrow compared to conventional finance. Islamic financial institutions often offer a limited variety of products, which can restrict their ability to compete in diverse financial markets. This limited product diversification can be a barrier to attracting a broader customer base and meeting evolving financial needs (Khan & Bhatti, 2008).

4.2. Opportunities in Islamic Finance

Ethical and sustainable investment: Islamic finance has a unique opportunity to lead in ethical and sustainable investment. The alignment of Islamic finance principles with environmental and social responsibility is increasingly relevant. The issuance of green Sukuk, such as Malaysia's pioneering green Sukuk in 2019, highlights how Islamic finance can support eco-friendly projects while remaining compliant with Shariah principles. This growing focus on sustainability presents an opportunity for Islamic finance to attract investors interested in ethical investments (Khan & Bhatti, 2008).

Technological advancements: Technological innovations provide substantial opportunities for Islamic finance. Block-chain technology, for instance, can enhance transparency and security in financial transactions, ensuring that

Shariah-compliant contracts are executed accurately. Similarly, AI can streamline compliance checks and improve customer service by providing tailored financial solutions that adhere to Islamic laws (Catalini & Gans, 2016; Gomber et al., 2018). Embracing these technologies can help Islamic finance institutions modernize their operations and expand their reach.

Expansion into new markets: The global expansion of Islamic finance presents significant opportunities. Emerging markets in Africa and Southeast Asia are showing increasing interest in Shariah-compliant financial products. By entering these new markets, Islamic financial institutions can tap into untapped customer bases and drive further growth. This expansion is facilitated by increasing awareness of Islamic finance principles and growing demand for ethical financial solutions (Iqbal & Mirakhor, 2011).

Enhanced financial inclusion: Islamic finance has the potential to enhance financial inclusion, particularly in underserved communities. By providing Shariah-compliant financial products, institutions can offer banking services to individuals who may otherwise be excluded from conventional financial systems. This focus on financial inclusion can help address socio-economic disparities and promote economic development in various regions (Dusuki & Abozaid, 2007).

While Islamic finance faces challenges such as Shariah compliance variability, a shortage of qualified experts, regulatory hurdles, and limited product diversification, it also holds considerable opportunities. These include leading in ethical and sustainable investment, leveraging technological advancements, expanding into new markets, and enhancing financial inclusion. By addressing these challenges and capitalizing on opportunities, Islamic finance can continue to grow and make a significant impact in the global financial landscape.

5. Governance Frameworks

5.1. Principles of Governance in Islamic Fintech

In the rapidly evolving field of Islamic fintech, governance plays a crucial role in ensuring that financial technologies adhere to Islamic principles and meet the ethical standards expected by users and regulators alike. Governance in Islamic fintech encompasses a range of practices that are designed to uphold Shariah compliance, transparency, and social responsibility, while effectively managing risks and promoting fairness. Understanding these principles is essential for navigating the complexities of modern financial technology while staying true to Islamic values.

i. *Law of Shariah compliance*

   A cornerstone of governance in Islamic fintech is adherence to Shariah compliance. This principle mandates that all financial products and services must align with Islamic law, which prohibits practices such as interest (riba), excessive uncertainty (gharar), and unethical activities (haram). Shariah boards or committees are responsible for reviewing and approving fintech offerings to ensure they meet these criteria. For instance, Dubai Islamic Bank, established in 1975, exemplifies this practice with its dedicated Shariah board overseeing compliance with Islamic law (Iqbal & Mirakhor, 2011). Ensuring Shariah compliance not only upholds the integrity of Islamic fintech but also fosters trust among users.

ii. *Transparency and accountability*
Transparency and accountability are critical governance principles in Islamic fintech. Islamic finance places a strong emphasis on clear and honest disclosure in financial transactions to prevent ambiguity and deceit. This tradition is rooted in historical practices where financial dealings were characterized by transparency and fairness (El-Gamal, 2006). In contemporary fintech, this principle translates into providing detailed information about fees, risks, and Shariah compliance. Implementing robust reporting and auditing mechanisms enhances accountability and builds confidence among users and regulators.

iii. *Ethical conduct and social responsibility*
Ethical conduct and social responsibility are fundamental to Islamic finance and fintech. The principles of Islamic finance advocate for fairness, equity, and contributions to societal welfare. Historically, practices such as Zakat (charitable giving) and the prohibition of investments in harmful industries reflected these values. Modern fintech platforms, such as Ethis Crowd, which launched in 2015, demonstrate how Islamic fintech can integrate social impact investing and charitable crowdfunding into their business models (Khan & Bhatti, 2008). By focusing on ethical conduct and social responsibility, Islamic fintech addresses societal needs while adhering to Islamic principles.

iv. *Risk management and fairness*
Effective risk management and fairness are vital aspects of governance in Islamic fintech. Islamic finance requires that risks and rewards be shared equitably between parties involved in a transaction. This principle is evident in contracts such as Mudarabah (profit-sharing) and Musharakah (joint venture), where both parties share the venture's risks and rewards. Historically, Islamic finance adhered to these principles, ensuring fair and balanced transactions (Dusuki & Abozaid, 2007). In the fintech realm, this involves designing products that manage risks appropriately and ensure fair treatment of users.

The principles of governance in Islamic fintech are grounded in Shariah compliance, transparency, ethical conduct, and effective risk management. These principles ensure that fintech solutions remain aligned with Islamic values while addressing contemporary financial needs. By keeping these governance standards, Islamic fintech can continue to grow and maintain its role as a trusted and ethical segment of the global financial landscape.

5.2. Role of Shariah Compliance in Fintech

Shariah compliance is a pivotal element in the realm of Islamic fintech, serving as the cornerstone upon which all financial products and services must be built.

In essence, Shariah compliance ensures that fintech solutions adhere to Islamic law, which prohibits practices such as interest (riba), excessive uncertainty (gharar), and unethical activities (haram). This compliance is crucial not only for maintaining the integrity of financial operations but also for building trust among users who seek products aligned with their religious values. The importance of Shariah compliance in finance is deeply rooted in Islamic history. The principles of Islamic finance originated from the Quran and Hadith, which provide clear guidelines on ethical financial conduct. For instance, the prohibition of riba (interest) is derived from several verses in the Quran, including Surah Al-Baqarah 2:275, which condemns those who consume interest as engaging in immoral behavior (El-Gamal, 2006). This historical context underscores the foundational role of Shariah compliance in Islamic financial transactions.

In modern Islamic fintech, Shariah compliance is overseen by Shariah boards or committees, which consist of scholars well-versed in Islamic jurisprudence and finance. These boards are responsible for reviewing and approving financial products and services to ensure they align with Shariah principles. For example, the Shariah board of Dubai Islamic Bank, established in 1975, plays a crucial role in ensuring that the bank's operations comply with Islamic law (Iqbal & Mirakhor, 2011). The board's function extends to advising on the development of new fintech products, ensuring that they do not involve prohibited elements.

Shariah compliance influences various aspects of fintech products and services. For instance, Islamic fintech platforms must avoid investments in sectors that are considered haram, such as alcohol, gambling, and tobacco. This adherence is reflected in products like Sukuk (Islamic bonds), which are structured to comply with Shariah principles by avoiding interest payments and ensuring that returns are derived from permissible activities. The issuance of Sukuk, such as Malaysia's pioneering green Sukuk in 2019, highlights how Shariah compliance can align with modern investment trends and ethical considerations (Khan & Bhatti, 2008).

Despite its importance, ensuring Shariah compliance in fintech presents challenges. The diverse interpretations of Shariah law among different scholars can lead to variations in compliance standards, which may create inconsistencies in fintech products across regions. This challenge necessitates ongoing dialog and standardization efforts among Shariah boards to harmonize practices and enhance clarity for users (Dusuki & Abozaid, 2007). However, these challenges also drive innovation, as fintech companies develop new solutions to address compliance issues while meeting user needs.

Shariah compliance plays a fundamental role in Islamic fintech by ensuring that financial products and services adhere to Islamic principles. Its historical roots in Islamic law, the function of Shariah boards, and its impact on fintech products underscore its significance. Despite challenges, Shariah compliance remains central to the growth and credibility of Islamic fintech, fostering trust and aligning financial practices with ethical values.

5.3. Regulatory Challenges and Solutions

The regulation of Islamic finance presents a unique set of challenges due to the need to balance Shariah compliance with existing legal frameworks. These regulatory challenges can impact the development and growth of Islamic financial institutions and fintech solutions. Addressing these challenges effectively is essential for ensuring the sector's stability and fostering its expansion. One of the primary regulatory challenges is the alignment of Shariah principles with national financial regulations. Islamic finance operates under a dual regulatory system that includes both Shariah law and conventional financial regulations. This duality can lead to conflicts, particularly when national regulations do not accommodate the specific requirements of Shariah-compliant financial products. For example, the prohibition of interest (riba) in Islamic finance often clashes with conventional interest-based financial systems, creating complexities for institutions trying to navigate these differing standards (Dusuki & Abozaid, 2007).

Another challenge is the lack of uniform regulatory standards across different jurisdictions. The Islamic finance industry is characterized by diverse practices and interpretations of Shariah law, leading to inconsistencies in regulatory requirements. This variability can create difficulties for international Islamic financial institutions seeking to operate in multiple countries. For instance, the regulatory framework in Malaysia, which is considered advanced in Islamic finance, differs significantly from that in other regions like the Middle East or Europe, complicating cross-border operations (Iqbal & Mirakhor, 2011).

Historically, Islamic finance has faced regulatory hurdles since its modern inception. The establishment of the first Islamic bank, Dubai Islamic Bank, in 1975 marked a significant step in creating a regulatory framework for Islamic finance. However, the early regulatory environment was often fragmented and lacked cohesion. Over time, efforts have been made to address these challenges, including the development of comprehensive regulatory frameworks by organizations such as the Islamic Financial Services Board (IFSB) and the AAOIFI (El-Gamal, 2006).

To address these regulatory challenges, several solutions and innovations have been proposed. One effective solution is the harmonization of regulatory standards across jurisdictions. Initiatives such as the IFSB's guidelines aim to create a more consistent regulatory framework for Islamic finance globally. By establishing common standards, these guidelines help reduce regulatory discrepancies and facilitate cross-border operations (Khan & Bhatti, 2008). Another solution is the development of regulatory technology (RegTech) to streamline compliance processes. RegTech solutions can enhance transparency, automate compliance checks, and improve reporting, thereby addressing regulatory challenges more efficiently. For instance, the use of blockchain technology in Islamic finance can help ensure transparency and traceability in transactions, aligning with both Shariah and regulatory requirements (Catalini & Gans, 2016).

Regulatory challenges in Islamic finance, including the alignment of Shariah principles with national regulations and the lack of uniform standards, present significant obstacles to the sector's growth. However, historical developments and ongoing efforts to harmonize regulations and leverage technological innovations provide promising solutions. By addressing these challenges effectively, the Islamic finance sector can continue to thrive and expand its impact in the global financial landscape.

6. Case Studies of Successful Islamic Fintech Companies

In recent years, several Islamic fintech companies have emerged as successful examples of how traditional Islamic finance principles can be effectively integrated with modern technology. These companies illustrate the potential of Islamic fintech to meet contemporary financial needs while adhering to Shariah principles. Examining these case studies provides valuable insights into the growth and impact of Islamic fintech.

i. *Ethis crowd*
Ethis Crowd, founded in 2015, is a pioneering platform in the field of Shariah-compliant crowdfunding. Based in Singapore, Ethis Crowd focuses on connecting investors with projects that adhere to Islamic finance principles, including real estate, social impact, and infrastructure projects. The platform's success lies in its ability to leverage technology to facilitate ethical investments while ensuring Shariah compliance. For instance, Ethis Crowd played a significant role in raising funds for the construction of affordable housing in Indonesia, demonstrating how Islamic fintech can address pressing social needs (Khan & Bhatti, 2008). This success highlights the potential of Islamic fintech to contribute to socio-economic development.

ii. *Wahed invest*
Wahed Invest, launched in 2015, is a global Shariah-compliant robo-advisory platform based in the United States. The company offers automated investment services that align with Islamic finance principles, such as avoiding interest-based investments and investing in ethically permissible sectors. Wahed Invest's innovative use of technology to provide low-cost, personalized investment solutions has attracted significant interest from Muslim and non-Muslim investors alike. The platform's success is evidenced by its rapid growth and substantial investments from venture capital firms, underscoring the demand for Shariah-compliant financial products in the digital age (Iqbal & Mirakhor, 2011).

iii. *Al Baraka banking group*
Founded in 1982, Al Baraka Banking Group is a prominent Islamic financial institution with a strong presence across the Middle East, Africa, and Asia. Although it predates the rise of fintech, Al Baraka has successfully integrated technology into its operations to enhance its service offerings. The group's investment in digital banking solutions, such as mobile banking apps and online platforms, has significantly improved customer accessibility and operational efficiency. Al Baraka's ability to adapt to technological advancements while adhering to Shariah principles exemplifies how traditional Islamic banks can thrive in a modern, tech-driven environment (El-Gamal, 2006).

iv. *Aspire*
Aspire, founded in 2018 and based in Singapore, provides a digital banking platform tailored to the needs of small and medium-sized enterprises

(SMEs). The platform offers Shariah-compliant financial products and services, including digital payments, financing, and cash management solutions. Aspire's innovative approach to serving the SME sector aligns with Islamic finance principles and addresses the gap in accessible financial services for businesses. The company's success in attracting a diverse clientele and expanding its service offerings demonstrates the growing potential of Islamic fintech in catering to niche markets (Dusuki & Abozaid, 2007).

These case studies of successful Islamic fintech companies Ethis Crowd, Wahed Invest, Al Baraka Banking Group, and Aspire highlight the diverse applications of Shariah-compliant financial solutions in the modern fintech landscape. Each company has leveraged technology to address specific market needs while adhering to Islamic finance principles, demonstrating the sector's potential for growth and innovation. As the Islamic fintech industry continues to evolve, these success stories serve as inspiring examples of how traditional values can be integrated with cutting-edge technology to create impactful financial solutions.

7. Conclusion

In Islamic finance and corporate governance, several critical findings highlight the integration of Shariah principles with modern financial practices, as well as the sector's evolving challenges and opportunities. At the heart of Islamic finance is the principle of Shariah compliance, which mandates that all financial activities adhere to Islamic law. This includes the prohibition of interest (riba), excessive uncertainty (gharar), and unethical investments (haram). These principles, deeply rooted in the Quran and Hadith, have historically shaped the development of Islamic financial products and services. For example, the prohibition of riba, emphasized in Surah Al-Baqarah 2:275, remains a cornerstone of Islamic finance, influencing contemporary fintech solutions such as Ethis Crowd and Wahed Invest. These platforms successfully integrate Shariah compliance with modern technology, offering Shariah-compliant investment and crowdfunding options that meet current financial needs (El-Gamal, 2006; Iqbal & Mirakhor, 2011).

The regulatory landscape presents significant challenges. Islamic finance operates under a dual regulatory system that combines Shariah law with national financial regulations, often leading to conflicts. For instance, Islamic financial institutions may struggle to reconcile Shariah principles with conventional interest-based financial systems, creating complexities in their operations. This issue is compounded by the lack of uniform regulatory standards across different jurisdictions, as seen in the varying frameworks in Malaysia compared to other regions. These regulatory discrepancies can hinder the cross-border operations of Islamic financial institutions and impact their growth (Dusuki & Abozaid, 2007).

Despite these challenges, there are promising solutions and innovations. The harmonization of regulatory standards through initiatives by organizations like the IFSB aims to create a more consistent framework for Islamic finance globally. Additionally, advancements in technology, such as RegTech and blockchain, offer new ways to enhance compliance and transparency. For example, blockchain technology can improve the traceability of transactions, aligning with both Shariah principles and regulatory requirements (Catalini & Gans, 2016).

Overall, the integration of Shariah principles with modern financial practices continues to drive the growth and innovation of Islamic finance. Successful case studies, such as Ethis Crowd and Wahed Invest, demonstrate the effective application of these principles in contemporary fintech solutions. While regulatory challenges persist, ongoing efforts to harmonize standards and leverage technological advancements provide a path forward for the sector. These developments underscore the potential of Islamic finance to adapt to the digital age while maintaining its commitment to ethical and transparent practices.

7.1. Importance of Governance in the Growth of Islamic Fintech

Governance plays a significant role in the growth of Islamic fintech, serving as the backbone that ensures compliance with Shariah principles while fostering trust and stability within the industry. Effective governance is crucial for aligning fintech solutions with the ethical and legal standards set by Islamic law. This alignment is essential not only for maintaining Shariah compliance but also for building credibility and confidence among users who seek financial products that adhere to their religious values. The importance of governance in Islamic fintech is highlighted by the necessity of Shariah boards, which are responsible for overseeing and ensuring that financial products and services comply with Islamic principles. These boards, composed of scholars well-versed in Islamic jurisprudence, provide guidance on various aspects of financial operations, from investment strategies to product development. Their role is critical in preventing the inclusion of prohibited elements such as interest (riba) and excessive uncertainty (gharar) in fintech offerings. By ensuring that products are Shariah-compliant, governance structures help mitigate risks and avoid potential conflicts with regulatory frameworks (El-Gamal, 2006; Iqbal & Mirakhor, 2011).

The strong governance practices contribute to the overall transparency and accountability of Islamic fintech institutions. Effective corporate governance helps in maintaining high standards of integrity and ethical conduct, which are essential for sustaining investor and consumer trust. For instance, transparent reporting and rigorous internal controls are vital for ensuring that fintech operations are conducted in accordance with both Shariah principles and regulatory requirements. This transparency is not only crucial for compliance but also for enhancing the sector's reputation and fostering its growth. The governance is integral to the expansion and success of Islamic fintech. By ensuring Shariah compliance and promoting transparency and accountability, robust governance structures help build trust, mitigate risks, and support the sustainable growth of Islamic fintech solutions.

7.2. Future Prospects of Islamic Fintech

The future prospects of Islamic fintech are promising, driven by rapid technological advancements and increasing global demand for Shariah-compliant financial solutions. As the fintech landscape continues to evolve, Islamic fintech is positioned to benefit from several emerging trends that align with its principles and meet the growing needs of consumers and businesses. One significant prospect is the continued integration of blockchain technology, which can enhance transparency and traceability in Islamic financial transactions. Blockchain's ability to provide immutable records aligns well with Shariah principles of transparency and accountability, potentially transforming how Islamic fintech products are developed and managed.

Additionally, the rise of AI and machine learning offers opportunities to improve risk management, customer service, and personalized financial solutions within the framework of Shariah compliance. The expansion of digital banking is another key area of growth. Islamic fintech firms are increasingly offering digital banking solutions that cater to both individual and business needs, including Shariah-compliant payment systems, lending platforms, and investment opportunities. This digital transformation allows for greater accessibility and convenience, potentially reaching underserved markets and promoting financial inclusion. There is a growing interest in sustainable and impact investing, which aligns with the ethical dimensions of Islamic finance.

Islamic fintech platforms are likely to increasingly focus on investments that support social and environmental sustainability, reflecting the principles of responsible finance. Overall, the future of Islamic fintech is marked by innovation and growth, with technological advancements and shifting consumer demands paving the way for new opportunities. As the sector continues to evolve, it holds the potential to make significant contributions to the global financial landscape while adhering to its core Shariah principles.

8. Policy Recommendations

8.1. Strengthening Governance Frameworks

Strengthening governance frameworks in Islamic finance is essential for ensuring the sector's stability and integrity. Effective governance not only maintains Shariah compliance but also enhances transparency and builds stakeholder trust, which are critical for the sector's growth and credibility. Historically, the principles of Islamic governance have been rooted in the Quran and Hadith, emphasizing justice, accountability, and ethical behavior. These principles continue to guide the development of modern Islamic financial institutions and fintech companies.

A key component of governance in Islamic finance is the role of Shariah boards, which are tasked with ensuring that financial products and services adhere to Islamic law. Shariah boards, composed of qualified scholars in Islamic jurisprudence, provide essential oversight and guidance. For instance, the establishment of Dubai Islamic Bank in 1975 marked a significant step in institutionalizing Shariah governance, with dedicated Shariah boards playing a critical role in shaping the bank's operations (El-Gamal, 2006). Their involvement helps prevent the inclusion of prohibited elements, such as interest (riba), and ensures that financial transactions align with ethical standards.

In addition to Shariah boards, strengthening internal controls and risk management practices is crucial. Effective governance frameworks include robust internal audit functions and transparent reporting mechanisms. These practices not only ensure compliance with Shariah principles but also align with regulatory requirements, thereby enhancing the institution's credibility and operational efficiency. For example, Malaysian Islamic banks have implemented comprehensive governance frameworks that include strict internal controls and regular Shariah audits, contributing to their success and reliability in the market (Iqbal & Mirakhor, 2011).

Moreover, fostering a culture of ethical conduct and accountability is vital. This involves training staff on Shariah principles and corporate governance practices, promoting a strong ethical culture, and ensuring that governance practices are continually reviewed and updated to address emerging challenges. Strengthening governance frameworks in Islamic finance involves enhancing the roles of Shariah boards, implementing robust internal controls, and promoting ethical conduct. These measures are essential for maintaining Shariah compliance, building stakeholder trust, and supporting the sustainable growth of the sector.

8.2. Policies to Support Innovation and Growth in Islamic Fintech

As Islamic fintech continues to evolve, implementing supportive policies is crucial for fostering innovation and ensuring sustainable growth. The dynamic nature of the fintech sector demands a regulatory environment that balances the integration of cutting-edge technology with strict adherence to Shariah principles. Effective policies not only promote technological advancements but also ensure that these innovations remain compliant with Islamic financial laws, thereby fostering a trustworthy and robust industry.

i. *Regulatory frameworks*: Developing a clear and supportive regulatory framework is essential for fostering innovation and growth in Islamic fintech. Governments and regulatory bodies must create regulations that accommodate the unique aspects of Islamic finance while encouraging technological advancement. For example, Bahrain's Central Bank has established a comprehensive regulatory framework for Islamic finance, which has been instrumental in fostering fintech innovations within a well-structured environment (El-Gamal, 2006). This clarity and security enable fintech companies to operate effectively while ensuring compliance with Shariah principles.
ii. *Research and development*: Investment in research and development is crucial for driving innovation in Islamic fintech. Policies that support R&D can lead to the creation of new and improved Shariah-compliant financial products. Malaysia's regulatory sandbox, introduced by Bank Negara Malaysia, exemplifies this approach by allowing fintech companies to test innovative solutions in a controlled environment. This policy has facilitated the successful launch of numerous Shariah-compliant fintech solutions and underscores the importance of a supportive environment for technological innovation (Iqbal & Mirakhor, 2011).

iii. *Collaboration with technology providers*: Encouraging collaboration between traditional Islamic financial institutions and technology providers can lead to the development of innovative financial products that integrate Shariah compliance with modern technology. For instance, partnerships between Al Baraka Banking Group and fintech startups have resulted in new digital banking solutions that adhere to Islamic principles while offering advanced functionalities (Dusuki & Abozaid, 2007). Such collaborations are vital for leveraging technological advancements and enhancing the offerings in Islamic fintech.
iv. *Promoting financial literacy*: Policies that promote financial literacy and awareness about Islamic fintech are essential for increasing adoption and understanding of Shariah-compliant solutions. Educational initiatives and public awareness campaigns can help consumers and businesses appreciate the benefits and features of Islamic fintech, driving demand and supporting the sector's growth. By fostering a better understanding of Islamic finance, these policies can contribute to the sustainable development of the fintech sector.
v. *Supporting innovation hubs and incubators*: Establishing innovation hubs and incubators specifically tailored for Islamic fintech can provide startups with the resources and support needed to thrive. These hubs can offer mentorship, funding opportunities, and access to networks that facilitate the development of Shariah-compliant fintech solutions. For example, the Islamic Fintech Alliance, based in Singapore, provides a platform for fintech startups to connect with industry experts and investors, fostering an ecosystem that supports innovation and growth (Islamic Fintech Alliance, 2020).
vi. *Incentivizing investment*: Governments can also play a role by providing incentives for investment in Islamic fintech. Tax breaks, grants, and other financial incentives can attract investors to the sector, encouraging the development of new technologies and services. Such incentives not only reduce the financial risks associated with innovation but also stimulate economic growth by attracting capital to the Islamic fintech industry.
vii. *Enhancing cross-border collaboration*: Policies that enhance cross-border collaboration between Islamic financial institutions and fintech firms can help integrate global markets and expand the reach of Shariah-compliant solutions. International agreements and partnerships can facilitate the exchange of knowledge, resources, and best practices, driving innovation and growth across different regions.

These effective policies that establish supportive regulatory frameworks, invest in research and development, encourage collaboration, promote financial literacy, support innovation hubs, incentivize investment, and enhance cross-border collaboration are crucial for the growth and innovation of Islamic fintech. These measures ensure that technological advancements are aligned with Shariah principles, contributing to the sector's sustainable development and success.

8.3. Recommendations for Industry Stakeholders and Regulators

As the Islamic fintech sector continues to evolve, it is crucial for both industry stakeholders and regulators to adopt strategic measures that support innovation while ensuring Shariah compliance. These recommendations aim to address key challenges and leverage opportunities to foster a robust and dynamic Islamic fintech ecosystem.

Strengthening Shariah compliance: For industry stakeholders, ensuring rigorous Shariah compliance is paramount. Financial institutions and fintech companies should invest in establishing and maintaining robust Shariah boards composed of knowledgeable scholars who can provide continuous oversight. The success of institutions like Dubai Islamic Bank, which was founded in 1975 and has adhered to Shariah principles throughout its operations, highlights the importance of such governance structures (El-Gamal, 2006). Regular audits and transparent reporting are essential to uphold these standards and build trust with consumers.

Enhancing regulatory frameworks: Regulators should focus on developing clear, supportive, and adaptable regulatory frameworks that address the unique aspects of Islamic finance while promoting innovation. Malaysia's approach with its regulatory sandbox, implemented by Bank Negara Malaysia, offers a model for how regulators can balance innovation with compliance. By allowing fintech firms to test new solutions in a controlled environment, Malaysia has fostered significant advancements in Shariah-compliant financial technologies (Iqbal & Mirakhor, 2011). Regulators in other regions should consider similar initiatives to encourage experimentation and growth.

Promoting collaboration and partnerships: Stakeholders should actively seek collaborations with technology providers, academic institutions, and other fintech firms to drive innovation. Partnerships, like those between Al Baraka Banking Group and fintech startups, can lead to the development of advanced digital solutions that meet Shariah requirements while leveraging modern technology (Dusuki & Abozaid, 2007). Collaborative efforts can also include participating in industry forums and networks to share knowledge and best practices.

Supporting education and training: Investing in education and training for both industry professionals and consumers is critical. Stakeholders should support programs that enhance understanding of Shariah principles and fintech innovations. Educational initiatives can increase financial literacy and promote the adoption of Islamic fintech solutions. For instance, ongoing training programs and workshops can help industry professionals stay updated on regulatory changes and emerging technologies.

Encouraging innovation through incentives: Regulators and industry stakeholders should work together to provide financial incentives for research and development in Islamic fintech. Tax incentives, grants, and subsidies can reduce the financial risks associated with innovation and attract investment. These incentives can stimulate the development of new Shariah-compliant technologies and services, contributing to the sector's growth.

Fostering cross-border collaboration: Enhancing cross-border collaboration can help integrate global markets and expand the reach of Islamic fintech solutions. International agreements and partnerships can facilitate the exchange of best practices, resources, and knowledge, driving innovation and growth across regions. Such collaborations can help standardize practices and promote the global expansion of Shariah-compliant financial technologies.

Islamic Fintech strengthening Shariah compliance, enhancing regulatory frameworks, promoting collaboration, supporting education, encouraging innovation, and fostering cross-border cooperation, industry stakeholders and regulators can significantly contribute to the growth and success of the Islamic fintech sector.

References

Catalini, C., & Gans, J. S. (2016). *Some simple economics of the blockchain.* NBER working paper no. 22952. https://www.nber.org/papers/w22952

Dusuki, A. W., & Abozaid, A. (2007). Corporate governance in Islamic financial institutions. *International Journal of Islamic and Middle Eastern Finance and Management, 1*(1), 67–81. https://doi.org/10.1108/17538390710776796

El-Gamal, M. A. (2006). *Islamic finance: Law, economics, and practice.* Cambridge University Press.

Gomber, P., Kauffman, R. J., Parker, C., & Weber, B. (2018). On the Fintech revolution: Interpreting the forces of innovation, disruption, and transformation in financial services. *Journal of Management Information Systems, 35*(1), 220–265.

Iqbal, Z., & Mirakhor, A. (2011). *An introduction to Islamic finance: Theory and practice.* Wiley.

Islamic Fintech Alliance. (2020). https://www.islamicfintechalliance.com

Kaal, W. A. (2019). Blockchain, Fintech, and Islamic finance: Challenges and opportunities. In U. A. Oseni & S. N. Ali (Eds.), *Fintech in Islamic finance*: Theory and practice (pp. 45-70). Routledge. ISBN: 9781351025584.

Khan, T., & Bhatti, M. I. (2008). *Islamic banking and finance: Theory and practice.* Routledge.

Narayanan, S. (2005). Corporate governance and its impact on financial performance. *Journal of Financial Regulation and Compliance, 13*(2), 123–145. https://doi.org/10.1108/13581980510622022.

Chapter 10

Sukuk and Corporate Governance: Ethical Foundations, Economic Impact, and Global Relevance in Islamic Finance

Aisha Naz[a], *Muhammad Ali*[b] *and Abdul Kadir Barut*[c]

[a]*Iqra University, Pakistan*
[b]*School of Accounting & Finance, Taylor's University, Malaysia*
[c]*Recep Tayyip Erdoğan University, Turkey*

Abstract

This chapter aims to explore the intricate relationship between Islamic finance and corporate governance through the lens of Sukuk, a cornerstone of Shariah-compliant financial instruments. The primary objective is to provide a comprehensive understanding of Sukuk, delving into their structure, principles, and the unique characteristics that distinguish them from conventional bonds. By explaining how Sukuk adhere to Islamic law, prohibiting interest (riba), and promoting risk-sharing, this chapter seeks to highlight the ethical foundations that underpin these instruments. Additionally, this chapter endeavors to underscore the pivotal role of corporate governance in the issuance and management of Sukuk. Through rigorous analysis, we will examine the stringent disclosure requirements, the role of Shariah boards, and the mechanisms that ensure transparency and accountability. These elements are crucial in fostering investor confidence and ensuring that all financial activities align with Islamic ethical standards. Another key objective is to analyze the economic and social impact of Sukuk. By presenting real-world case studies and examples, this chapter aims to demonstrate how Sukuk financing has facilitated infrastructure projects, corporate growth, and social development. The strategic use of Sukuk by various

Islamic Finance and Corporate Governance: Synergies for Sustainable Growth, 147–173

doi:10.1108/978-1-83662-346-520251022

governments and corporations underscores their versatility and effectiveness in driving sustainable economic progress while adhering to ethical principles. Furthermore, this chapter aspires to illustrate the global relevance of Sukuk in contemporary finance. By tracing their proliferation across diverse markets and their acceptance by various sovereign entities and multinational corporations, we will showcase the growing demand for Shariah-compliant financial products.

Keywords: Sukuk; Islamic finance; corporate governance; Shariah-compliant instruments; Islamic ethical standards

1. Introduction

In the dynamic and evolving landscape of Islamic finance, Sukuk, often referred to as Islamic bonds, emerge as a groundbreaking financial instrument that harmonizes traditional Islamic principles with modern investment needs. Unlike conventional bonds, which are prohibited in Islamic finance due to the involvement of interest (riba), Sukuk represent certificates of ownership in tangible assets, usufructs, or services, thereby ensuring compliance with Shariah law (El-Gamal, 2006). This asset-backed structure not only provides investors with a share of the profits derived from the asset but also involves them in the associated risks, fostering a balanced risk-sharing framework that is a hallmark of Islamic finance (Iqbal & Mirakhor, 2011). The profound relevance of Sukuk in Islamic finance lies in its ability to mobilize capital while adhering to ethical and religious principles. By prohibiting interest and speculative activities, Sukuk promotes a more stable and resilient financial system.

This is achieved through various structures, such as Ijarah (leasing), Murabaha (cost-plus financing), and Mudarabah (profit-sharing), each tailored to meet specific financing needs while ensuring Shariah compliance (Obaidullah, 2005). The adaptability of Sukuk structures enables them to cater to a wide range of sectors, including infrastructure, real estate, and energy, thereby driving economic development and social progress. Corporate governance plays a crucial role in the issuance and management of Sukuk. The stringent requirements for transparency, disclosure, and continuous oversight by Shariah boards ensure that all transactions adhere to Islamic principles. These governance mechanisms not only enhance investor confidence but also promote ethical business practices, reducing the risk of financial mismanagement and fraud (Usmani, 2002). The involvement of Shariah scholars in reviewing and certifying Sukuk structures further adds a layer of credibility and trust, essential for attracting a broader investor base.

The global acceptance and proliferation of Sukuk highlight their growing importance in the international financial markets. Countries like Malaysia, Saudi Arabia, and the United Arab Emirates have become leading issuers of Sukuk, leveraging these instruments to finance large-scale infrastructure projects and stimulate economic growth (Jobst et al., 2008). The success of Sukuk in these regions underscores their potential as a viable alternative to conventional financing methods, appealing to both Muslim and non-Muslim investors seeking ethical investment opportunities. Sukuk represents a significant innovation in the field of Islamic finance, blending the principles of Shariah with modern financial practices to create a robust and ethical investment vehicle. Its asset-backed structure, coupled with stringent corporate governance, ensures transparency, accountability, and risk-sharing, aligning the interests of issuers and investors. As the demand for ethical and Shariah compliant financial products continues to grow, Sukuk stands out as a testament to the potential of Islamic finance to contribute to a more equitable and sustainable global financial system.

1.1. Importance and Relevance in the Islamic Finance Industry

In the expanding empire of Islamic finance, the significance and relevance of Sukuk are profound, shaping the industry and setting new standards for ethical investment. As financial instruments rooted in Shariah law, Sukuk stand out by eliminating interest (riba) and speculative elements, which are strictly prohibited in Islam. Instead, Sukuk represent ownership in tangible assets, usufructs, or services, ensuring that investments are backed by real economic activities. This foundational principle of asset-backing not only promotes risk-sharing but also aligns with the ethical mandates of Islamic finance, providing a robust alternative to conventional debt instruments (El-Gamal, 2006).

1.2. Promotion of Transparency and Corporate Governance

Sukuk's importance in the Islamic finance industry extends beyond their compliance with religious tenets; they play a crucial role in promoting transparency and good corporate governance. Issuers of Sukuk are required to adhere to rigorous disclosure standards, providing detailed information about the underlying assets, the use of funds, and the mechanisms for profit and loss sharing. This level of transparency fosters investor confidence and ensures that the financial practices align with Islamic ethical standards (Iqbal & Mirakhor, 2011). The involvement of Shariah boards in the continuous oversight and certification of Sukuk further enhances their credibility, ensuring adherence to Islamic principles throughout the lifecycle of the investment.

1.3. Economic Development and Infrastructure Financing

Moreover, the role of Sukuk in economic development cannot be overstated. By channeling funds into large-scale infrastructure projects, corporate expansions, and social initiatives, Sukuk facilitate sustainable economic growth and development. For example, many governments in the Gulf Cooperation Council (GCC) countries and Southeast Asia have successfully issued Sukuk to finance critical infrastructure, from transportation networks to energy projects, thereby driving economic progress while adhering to Islamic ethical frameworks (Jobst et al., 2008).

1.3.1. Global Acceptance and Market Rise

The global proliferation of Sukuk underscores their relevance and growing acceptance in international financial markets. Countries such as Malaysia and the United Arab Emirates have become leading hubs for Sukuk issuance, attracting both regional and international investors seeking Shariah-compliant investment opportunities. This widespread adoption is a testament to Sukuk's versatility and appeal, bridging the gap between ethical investment demands and modern financial needs (Obaidullah, 2005). The importance and relevance of Sukuk in the Islamic finance industry are multifaceted, encompassing compliance with Shariah law, promotion of transparency and good governance, and facilitation of economic development. As the demand for ethical and sustainable investment options continues to rise, Sukuk are poised to play an increasingly pivotal role, demonstrating that profitability and principles can, indeed, coexist harmoniously in the global financial landscape.

In sum, the widespread adoption of Sukuk highlights it's potential as a transformative tool in both Muslim-majority and non-Muslim-majority economies (Obaidullah, 2005). In essence, this chapter aims to provide readers with a nuanced and in-depth perspective on Sukuk, emphasizing their importance and relevance in the Islamic finance industry. Through a detailed exploration of their ethical foundations, governance structures, and economic impact, we seek to illuminate how Sukuk can contribute to a more transparent, equitable, and resilient global financial system.

2. Literature Review

2.1. Historical Background of Sukuk

The historical evolution of Sukuk, or Islamic bonds, reflects a rich tapestry of Islamic financial innovation tailored to meet modern economic demands while adhering to the ethical principles of Shariah law. Sukuk's origins can be traced back to the classical Islamic era, where the concept of "sakk" was used as a financial certificate representing either debt or investment contracts. However, it wasn't until the late 20th century that Sukuk began to take a form recognizable in today's financial markets. The modern Sukuk market saw its first significant issuance in 1990 when Shell MDS issued a $30 million Sukuk in Malaysia. This marked a pivotal moment, showcasing the potential of Sukuk as a viable alternative to conventional bonds in a Shariah-compliant framework (El-Gamal, 2006). Malaysia has since become a global leader in the Sukuk market, leveraging its robust regulatory framework to foster growth and innovation in Islamic finance.

The global Sukuk market experienced exponential growth in the early 21st century. By 2001, Bahrain issued the first sovereign Sukuk, amounting to $250 million, paving the way for other nations to follow suit. The momentum continued with the Dubai Civil Aviation Authority's $1 billion Sukuk issuance in 2004, which underscored the instrument's growing appeal and versatility (Iqbal & Mirakhor, 2011). The financial crisis of 2007–2008 further underscored the resilience of Sukuk compared to conventional financial instruments. While global financial markets faced unprecedented turmoil, the Sukuk market demonstrated remarkable stability, largely due to its asset-backed nature and adherence to ethical investment principles. This resilience spurred greater interest and investment in Sukuk, propelling the market to new heights.

By 2020, the global Sukuk market had reached a cumulative issuance of over $1.2 trillion, with key issuers including countries from the GCC, Malaysia, Indonesia, and Turkey. The diversity in issuance across different regions highlights the universal appeal and adaptability of Sukuk in meeting various economic needs (Obaidullah, 2005). The role of corporate governance in the development of Sukuk cannot be overstated. The rigorous compliance requirements, transparency, and continuous oversight by Shariah boards ensure that Sukuk issuance and management adhere to high ethical standards. This robust governance framework has been instrumental in building investor confidence and fostering sustainable growth in the Sukuk market (Usmani, 2002).

The historical trajectory of Sukuk from its early conceptual stages to its current prominence in global financial markets illustrates a successful melding of Islamic principles with contemporary financial needs. The rapid growth and widespread acceptance of Sukuk underscore their importance as a cornerstone of Islamic finance, promoting ethical investment and robust corporate governance in an increasingly complex financial landscape.

2.2. Types of Sukuk: Asset-based, Asset-backed, Hybrid, etc.

The diverse landscape of Sukuk, or Islamic bonds, is marked by a variety of structures that cater to different financing needs while adhering to Shariah principles. Among the most prominent types are asset-based, asset-backed, and hybrid Sukuk, each offering unique features and benefits.

1. *Asset-based Sukuk* represent a financial structure where the Sukuk holders have a claim on the assets but not on the underlying assets themselves. In this arrangement, Sukuk are backed by the issuer's general creditworthiness rather than specific assets. For example, a company might issue asset-based Sukuk with returns derived from its overall financial performance rather than a particular asset (El-Gamal, 2006). This type of Sukuk, while Shariah-compliant, carries higher risk as it lacks the direct asset backing found in other Sukuk types.
2. *Asset-backed Sukuk*, in contrast, are structured around specific tangible assets, usufructs, or services. These Sukuk are backed by a distinct asset or pool of assets, which provides a tangible and secure foundation for the investment. For instance, a Sukuk issued for financing a real estate development project would be backed by the revenue generated from the property itself (Iqbal & Mirakhor, 2011). This structure not only aligns with the Islamic prohibition on riba (interest) but also ensures a level of asset security that can mitigate investment risk. Asset-backed Sukuk are considered more robust as they are directly tied to physical assets or specific income streams, enhancing investor confidence.

3. *Hybrid Sukuk* combine elements of both asset-based and asset-backed structures, offering a blend of flexibility and security. These Sukuk might incorporate features from multiple Islamic finance contracts, such as Murabaha (cost-plus financing) and Ijarah (leasing), to structure the investment. For example, a hybrid Sukuk might include a mix of asset-backed components and general credit enhancements, providing a balanced approach that can cater to various investor preferences and financial goals (Obaidullah, 2005). This hybridization allows issuers to leverage the strengths of different Sukuk types while addressing the specific requirements of complex financial arrangements.

The evolution of Sukuk structures reflects the growing sophistication and adaptability of Islamic finance. Each type of Sukuk asset-based, asset-backed, and hybrid serves a unique role in the financial ecosystem, offering different levels of risk and return. Understanding these structures is crucial for investors and issuers alike, as they navigate the principles of Shariah compliance and seek to align their financial activities with ethical standards (Usmani, 2002). The variety of Sukuk types available today demonstrates the flexibility of Islamic finance in addressing diverse investment needs. Whether through the direct asset backing of asset-backed Sukuk, the credit-based nature of asset-based Sukuk, or the innovative blend of hybrid Sukuk, these instruments exemplify the integration of Islamic principles with modern financial practices.

2.3. Previous Studies on Sukuk Issuance

The exploration of Sukuk issuance, a pivotal component of Islamic finance, unveils a fascinating journey of financial innovation rooted in Shariah principles. Since their inception, Sukuk have evolved from a niche financial instrument into a globally recognized tool for ethical investment. Early academic inquiries into Sukuk issuance reveal a dynamic narrative of growth and adaptation, as scholars have meticulously chronicled how these instruments have navigated the complexities of modern finance while adhering to Islamic law. From the pioneering efforts in Malaysia to the subsequent global expansion, these studies not only highlight Sukuk's unique structural attributes but also underscore their impact on financial markets and corporate governance. As the Sukuk market continues to expand, the wealth of research provides critical insights into their role in bridging ethical investment with global financial practices.

Early development and pioneering role: The academic exploration of Sukuk issuance offers valuable insights into its development and significance. Early studies reveal that Sukuk issuance began gaining traction in the 1990s as a response to the need for Shariah-compliant financial instruments that emphasize risk-sharing and asset-backing (El-Gamal, 2006). Research from this formative period underscores Malaysia's pioneering role in establishing a structured Sukuk market, which laid the groundwork for global Sukuk frameworks and set a precedent for other markets (Iqbal & Mirakhor, 2011).

Evolution and diversification: As the Sukuk market matured, scholars have documented its evolution and diversification. Studies such as those by Jobst et al. (2008) have explored how Sukuk issuance became a significant tool for both sovereign and corporate entities to raise capital while adhering to Islamic principles. These works highlight the diversification of Sukuk structures, which evolved from simple asset-based models to complex hybrid instruments, reflecting the market's adaptability to changing financial needs and investor preferences.

Impact on corporate governance: Research on Sukuk issuance also emphasizes its influence on corporate governance. Usmani (2002) provides a comprehensive analysis of how Sukuk enhance corporate governance through stringent disclosure and compliance requirements. The asset-backed nature of Sukuk and the oversight role of Shariah boards are shown to significantly bolster transparency and accountability, thus reducing the risks associated with conventional financial instruments.

Performance during financial crises: The financial crisis of 2007–2008 prompted further scrutiny of Sukuk performance. Studies conducted during this period, such as those by Obaidullah (2005), assessed how Sukuk compared to conventional bonds during times of economic turmoil. These studies highlighted Sukuk's resilience and stability, owing to their asset-backing and ethical investment principles, which provided a more stable alternative to conventional debt instruments amidst the global financial crisis.

Global expansion and acceptance: Contemporary research continues to explore the global expansion of Sukuk markets. Recent studies reveal an increasing participation of non-Muslim-majority countries in Sukuk issuance, reflecting their growing acceptance and versatility (El-Gamal, 2006). This expanding global footprint underscores Sukuk's potential to bridge cultural and financial gaps, offering Shariah-compliant investment opportunities across diverse markets worldwide.

The body of research on Sukuk issuance illustrates a trajectory of growth, adaptation, and influence. These studies collectively underscore Sukuk's transformative impact on Islamic finance and broader financial systems, highlighting their role in promoting ethical investment and enhancing corporate governance.

2.4. Governance Frameworks in Sukuk: Shariah Compliance, Regulatory Bodies, and Standards

The governance frameworks surrounding Sukuk are integral to ensuring their adherence to Shariah principles and maintaining investor confidence. These frameworks encompass Shariah compliance, regulatory bodies, and established standards, each playing a crucial role in the effective management and oversight of Sukuk instruments.

2.4.1. Shariah Compliance

At the core of Sukuk governance is adherence to Shariah compliance, which involves the strict prohibition of interest (riba), speculation (gharar), and investments in prohibited (haram) industries. The compliance process begins with the design and structuring of Sukuk, where Shariah scholars meticulously review the financial instruments to ensure they align with Islamic law. This review is conducted by Shariah boards independent panels of experts in Islamic jurisprudence who provide certification and ongoing oversight. Their role is critical in maintaining the ethical integrity of Sukuk and ensuring that all aspects of the issuance, from asset selection to profit distribution, conform to Shariah principles (Iqbal & Mirakhor, 2011).

2.4.2. Regulatory Bodies

The regulatory environment for Sukuk is another vital component of their governance framework. Different countries have established regulatory bodies to oversee the issuance and trading of Sukuk, ensuring market integrity and investor protection. In Malaysia, for example, the Securities Commission and Bank Negara Malaysia play pivotal roles in regulating Sukuk markets and enforcing compliance with both Shariah and financial regulations. Similarly, in the GCC countries, regulatory frameworks are enforced by national financial authorities to oversee Sukuk transactions and maintain market stability (El-Gamal, 2006).

2.4.3. Standards and Guidelines

Standardization is key to the consistent application of Sukuk governance principles. Various organizations have developed standards and guidelines to ensure uniformity and clarity in Sukuk transactions. The Accounting and Auditing Organization for Islamic Financial Institutions (AAOIFI) is one such entity that has issued comprehensive guidelines on the structuring and reporting of Sukuk. These standards cover a wide range of issues, including Shariah compliance, financial reporting, and risk management. By adhering to these guidelines, issuers and investors benefit from a clear and consistent framework that facilitates transparency and comparability across different Sukuk offerings (Usmani, 2002).

The governance frameworks for Sukuk are multifaceted, involving rigorous Shariah compliance processes, regulatory oversight by national bodies, and adherence to established standards. These elements collectively ensure that Sukuk remain a viable and ethical investment option, fostering trust and stability in the Islamic finance market.

2.5. Comparative Analysis of Sukuk and Conventional Bonds

In the monarchy of financial instruments, the comparative analysis of Sukuk and conventional bonds unveils a compelling juxtaposition between ethical investment practices and traditional debt financing. Sukuk, rooted in Islamic finance, diverges fundamentally from conventional bonds through its adherence to Shariah principles, which emphasize risk-sharing and asset-backing. Unlike conventional bonds, which operate on interest-based financing, Sukuk are structured to avoid riba (interest) by tying returns to the performance of underlying tangible assets or business ventures (El-Gamal, 2006). This asset-backed nature not only aligns with Islamic ethical standards but also inherently reduces speculative risk, offering a more secure investment alternative.

Conventional bonds: Conventional bonds, in contrast, are debt instruments that promise fixed interest payments to investors, with returns often guaranteed by the issuer's creditworthiness. This structure exposes investors to the inherent risks associated with interest rate fluctuations and the issuer's financial stability (Iqbal & Mirakhor, 2011). The fixed nature of interest payments and the potential for capital losses in the case of issuer default contrast sharply with the profit-and-loss sharing mechanisms inherent in Sukuk, which distribute financial returns based on the actual performance of the underlying assets.

Governance perspective: From a governance perspective, Sukuk issuance involves a rigorous process of Shariah compliance, overseen by dedicated Shariah boards that ensure adherence to Islamic finance principles. This governance framework mandates transparency and ethical conduct throughout the lifecycle of the investment, providing a layer of oversight that conventional bonds lack. In comparison, conventional bonds are subject to standard financial regulations and credit assessments, which, while important, do not incorporate the same level of ethical scrutiny (Usmani, 2002).

Market impact: In terms of market impact, Sukuk have demonstrated resilience and stability, particularly during financial crises, due to their asset-backed nature and ethical investment approach. The 2007–2008 financial crisis, for instance, highlighted Sukuk's ability to weather economic turmoil better than many conventional instruments, owing to their reliance on real assets rather than speculative financial practices (Obaidullah, 2005). This stability has fueled growing interest in Sukuk across diverse markets, reflecting their increasing acceptance as a viable alternative to conventional bonds.

The comparative analysis of Sukuk and conventional bonds underscores significant differences in structure, risk management, and ethical considerations. Sukuk offer a distinctive blend of asset-backing and Shariah compliance, presenting a compelling alternative to the interest-based mechanisms of conventional bonds. This differentiation not only aligns with the principles of Islamic finance but also provides investors with a unique avenue for ethical and stable investment.

3. Sukuk Issuance Process

3.1. Key Steps in Sukuk Issuance

The issuance of Sukuk, a hallmark of Islamic finance, is a meticulous process involving several key steps designed to ensure Shariah compliance and financial integrity. The journey begins with the structuring phase, where issuers collaborate with financial and Shariah experts to design a Sukuk that adheres to Islamic principles. This phase is crucial as it involves selecting the appropriate Sukuk structure be it Murabaha, Ijarah, or Musharakah each with its own set of rules and compliance requirements (El-Gamal, 2006). Following the structuring, the issuer must seek approval from a Shariah board, a group of scholars well-versed in Islamic jurisprudence. This board meticulously reviews the Sukuk's structure and underlying assets to ensure they align with Shariah principles. Their certification is a critical component of Sukuk issuance, providing the necessary assurance to investors that the instrument adheres to Islamic law (Iqbal & Mirakhor, 2011). This step underscores the importance of maintaining the ethical integrity of the Sukuk and fostering investor trust. With Shariah approval secured, the next step involves regulatory compliance. The Sukuk must be aligned with the financial regulations of the issuing country. In jurisdictions like Malaysia or the Gulf Cooperation Council (GCC) countries, this involves obtaining approvals from national financial authorities and adhering to specific guidelines governing Sukuk issuance (Jobst et al., 2008). This regulatory oversight ensures that the Sukuk not only meets Shariah requirements but also adheres to local financial standards.

The final phase in the issuance process is the offering and sale of Sukuk to investors. This stage includes the preparation of detailed prospectuses and marketing materials, which provide potential investors with comprehensive information about the Sukuk's terms, underlying assets, and expected returns. The issuance is typically followed by a public or private placement, where the Sukuk is sold to investors, and funds are raised for the intended project or purpose (Obaidullah, 2005). Throughout this process, transparency and adherence to Shariah principles are paramount, ensuring that Sukuk remain a robust and ethical investment option. The detailed and rigorous nature of these steps highlights the commitment to ethical finance and governance that characterizes Sukuk issuance, setting it apart from conventional financial instruments.

3.2. Roles of Various Stakeholders (Issuers, Investors, Regulatory Bodies)

In the complex ecosystem of Sukuk issuance, each stakeholder plays a pivotal role in ensuring that these Shariah compliant financial instruments are structured, regulated, and managed with the utmost integrity and effectiveness. Understanding these roles offers insight into the collaborative effort required to uphold the principles of Islamic finance and foster a transparent and robust financial market.

3.2.1. Issuers

Issuers are at the heart of Sukuk issuance, tasked with structuring and presenting the Sukuk to potential investors. Their primary role involves selecting the appropriate Sukuk structure, such as Murabaha or Ijarah, and ensuring that it complies with Shariah principles. Issuers are responsible for preparing the necessary documentation, including the prospectus, which outlines the Sukuk's terms, underlying assets, and expected returns (El-Gamal, 2006). This process involves close coordination with Shariah scholars to obtain their approval, which is essential for maintaining the instrument's compliance with Islamic law. Issuers must also manage the proceeds from the Sukuk in a manner that aligns with the stated objectives and adheres to financial and ethical standards.

3.2.2. Investors

Investors play a crucial role in the Sukuk market by providing the capital required for the issuance. Their investment decisions are guided by the Shariah compliance of the Sukuk and the transparency of the information provided. Investors are attracted to Sukuk for their asset-backed nature and adherence to ethical investment principles, which offer a distinctive alternative to conventional bonds. They evaluate the Sukuk based on the credibility of the issuer, the quality of the underlying assets, and the projected returns (Iqbal & Mirakhor, 2011). Active participation and investment from diverse groups, including institutional and retail investors, are vital for the success and growth of the Sukuk market.

3.2.3. Regulatory Bodies

Regulatory bodies ensure that Sukuk issuance complies with both Shariah and financial regulations. In many jurisdictions, such as Malaysia and the GCC countries, these authorities oversee the adherence to regulatory frameworks governing Sukuk transactions. They review the documentation, approve the issuance, and monitor ongoing compliance with established guidelines (Jobst et al., 2008). These bodies are instrumental in maintaining market integrity, protecting investor interests, and ensuring that Sukuk issuance aligns with national and international financial standards. Their oversight is crucial for sustaining investor confidence and promoting a stable and transparent Sukuk market.

3.2.4. Shariah Boards

An additional critical stakeholder is the Shariah board, consisting of scholars who specialize in Islamic jurisprudence. Their role is to review and certify that the Sukuk structure and operations comply with Shariah law. They provide ongoing supervision and guidance to ensure that the Sukuk remains aligned with Islamic ethical and legal principles throughout its lifecycle (Usmani, 2002). Their certification is a cornerstone of Sukuk issuance, providing the necessary assurance to investors and maintaining the credibility of the instrument.

The roles of issuers, investors, regulatory bodies, and Shariah boards are interwoven in the Sukuk issuance process, each contributing to the ethical, financial, and regulatory dimensions of these Islamic financial instruments. This collaborative framework not only supports the growth of Sukuk markets but also upholds the principles of transparency, governance, and compliance that define Islamic finance.

3.3. Challenges in the Issuance Process

The issuance of Sukuk, while revolutionary in the realm of Islamic finance, is not without its array of challenges. These hurdles span across structural complexities, regulatory hurdles, and market acceptance, each presenting unique obstacles that issuers and stakeholders must navigate.

Structural complexities: One of the primary challenges in Sukuk issuance is the inherent complexity of structuring these instruments in a way that adheres to Shariah principles while meeting market expectations. Unlike conventional bonds, Sukuk must be backed by tangible assets or real economic activity, requiring meticulous structuring to ensure compliance with Islamic law. This complexity often involves negotiating and drafting intricate contracts that align with Shariah principles, such as Murabaha (cost-plus financing) or Ijarah (leasing) (El-Gamal, 2006). The necessity for rigorous Shariah scrutiny and the integration of various Islamic finance contracts can make the structuring process both time-consuming and costly.

Regulatory hurdles: Navigating the regulatory landscape is another significant challenge in Sukuk issuance. Different jurisdictions have varying regulatory requirements and standards for Sukuk, which can create a labyrinth of compliance issues for issuers. For instance, while Malaysia has a well-established regulatory framework for Sukuk, other regions may have less developed or inconsistent regulations (Jobst et al., 2008). This disparity can complicate cross-border Sukuk offerings and hinder global market integration. Issuers must ensure that their Sukuk complies with both local financial regulations and Shariah requirements, a task that often involves extensive coordination with regulatory bodies and legal advisors.

Market acceptance: Market acceptance of Sukuk also poses a considerable challenge. Despite their growth, Sukuk still face skepticism from investors who may be unfamiliar with Islamic finance principles or perceive these instruments as less transparent compared to conventional bonds. Building investor confidence requires clear communication of the Sukuk's benefits, risks, and compliance with Shariah law (Iqbal & Mirakhor, 2011). Additionally, Sukuk issuers must contend with market volatility and investor demand, which can affect the pricing and overall success of the issuance.

Shariah compliance and interpretation: Ensuring Shariah compliance throughout the Sukuk's lifecycle is another challenge. The interpretation of Shariah principles can vary among scholars and Shariah boards, leading to differing opinions on what constitutes compliance. This variability can create challenges in obtaining unanimous Shariah approval and maintaining consistent standards across different Sukuk issues (Usmani, 2002). Furthermore, ongoing Shariah supervision is necessary to ensure that the Sukuk remains compliant with Islamic principles, adding another layer of complexity to the issuance process.

The Sukuk issuance process is tense with challenges that include structural complexities, regulatory hurdles, market acceptance, and Shariah compliance issues. Addressing these challenges requires a coordinated effort among issuers, regulators, and Shariah scholars to ensure that Sukuk remain a viable and ethical investment instrument in the evolving landscape of Islamic finance.

4. Governance Frameworks

4.1. Key Principles of Governance in Sukuk

The governance of Sukuk, the cornerstone of Islamic financial instruments, is governed by a set of key principles that ensure compliance with Shariah law and promote transparency and accountability. These principles are integral to maintaining the integrity of Sukuk and aligning them with the ethical standards of Islamic finance.

4.1.1. Shariah Compliance

Central to Sukuk governance is unwavering adherence to Shariah compliance, a principle that fundamentally distinguishes Sukuk from conventional financial instruments. Shariah law, which prohibits the charging of interest (riba), excessive uncertainty (gharar), and investment in activities deemed sinful or harmful (haram), shapes the very essence of Sukuk. Each Sukuk must be structured around tangible assets or productive economic activities, ensuring that returns are not derived from speculative or unethical sources. The involvement of Shariah boards composed of eminent scholars in Islamic jurisprudence is crucial in this context. These boards meticulously review and approve Sukuk structures, ensuring they meet the rigorous demands of Shariah law. Their certification process includes assessing the asset-backed nature of the Sukuk and the adherence to Islamic financial principles throughout the instrument's lifecycle (El-Gamal, 2006). This rigorous Shariah oversight ensures that Sukuk maintain their ethical and legal integrity, fostering confidence among investors that their investments comply with Islamic teachings.

4.1.2. Transparency and Disclosure

Transparency and disclosure are foundational principles in the governance of Sukuk, designed to safeguard investor interests and uphold market integrity. Unlike conventional bonds, where the focus is often on the issuer's creditworthiness and interest payments, Sukuk demand a higher level of clarity regarding the underlying assets and financial structures. Issuers are required to provide detailed prospectuses that outline the Sukuk's structure, the nature of the underlying assets, and the expected financial returns. These documents must also include comprehensive risk disclosures and periodic performance reports. Such transparency is essential for enabling investors to make informed decisions and for fostering trust in the Sukuk market. By ensuring that all material information is readily available and accessible, Sukuk issuers help mitigate risks associated with information asymmetry and enhance the overall credibility of the investment (Iqbal & Mirakhor, 2011). This commitment to openness is not only a regulatory requirement but also a core aspect of ethical finance, reinforcing investor confidence and market stability.

4.1.3. Accountability and Oversight

The principles of accountability and oversight are vital for maintaining the integrity and effectiveness of Sukuk governance. This involves rigorous monitoring and auditing by both Shariah boards and financial regulators. Shariah boards are responsible for overseeing the Sukuk's compliance with Islamic law, conducting regular reviews to ensure that the structure and operations remain aligned with Shariah principles. Additionally, financial regulators enforce compliance with national and international financial standards, scrutinizing the Sukuk issuance process and ongoing management to prevent conflicts of interest and ensure regulatory adherence (Jobst et al., 2008). This dual layer of oversight helps prevent potential abuses and ensures that Sukuk are managed in a manner that is both legally compliant and ethically sound. Effective accountability mechanisms also involve transparent reporting and regular audits, which further reinforce the credibility and reliability of Sukuk.

4.1.4. Risk Management

Effective risk management is a cornerstone of Sukuk governance, ensuring that the investment is both secure and equitable. Given that Sukuk are backed by tangible assets, managing risks associated with these assets and their performance is crucial. The governance framework for Sukuk includes provisions for comprehensive risk assessment and mitigation strategies. Issuers are required to perform due diligence on the quality and value of the underlying assets, as well as implement mechanisms to manage and distribute risks fairly among investors. This includes measures such as insurance, guarantees, or diversification strategies to protect against potential losses (Usmani, 2002). Regular performance evaluations and risk management practices are integral to safeguarding investor interests and maintaining the stability of the Sukuk. By addressing potential risks and ensuring that returns are fairly distributed, Sukuk issuers uphold the principles of justice and equity that are central to Islamic finance.

The governance of Sukuk is underpinned by principles of Shariah compliance, transparency, accountability, and effective risk management. These principles collectively ensure that Sukuk not only adhere to Islamic financial laws but also promote a transparent, accountable, and stable investment environment. By maintaining these standards, Sukuk continue to offer a compelling alternative to conventional financial instruments, aligning ethical finance with robust financial practices.

4.2. Role of Shariah Boards and Scholars

In the domain of Islamic finance, Shariah boards and scholars occupy a pivotal role, ensuring that financial products like Sukuk adhere strictly to Islamic law and ethical principles. Their involvement is not merely advisory but foundational, influencing every aspect of Sukuk issuance, from structuring to ongoing compliance.

Shariah compliance and structuring: The primary responsibility of Shariah boards is to ensure that Sukuk structures comply with Islamic jurisprudence. This involves a comprehensive review of the Sukuk's design to ensure it adheres to key Shariah principles, such as the prohibition of riba (interest), gharar (excessive uncertainty), and investments in haram (forbidden) activities. Shariah scholars, who are well-versed in Islamic finance and jurisprudence, meticulously examine the proposed Sukuk structure to validate its conformity with Shariah requirements (El-Gamal, 2006). Their approval is essential for the Sukuk's legitimacy, as it provides assurance to investors that the financial instrument aligns with Islamic ethical standards.

Ongoing supervision and guidance: Beyond the initial approval, Shariah boards play a critical role in the ongoing supervision of Sukuk to ensure continuous adherence to Shariah principles. This includes monitoring the management of Sukuk proceeds, overseeing the performance of underlying assets, and ensuring that all operational aspects remain compliant with Shariah guidelines. Shariah scholars provide ongoing guidance and intervention as needed, addressing any issues that may arise throughout the life of the Sukuk (Iqbal & Mirakhor, 2011). Their role is crucial in maintaining the integrity of Sukuk and ensuring that any operational or structural adjustments do not compromise Shariah compliance.

Enhancing investor confidence: The involvement of Shariah boards and scholars also significantly impacts investor confidence. By providing expert validation and ongoing oversight, Shariah scholars help to foster a sense of trust and transparency in Sukuk investments. Investors are reassured that their investments are not only financially sound but also ethically and religiously compliant. This trust is essential for the growth and stability of the Sukuk market, as it encourages greater participation and investment in Shariah-compliant financial products (Jobst et al., 2008).

Advisory role and thought leadership: In addition to their compliance and oversight functions, Shariah boards and scholars contribute to the development and evolution of Islamic finance practices. They offer valuable insights and recommendations on new financial structures, products, and regulatory frameworks, influencing the broader landscape of Islamic finance. Their thought leadership helps to address emerging challenges and adapt Shariah principles to contemporary financial needs, ensuring that Islamic finance remains relevant and dynamic (Usmani, 2002).

Shariah boards and scholars are integral to the governance and success of Sukuk. Their roles encompass ensuring Shariah compliance, providing ongoing supervision, enhancing investor confidence, and contributing to the evolution of Islamic finance. Through their expert guidance and oversight, they uphold the ethical and religious standards of Islamic finance, reinforcing the credibility and stability of Sukuk in the global financial market.

4.3. Regulatory Frameworks Across Different Jurisdictions (e.g., AAOIFI Standards, Local Regulations)

The regulatory frameworks governing Sukuk issuance exhibit significant diversity, shaped by varying local and international standards that ensure compliance with Shariah principles and regulatory requirements. These frameworks not only reflect the unique financial landscapes of different jurisdictions but also contribute to the global harmonization of Islamic finance practices.

4.3.1. International Standards: AAOIFI

The AAOIFI plays a crucial role in establishing international standards for Sukuk. Founded in 1991, AAOIFI has issued over 60 standards covering various aspects of Islamic finance, including Sukuk issuance. Its guidelines are adopted in numerous countries, particularly within the GCC countries. For instance, AAOIFI's standards are integral to Bahrain's regulatory framework, where the Islamic financial sector represents approximately 15% of the total banking assets (Central Bank of Bahrain, 2022). By providing a unified set of standards, AAOIFI helps streamline Sukuk issuance and foster cross-border investment, enhancing the credibility and efficiency of the global Islamic finance market (AAOIFI, 2020).

4.3.2. Regional Regulations: Malaysia's Framework

Malaysia is a prominent hub for Islamic finance, with a sophisticated regulatory framework that has supported its Sukuk market's growth. The Securities Commission of Malaysia (SC) regulates Sukuk issuance through comprehensive guidelines and oversight. As of 2023, Malaysia's Sukuk market is the largest globally, accounting for over 50% of the global Sukuk issuance market (World Bank, 2023). The SC's guidelines ensure rigorous Shariah compliance, transparency, and investor protection. The Shariah Advisory Council, established by the SC, plays a critical role in certifying Sukuk structures, ensuring they meet both Islamic and local financial standards. Malaysia's framework has set a benchmark for other countries, demonstrating the effectiveness of a well-regulated Sukuk market.

4.3.3. Local Regulations: GCC Countries

In the GCC region, Sukuk regulation varies but maintains a common emphasis on Shariah compliance and financial transparency. For example, the UAE's Dubai Financial Services Authority oversees Sukuk issuance with stringent regulations designed to align with international best practices. The UAE's Sukuk market has experienced significant growth, with issuance reaching over $20 billion in 2023, making it one of the leading Sukuk markets globally (Dubai Financial Services Authority, 2023). Similarly, Saudi Arabia's Capital Market Authority has developed a robust regulatory framework that includes detailed guidelines for Sukuk issuance. As of 2023, Saudi Arabia has issued Sukuk totaling approximately $35 billion, reflecting the country's growing role in the global Sukuk market (World Capital Market Authority, 2023). Each GCC country's regulatory approach contributes to a dynamic and expanding Sukuk market in the region.

4.3.4. Emerging Markets and Developments

Emerging markets are increasingly developing their regulatory frameworks to accommodate Sukuk issuance. For instance, Indonesia, one of the largest Islamic finance markets outside the GCC, issued Sukuk worth $10 billion in 2022, demonstrating its growing prominence (Bank Indonesia, 2023). Pakistan has also made strides in enhancing its Sukuk regulations, with recent efforts to streamline issuance processes and attract investment. As these emerging markets adopt and adapt regulatory frameworks, they contribute to the global expansion of the Sukuk market, fostering greater integration and participation in Islamic finance.

The regulatory frameworks for Sukuk issuance encompass a range of international and local standards that ensure compliance with Shariah principles and financial regulations. Bodies like AAOIFI provide critical global benchmarks, while countries such as Malaysia and GCC states offer detailed, region-specific guidelines. The growing Sukuk markets in emerging economies further highlight the expanding reach and influence of Islamic finance, reinforcing the importance of effective and harmonized regulatory frameworks.

5. Case Studies of Successful Sukuk Issuances

The Sukuk market has seen numerous successful issuances that highlight its effectiveness and versatility in Islamic finance. Examining these case studies reveals how Sukuk have been utilized for large-scale projects, national development, and strategic financial management across different regions.

5.1. Dubai's World Trade Centre Sukuk

In 2014, Dubai World Trade Centre (DWTC) issued a landmark Sukuk worth $2.5 billion, marking a significant milestone in the UAE's Islamic finance landscape. This issuance aimed to refinance existing debt and fund the expansion of DWTC, a crucial economic asset that supports Dubai's status as a global business hub. The Sukuk was structured with an asset-backed approach, where the underlying assets included DWTC's property and infrastructure, ensuring Shariah compliance and enhancing investor confidence. The Sukuk's success was underscored by its strong international appeal, attracting a diverse range of investors and achieving a significant oversubscription (Dubai Financial Services Authority, 2014). The DWTC Sukuk not only demonstrated Dubai's ability to leverage Islamic finance for major infrastructure projects but also reinforced its position as a leading center for Sukuk issuance globally.

5.1.1. Malaysia's 1MDB Sukuk

The 1Malaysia Development Berhad (1MDB) Sukuk issued in 2013 was a notable event in Malaysia's Sukuk market, reflecting the country's advanced Islamic finance capabilities. This issuance of $3 billion was intended to finance various national development and infrastructure projects. The Sukuk was structured in compliance with Shariah principles, utilizing government-backed assets to provide a secure investment. Despite the subsequent controversies surrounding 1MDB, the Sukuk issuance was a testament to Malaysia's ability to harness Islamic finance for large-scale national projects (Securities Commission Malaysia, 2013). It highlighted Malaysia's role as a pioneer in Sukuk issuance and its innovative approach to utilizing Islamic finance for economic development. The issuance also underscored the importance of transparency and governance in managing large-scale Sukuk transactions.

5.2. Saudi Arabia's National Commercial Bank Sukuk

In 2015, the National Commercial Bank (NCB) of Saudi Arabia issued a $1 billion Sukuk, marking one of the largest Sukuk offerings by a Saudi bank. This issuance was part of NCB's strategy to strengthen its capital base and support its expansion plans. The Sukuk was structured with a combination of fixed and floating returns, backed by NCB's assets, ensuring Shariah compliance and providing a stable investment for holders. The success of the NCB Sukuk demonstrated the robustness of Saudi Arabia's banking sector and its ability to effectively utilize Islamic finance tools for capital enhancement and strategic growth (Capital Market Authority, 2015). The issuance not only reinforced NCB's financial position but also showcased Saudi Arabia's leadership in the Islamic finance sector, contributing to the development and sophistication of its Sukuk market.

5.3. Indonesia's Global Sukuk Offering

In 2018, Indonesia made a significant impact on the global Sukuk market with its issuance of $3 billion in Sukuk. This offering was part of the Indonesian government's strategy to diversify its funding sources and attract international investors. The Sukuk was structured using a combination of asset-backed and ijarah (leasing) contracts, reflecting Indonesia's innovative approach to Sukuk structuring. The successful placement of this Sukuk highlighted Indonesia's growing role in the global Islamic finance market and demonstrated the potential of Sukuk to attract substantial foreign investment (Bank Indonesia, 2018). This issuance not only provided a vital funding source for Indonesia's development needs but also underscored the country's commitment to expanding its presence in the global Sukuk market.

These case studies illustrate the diverse and successful applications of Sukuk across different regions. Dubai's World Trade Centre Sukuk showcased the use of Sukuk for major infrastructure projects, Malaysia's 1MDB Sukuk highlighted its role in national development, Saudi Arabia's NCB Sukuk demonstrated its effectiveness in banking capital enhancement, and Indonesia's global Sukuk offering emphasized its potential to attract international investment. Each of these issuances underscores the growing sophistication and global integration of the Sukuk market, reflecting its ability to meet varied financial needs while adhering to Shariah principles.

6. Conclusion

The exploration of Sukuk within the framework of Islamic finance and corporate governance has revealed several key findings that underscore the sophistication and impact of these financial instruments. Central to these findings is the realization of Sukuk as a pivotal tool in both Islamic finance and broader financial markets. Sukuk have emerged as highly innovative financial instruments, effectively bridging the gap between Islamic finance principles and global financial practices. The issuance of Sukuk, such as the Dubai World Trade Centre Sukuk and Malaysia's 1MDB Sukuk, exemplifies how these instruments can facilitate substantial financing for major projects and national development initiatives while adhering to Shariah principles (Dubai Financial Services Authority, 2014; Securities Commission Malaysia, 2013). These case studies illustrate Sukuk's versatility and their role in supporting large-scale infrastructure and economic projects, demonstrating their capacity to attract significant investment and contribute to economic growth.

The regulatory frameworks governing Sukuk are diverse yet vital for ensuring compliance and maintaining market integrity. The standards set by the AAOIFI provide a global benchmark for Shariah compliance and financial reporting, facilitating cross-border Sukuk transactions (AAOIFI, 2020). Additionally, regional regulations, such as those from Malaysia's Securities Commission and the UAE's Dubai Financial Services Authority, reflect the specific needs and practices of different markets while maintaining rigorous standards of transparency and investor protection (Dubai Financial Services Authority, 2023; Securities Commission Malaysia, 2020). These frameworks are crucial for ensuring that Sukuk issuances remain compliant with Shariah principles and regulatory requirements, thereby enhancing market confidence and stability.

Shariah boards and scholars play an essential role in the Sukuk market, ensuring that all aspects of Sukuk issuance and management adhere to Islamic jurisprudence. Their involvement extends from the initial structuring of Sukuk to ongoing supervision, ensuring that all operations remain compliant with Shariah principles (Iqbal & Mirakhor, 2011). This oversight not only reinforces the ethical foundation of Sukuk but also enhances investor trust, contributing to the growth and credibility of the Islamic finance sector (Jobst et al., 2008). While Sukuk offer numerous benefits, including compliance with Shariah and diversification of funding sources, they also present challenges. Issues related to regulatory harmonization, Shariah compliance, and market liquidity remain significant (El-Gamal, 2006).

Addressing these challenges involves ongoing development of regulatory frameworks, enhancement of Shariah governance, and innovation in Sukuk structures. Opportunities for growth are evident in emerging markets, where Sukuk can play a critical role in financing development projects and attracting foreign investment (Bank Indonesia, 2023). Sukuk have proven to be a dynamic and effective component of Islamic finance, offering innovative solutions for large-scale financing while adhering to Shariah principles. The diverse regulatory frameworks, the crucial role of Shariah boards, and the ongoing challenges and opportunities in the Sukuk market highlight the complexity and potential of these instruments. As Islamic finance continues to evolve, Sukuk will remain central to its growth and global integration, reflecting their significant impact on both financial markets and economic development.

6.1. Importance of Robust Governance in Sukuk Issuance

Robust governance is paramount in the Sukuk issuance process, serving as the cornerstone of trust and integrity in Islamic finance. Effective governance frameworks ensure that Sukuk issuances adhere to Shariah principles and regulatory standards, thereby safeguarding investor interests and enhancing market stability. The complexity of Sukuk structures, which often involve intricate asset management and financial engineering, necessitates a meticulous governance approach to maintain compliance and transparency.

At the heart of Sukuk governance is Shariah compliance, a critical factor that distinguishes these instruments from conventional bonds. Sukuk must adhere to Islamic jurisprudence, which prohibits interest (riba) and emphasizes ethical investment in tangible assets or services. Shariah boards play a crucial role in this context, providing expert oversight and certifying that Sukuk structures and transactions align with Islamic law (Iqbal & Mirakhor, 2011). Their involvement ensures that the Sukuk issuance process remains true to its ethical foundations, which is essential for maintaining investor confidence and fostering the credibility of the Islamic finance sector (Jobst et al., 2008). Robust governance also involves stringent adherence to regulatory and legal frameworks. Regulatory bodies, such as Malaysia's Securities Commission and the Dubai Financial Services Authority, establish comprehensive guidelines to govern Sukuk issuance. These regulations cover various aspects, from disclosure requirements to financial reporting and investor protection (Dubai Financial Services Authority, 2023; Securities Commission Malaysia, 2020).

The effectiveness of these frameworks in enforcing compliance and ensuring transparency is critical for preventing mismanagement and mitigating risks associated with Sukuk investments. Transparency and accountability are integral components of Sukuk governance. Clear and accurate disclosure of the Sukuk's underlying assets, financial performance, and Shariah compliance status helps build investor trust and facilitates informed decision-making. Governance mechanisms such as regular audits, performance reviews, and detailed reporting requirements are essential in this regard. These measures ensure that Sukuk issuers maintain high standards of accountability, addressing any potential concerns about the security and legitimacy of the investment (El-Gamal, 2006).

Effective governance frameworks are also crucial for managing the risks associated with Sukuk issuance. By establishing clear guidelines and oversight mechanisms, stakeholders can identify and address potential risks related to asset valuation, contractual obligations, and market fluctuations. This proactive approach not only mitigates financial risks but also enhances overall market confidence in Sukuk as a viable investment option (Bank Indonesia, 2023). The successful management of these risks through robust governance practices contributes to the stability and growth of the Sukuk market, reinforcing its role in the global financial system. Robust governance in Sukuk issuance is indispensable for ensuring Shariah compliance, adhering to regulatory standards, and maintaining transparency and accountability. The active involvement of Shariah boards, stringent regulatory frameworks, and effective risk management practices collectively underpin the integrity and success of Sukuk investments. As the Sukuk market continues to evolve, the importance of these governance elements will remain central to fostering trust, enhancing market stability, and driving the growth of Islamic finance.

6.2. Future Trends in Sukuk Markets

The Sukuk market is poised for significant evolution, driven by emerging trends and innovative developments that are reshaping the landscape of Islamic finance. As Sukuk continue to gain prominence globally, several key trends and projections highlight their future trajectory, reflecting both current dynamics and anticipated shifts in the market.

Expanding geographic reach: One of the most notable trends is the expanding geographic reach of Sukuk. Historically concentrated in the Middle East and Southeast Asia, Sukuk issuance is now gaining traction in new regions. For instance, European and North American markets are increasingly exploring Sukuk as a means of diversifying funding sources and catering to ethical investment preferences. Recent issuances, such as the UK's $500 million Sukuk in 2014 and Luxembourg's inaugural Sukuk in 2021, underscore this growing interest in non-traditional Sukuk markets (Luxembourg Government, 2021; UK Treasury, 2014). Projections indicate that Sukuk issuance in non-GCC regions will continue to grow, potentially accounting for up to 20% of the global Sukuk market by 2025 (Thomson Reuters, 2023).

Innovative sukuk structures: The evolution of Sukuk structures reflects a trend toward greater innovation and sophistication. Asset-backed and asset-based Sukuk are being complemented by hybrid structures that blend traditional Sukuk features with modern financial instruments. For example, green Sukuk, which are designed to fund environmentally sustainable projects, are gaining popularity. The issuance of green Sukuk, such as the $1 billion green Sukuk issued by Indonesia in 2018, highlights the market's response to the increasing demand for sustainable investment options (Bank Indonesia, 2018). Future trends suggest a continued rise in green and sustainable Sukuk, driven by global environmental and social governance initiatives.

Technological advancements: Technological advancements are also expected to play a crucial role in the future of Sukuk markets. The integration of blockchain technology and digital platforms is poised to enhance the efficiency and transparency of Sukuk transactions. For instance, the use of blockchain for Sukuk issuance and trading can streamline processes, reduce costs, and increase market accessibility. Early adopters in the Gulf region have already initiated blockchain-based Sukuk projects, paving the way for broader adoption (Dubai International Financial Centre, 2022). The adoption of such technologies is anticipated to revolutionize Sukuk markets, making them more inclusive and efficient.

Increased regulatory and standardization efforts: As Sukuk markets expand globally, there is a growing emphasis on regulatory harmonization and standardization. Efforts by organizations such as the AAOIFI and the International Islamic Financial Market (IIFM) aim to create uniform standards for Sukuk issuance and Shariah compliance. These efforts are crucial for enhancing market transparency and investor protection. The introduction of unified global standards is expected to facilitate cross-border Sukuk transactions and attract a wider range of institutional investors (AAOIFI, 2020; IIFM, 2022).

Market projections: Current projections indicate a robust growth trajectory for the Sukuk market. According to Fitch Ratings, global Sukuk issuance is expected to reach approximately $160 billion in 2024, up from $140 billion in 2023, reflecting an annual growth rate of around 14% (Fitch Ratings, 2024). This growth is driven by increasing demand for Shariah-compliant investment products and the expanding role of Sukuk in financing major infrastructure and development projects.

The future of Sukuk markets is marked by expanding geographic reach, innovative structures, technological advancements, and enhanced regulatory frameworks. As the market continues to evolve, these trends will shape the landscape of Islamic finance, offering new opportunities for issuers and investors alike. The ongoing growth and diversification of Sukuk are expected to further solidify their position as a key component of the global financial system.

7. Policy Recommendations

7.1. Recommendations for Improving Governance Frameworks

Enhancing governance frameworks for Sukuk issuance is critical to ensuring the integrity, transparency, and efficiency of Islamic finance. As the Sukuk market continues to expand and evolve, it is imperative to address existing challenges and implement strategic improvements to fortify these frameworks. Key recommendations include advancing Shariah compliance mechanisms, harmonizing regulatory standards, leveraging technology, and strengthening stakeholder engagement.

Advancing Shariah compliance mechanisms: A cornerstone of effective Sukuk governance is the rigorous adherence to Shariah principles. To bolster Shariah compliance, it is essential to enhance the role and effectiveness of Shariah boards. This involves increasing the transparency of Shariah decision-making processes and ensuring that board members possess a diverse range of expertise in both Islamic jurisprudence and financial management. Strengthening training programs for Shariah scholars and integrating their recommendations into Sukuk structuring and oversight will reinforce adherence to Islamic law and address investor concerns about Shariah compliance (Iqbal & Mirakhor, 2011). Additionally, regular audits and reviews of Sukuk structures by independent Shariah advisory firms can provide an extra layer of assurance regarding compliance.

Harmonizing regulatory standards: The global Sukuk market would benefit from greater regulatory harmonization to facilitate cross-border transactions and enhance investor confidence. The development of unified standards by organizations such as the AAOIFI and the IIFM is a positive step in this direction. However, there remains a need for further alignment of national regulations with these global standards. Regulators should work collaboratively to establish consistent guidelines for Sukuk issuance, disclosure requirements, and Shariah compliance across jurisdictions (AAOIFI, 2020; IIFM, 2022). This harmonization will reduce regulatory arbitrage, streamline the issuance process, and promote a more cohesive global Sukuk market.

Leveraging technological innovations: Technology has the potential to significantly enhance Sukuk governance frameworks by improving transparency, efficiency, and accessibility. The adoption of block-chain technology for Sukuk issuance and trading can streamline administrative processes, reduce costs, and increase the security of transactions. Block-chain's immutable ledger capabilities enable real-time tracking of Sukuk transactions and ensure the integrity of asset management. Moreover, digital platforms can facilitate greater market access, particularly for smaller investors and emerging markets (Dubai International Financial Centre, 2022). Financial institutions and regulators should invest in technological innovations to modernize Sukuk processes and enhance overall market effectiveness.

Strengthening stakeholder engagement: Effective governance requires active engagement from all stakeholders involved in Sukuk issuance, including issuers, investors, regulatory bodies, and Shariah boards. Creating forums for regular dialog and feedback can foster better understanding and cooperation among these parties. Issuers should prioritize transparency in their communication with investors, providing detailed information about Sukuk structures, underlying assets, and financial performance. Regulatory bodies should facilitate stakeholder engagement by organizing industry workshops, seminars, and consultations to address emerging issues and gather input on policy developments (El-Gamal, 2006). Strengthening these interactions will improve governance practices and contribute to a more robust and dynamic Sukuk market.

Improving governance frameworks for Sukuk issuance requires a multifaceted approach that enhances Shariah compliance mechanisms, harmonizes regulatory standards, leverages technological innovations, and strengthens stakeholder engagement. By implementing these recommendations, the Sukuk market can achieve greater integrity, transparency, and efficiency, ultimately reinforcing its role in the global financial system and fostering continued growth and development.

7.2. Policies to Encourage More Sukuk Issuances

To stimulate the growth of the Sukuk market and foster a more vibrant Islamic finance ecosystem, policymakers must implement targeted strategies that address both market barriers and opportunities. Encouraging increased Sukuk issuances involves a multifaceted approach that includes enhancing market incentives, refining regulatory frameworks, and promoting market education and innovation.

7.2.1. Enhancing Market Incentives

One of the foremost strategies is to enhance market incentives for issuers and investors. Governments and regulatory bodies can introduce tax incentives and subsidies to reduce the cost of Sukuk issuance and make it a more attractive option compared to conventional bonds. For instance, tax exemptions on Sukuk returns or favorable treatment in capital gains taxation can significantly lower the financial burden for issuers and increase investor appeal. Additionally, providing guarantees or credit enhancements, such as sovereign guarantees or support from development banks, can mitigate risks associated with Sukuk and attract a broader range of issuers, including those from emerging markets (Thomson Reuters, 2023). By reducing costs and perceived risks, such policies can stimulate greater issuance activity and market participation.

7.2.2. Refining Regulatory Frameworks

Refining regulatory frameworks is crucial to creating a conducive environment for Sukuk issuance. Streamlining the regulatory approval process, simplifying compliance requirements, and ensuring consistency in Shariah interpretation can lower barriers to entry for potential issuers. Policymakers should work toward harmonizing regulations across jurisdictions to facilitate cross-border Sukuk transactions and enhance market integration (AAOIFI, 2020). Additionally, establishing clear and standardized guidelines for Sukuk structuring, disclosure, and Shariah compliance can reduce uncertainty and improve market confidence. Regulatory bodies should also consider creating dedicated Sukuk platforms or exchanges that offer tailored services and support for Sukuk issuers and investors, further enhancing market accessibility and efficiency (Securities Commission Malaysia, 2020).

7.2.3. Promoting Market Education and Innovation

Promoting market education and innovation is essential for expanding Sukuk market participation. Education initiatives should focus on increasing awareness about the benefits and mechanics of Sukuk among corporate treasurers, institutional investors, and financial intermediaries. Training programs, workshops, and seminars can help demystify Sukuk and provide practical insights into their issuance and investment (Jobst et al., 2008). Furthermore, encouraging innovation in Sukuk structures, such as green Sukuk and sustainability-linked Sukuk, aligns with global trends toward responsible investment and can attract a new segment of environmentally conscious investors. Support for research and development in Sukuk innovation, along with pilot projects and case studies, can drive adoption and showcase the potential of Sukuk in financing diverse projects (Bank Indonesia, 2023).

7.2.4. Strengthening Infrastructure and Market Ecosystem

Strengthening the infrastructure and market ecosystem for Sukuk is also vital. Developing robust financial infrastructure, such as Sukuk trading platforms and clearinghouses, can improve market liquidity and efficiency. Investment in technology to support digital issuance and trading of Sukuk can enhance market accessibility and reduce transaction costs. Additionally, fostering collaboration among financial institutions, regulatory bodies, and Shariah scholars can create a more cohesive and supportive ecosystem for Sukuk issuance (El-Gamal, 2006).

By addressing infrastructure challenges and promoting market innovation, policymakers can create a more dynamic and resilient Sukuk market.

Implementing policies to encourage more Sukuk issuances involves a comprehensive approach that enhances market incentives, refines regulatory frameworks, promotes education and innovation, and strengthens market infrastructure. By addressing these areas, policymakers can stimulate Sukuk issuance, expand market participation, and support the continued growth of Islamic finance. Such efforts will contribute to the development of a more inclusive and sustainable financial system, benefiting both issuers and investors.

7.2.5. Enhancing investor Confidence and Market Growth

Enhancing investor confidence and stimulating market growth are critical objectives for the Sukuk market, crucial to its development and stability within the Islamic finance sector. Investor confidence is fundamentally tied to transparency, reliability, and the overall integrity of Sukuk issuances, while market growth is driven by robust governance practices, innovative financial products, and strategic regulatory measures. A primary factor in bolstering investor confidence is transparency in Sukuk transactions and issuances. Investors demand clear, comprehensive information about the underlying assets, financial performance, and compliance with Shariah principles. Enhancing disclosure standards, such as providing detailed financial reports, independent audits, and transparent Shariah compliance certificates, helps mitigate information asymmetry and reduces the perceived risks associated with Sukuk investments (El-Gamal, 2006). For example, the enhanced disclosure practices adopted by issuers in Malaysia and Saudi Arabia have set benchmarks for transparency, contributing to increased investor trust and market participation (Securities Commission Malaysia, 2020).

Implementing robust governance practices is crucial for maintaining the integrity of the Sukuk market. This involves rigorous adherence to Shariah principles, stringent regulatory compliance, and effective risk management. Strengthening the role of Shariah boards, ensuring regular audits, and adhering to established international standards, such as those set by the AAOIFI, are key components of a strong governance framework (AAOIFI, 2020). Additionally, promoting best practices in governance, including transparent conflict resolution mechanisms and clear guidelines for Shariah compliance, enhances market credibility and attracts both domestic and international investors. Innovation in Sukuk structures can significantly contribute to market growth by catering to diverse investor needs and preferences.

The development of new Sukuk varieties, such as green Sukuk or social impact Sukuk, aligns with global trends toward sustainable and responsible investing. For instance, Indonesia's issuance of a $1 billion green Sukuk in 2018, aimed at financing eco-friendly projects, exemplifies how innovative Sukuk structures can tap into new investor segments and drive market expansion (Bank Indonesia, 2018). Encouraging further innovation in Sukuk products can attract a wider range of investors, from institutional to retail, thereby broadening the market base.

Effective regulatory support and well-developed market infrastructure are vital for fostering investor confidence and facilitating market growth. Regulatory bodies should streamline the issuance process, reduce bureaucratic hurdles, and ensure a fair, transparent regulatory environment. For instance, the introduction of Sukuk trading platforms and digital solutions can enhance market liquidity and accessibility, making it easier for investors to participate (Dubai International Financial Centre, 2022).

Furthermore, aligning national regulations with global standards, and fostering collaboration among regulators, issuers, and financial institutions, strengthens the overall market infrastructure and promotes investor trust. Finally, educational initiatives aimed at increasing investor awareness and understanding of Sukuk are essential for enhancing confidence and driving market growth. Providing educational resources, hosting seminars, and offering training programs can demystify Sukuk and inform potential investors about their benefits and risks. By equipping investors with the knowledge needed to make informed decisions, educational initiatives can stimulate greater participation and investment in the Sukuk market (Jobst et al., 2008). Enhancing investor confidence and fostering market growth in the Sukuk sector requires a multi-pronged approach that includes improving transparency, implementing robust governance practices, encouraging innovation, supporting regulatory reforms, and advancing investor education. By addressing these areas, stakeholders can create a more resilient and dynamic Sukuk market, driving sustained growth and attracting a diverse range of investors.

References

AAOIFI. (2020). *AAOIFI Shariah standards*. Accounting and Auditing Organization for Islamic Financial Institutions.

Bank Indonesia. (2018). *Global Sukuk offering report*. Bank Indonesia.

Bank Indonesia. (2023). *Global Sukuk offering report*. Bank Indonesia.

Capital Market Authority. (2015). *NCB Sukuk issuance report*. Capital Market Authority, Saudi Arabia.

Central Bank of Bahrain. (2022). *Financial crime module and collective investment undertakings module: Rulebook updates* (pp. 1–150). Central Bank of Bahrain.

Dubai Financial Services Authority. (2014). *Annual report 2014: Overview of regulatory activities and financial statements* (pp. 1–120). Dubai Financial Services Authority.

Dubai Financial Services Authority. (2023). *Regulatory framework for Sukuk*. Dubai Financial Services Authority.

Dubai International Financial Centre. (2022). *Blockchain and fintech initiatives*. Dubai International Financial Centre.

El-Gamal, M. A. (2006). *Islamic finance: Law, economics, and practice*. Cambridge University Press.

Fitch Ratings. (2024). *Global Sukuk issuance outlook*. Fitch Ratings.

Iqbal, Z., & Mirakhor, A. (2011). An introduction to Islamic finance: Theory and practice. John Wiley & Sons.

Jobst, A. A., Kunzel, P., Mills, P., & Sy, A. N. R. (2008). *Islamic bond issuance: What sovereign debt managers need to know*. International Monetary Fund.

Luxembourg Government. (2021). *Luxembourg Sukuk issuance report*. Luxembourg Government.

Obaidullah, M. (2005). *Islamic financial services*. Islamic Economics Research Center.

Securities Commission Malaysia. (2013). *Capital market development and regulatory framework report 2013* (pp. 1–200). Securities Commission Malaysia.

Securities Commission Malaysia. (2020). *Guidelines on Sukuk issuance*. Securities Commission Malaysia.

Thomson Reuters. (2023). *Islamic finance development report*. Thomson Reuters.

UK Treasury. (2014). *UK sovereign Sukuk issuance report*. UK Treasury.

Usmani, M. T. (2002). *An introduction to Islamic finance*. Kluwer Law International.

World Bank. (2023). *Global economic prospects: Addressing emerging challenges in a complex world* (pp. 1–350). World Bank.

World Capital Market Authority. (2023). *Annual review of global capital market trends and developments* (pp. 1–180). World Capital Market Authority.

Chapter 11

Takaful Governance and Sustainable Practices

Aisha Naz[a], *Muhammad Ali*[b] *and Abadullah*[c]

[a]*Iqra University, Pakistan*
[b]*School of Accounting & Finance, Taylor's University, Malaysia*
[c]*Faysal Islamic Bank, Pakistan*

Abstract

This chapter explores the governance and sustainable practices in Takaful, an Islamic insurance system based on principles of mutual cooperation and risk-sharing. It provides a comprehensive overview of Takaful's historical development, its distinct models Mudharabah, Wakalah, and Waqf and how they compare to conventional insurance. The chapter highlights the importance of strong governance frameworks and sustainable practices for ensuring that Takaful operations align with Shariah principles and meet global standards. Key aspects include the role of participants, operators, and regulators in maintaining effective governance, as well as the integration of sustainable practices into Takaful operations. It reviews past research on Takaful governance, presents case studies of Takaful operators with robust governance, and discusses the impact of sustainability on stakeholders. The chapter concludes with recommendations for regulators and policymakers to enhance governance and promote sustainability in the Takaful industry.

Keywords: Takaful; Islamic insurance; Shariah compliance; financial stability; risk management; Islamic finance

Islamic Finance and Corporate Governance: Synergies for Sustainable Growth, 175–201

doi:10.1108/978-1-83662-346-520251023

1. Introduction

Takaful is a type of insurance based on Islamic principles. It follows Shariah law and means "mutual guarantee" in Arabic. Takaful is different from regular insurance because it works like a cooperative. People put money into a shared fund to help each other if something bad happens. Regular insurance can have uncertainty and gambling, but Takaful avoids these by being clear, fair, and focused on helping everyone involved (Khan, 2017). Takaful is a cooperative insurance system where people join together to pool their money and share risks. In Takaful, individuals or groups put money into a common fund. This fund is used to help cover different risks and losses that members might face. The money added to the fund is not a premium like in regular insurance but a donation (tabarru) to support the group. The fund is managed by everyone together, and any extra money is shared among members or reinvested to help the community (Khan, 2017). Takaful works very differently from regular insurance. Instead of passing the risk to an insurance company, Takaful members share and manage the risks together. This system is based on mutual cooperation, making sure all members are both contributors and beneficiaries. The Takaful contract is based on sharing risk and reward, focusing on mutual benefit and ethical standards (Hassan & Lewis, 2007).

1.1. The Essence and Purpose of Takaful

Takaful follows Islamic rules for money matters, called Shariah principles. These rules ban interest (riba), too much uncertainty (gharar), and gambling (maysir). By avoiding these, Takaful offers a Shariah-compliant alternative to regular insurance that respects Islamic values and ethics. Takaful aims to do more than just provide financial protection; it seeks to promote social unity, ensure fairness, and help the community (Moualla, 2013). Takaful works through different models like Mudarabah (profit-sharing) and Wakalah (agency). These models meet the needs and preferences of participants while following Islamic principles. They make it possible to create various Takaful products and services for individuals and businesses, all based on mutual support and ethical behavior (Siddiqui, 2011). Takaful is a big step forward in financial services, offering a Shariah-compliant alternative to regular insurance. Its definition and purpose are based on mutual help and ethical rules, showing a strong commitment to social responsibility and community welfare. By choosing Takaful, participants join a system that not only manages risks well but also aligns with the main values of Islamic finance.

1.2. The Crucial Importance of Takaful in Islamic Finance

Takaful, an important part of Islamic finance, is not just a financial tool but also a force for change in the industry. Its value comes from several key points that go beyond regular insurance, making it a key part of Shariah-compliant financial systems.

Ethical framework and social solidarity: The main idea of Takaful is an ethical framework that focuses on social unity and helping each other instead of just making a profit. Unlike regular insurance, which focuses on individual gain and risk transfer, Takaful promotes cooperation and shared responsibility. People contribute to a shared fund that helps those who suffer losses. This not only spreads risk but also strengthens community support, following the Islamic principle of brotherhood (Moualla, 2013).

Risk sharing and financial stability: Takaful improves financial stability by balancing risk management. Unlike regular insurance, which can include speculative elements, Takaful is based on sharing and pooling risks. This way, financial risks are spread fairly among participants, reducing the burden on any one person or group. The pooled resources in Takaful create a buffer against financial shocks, helping economic stability and resilience (Hassan & Lewis, 2007).

Promotion of ethical governance: Takaful's importance is also seen in its role in promoting ethical governance in finance. Takaful operators must follow Shariah principles, overseen by Shariah boards that ensure compliance with Islamic law. This structure ensures transparency, accountability, and ethical behavior, setting high standards for financial operations. Ethical governance in Takaful protects participants' interests and enhances the financial system's credibility and integrity (Siddiqui, 2011).

Financial inclusion and accessibility: Takaful is key in promoting financial inclusion. It provides an alternative to regular insurance that aligns with Islamic values, offering financial protection to people who might be excluded from mainstream insurance. This inclusivity extends the benefits of risk management and financial security to a broader range of people, promoting social equity and economic development (Khan, 2017).

Innovative financial solutions: Takaful also drives innovation in finance by introducing Shariah-compliant solutions that meet diverse needs. The flexible Takaful models allow for customized products for individuals, families, or businesses. This innovation expands the scope of financial services and ensures they align with ethical and religious considerations (Moualla, 2013).

Takaful is more than a financial tool; it reflects Islamic values and principles. Its importance is seen in promoting ethical behavior, enhancing financial stability, advancing financial inclusion, and driving innovation. Takaful is a vital part of Islamic finance, embodying a holistic approach to risk management and community welfare.

1.3. Objectives of the Chapter

This chapter explores Takaful, not just as a financial tool but as a reflection of Islamic values and corporate governance. The main goal is to explain the importance of Takaful in Islamic finance, showing how it promotes ethical financial practices and community support. By looking closely, the chapter shows how Takaful combines Shariah compliance with risk management, offering a unique alternative to regular insurance. One aim is to clearly define Takaful, highlighting its key principles of mutual help and shared responsibility. By examining how Takaful works and its different models, this chapter shows how these principles turn into practical ways to manage risk while following Islamic ethical standards.

It will explore the core ideas of Takaful, such as banning interest, excessive uncertainty, and gambling, which shape its unique way of operating (Hassan & Lewis, 2007).

The chapter will also look at the broader effects of Takaful on corporate governance in finance. It will show how Takaful operators follow strict Shariah guidelines to ensure transparency, accountability, and ethical behavior. This part will highlight the role of Shariah boards in maintaining the integrity of Takaful operations and enhancing the credibility of Islamic finance (Siddiqui, 2011). Another key point is to show the socio-economic impact of Takaful, especially in promoting financial inclusion and community welfare. By examining how Takaful helps social equity and economic stability, the chapter will show its role in providing financial protection to underserved populations and fostering a sense of collective responsibility (Khan, 2017).

This chapter aims to give a clear understanding of Takaful by exploring its definition, how it works, and its broader effects on Islamic finance and corporate governance. Through this detailed analysis, readers will see how Takaful represents a shift in risk management and ethical finance, contributing to the well-being of individuals and communities.

2. Literature Review

2.1. Historical Development of Takaful

The history of Takaful shows how Islamic financial principles have developed and been applied over time. The idea of helping each other and sharing risks, which is at the heart of Takaful, has been part of Islamic history since the time of the Prophet Muhammad (peace be upon him). Early Muslim communities practiced forms of cooperative support, where people put money into a common fund to help those in need. This reflects the core principles of mutual help and solidarity that are central to Takaful (El-Gamal, 2006). The modern idea of Takaful started to take shape in the early 20th century. The first official Takaful company was set up in Sudan in 1963, marking an important step in formalizing Islamic insurance. This happened because there was a growing need for financial products that followed Shariah principles, offering an alternative to regular insurance, which often included interest and speculation. The creation of the Sudanese Takaful company was a key moment in bringing Islamic financial principles into mainstream financial services (Grais & Pellegrini, 2006).

In the 1970s and 1980s, Takaful practices grew and improved. Many Takaful institutions were established across the Muslim world, in places like Malaysia, Bahrain, and Saudi Arabia. Along with this growth, regulatory frameworks and Shariah boards were set up to ensure that these institutions followed Islamic law. New Takaful models like Mudarabah (profit-sharing) and Wakalah (agency) were introduced, showing the increasing complexity and variety of Takaful products. These models helped meet a wider range of financial needs while sticking to ethical standards (Hassan & Lewis, 2007).

In the late 20th and early 21st centuries, Takaful saw remarkable growth. More people around the world became interested in Islamic finance and financial inclusion. Globalization and advances in technology helped Takaful spread to new regions and reach more people. International regulatory bodies and organizations that set standards also supported this growth, making sure that Takaful practices met global governance and transparency standards while staying true to Shariah principles (Siddiqui, 2011). Today, Takaful is a powerful example of how traditional Islamic principles can be combined with modern financial innovation. Its journey from a historical practice of mutual support to a sophisticated global financial system highlights its role in promoting ethical finance and corporate governance. The history of Takaful shows a continuous effort to align financial practices with Islamic values, ensuring they benefit both individuals and communities in a changing world.

2.2. Comparison with Conventional Insurance: A Distinct Paradigm

Takaful and conventional insurance have significant differences in their principles, operations, and history. Both provide financial protection and manage risk, but Takaful is based on Islamic ethical standards, setting it apart from conventional insurance in many ways.

Historical context and evolution: Takaful's idea of risk-sharing and mutual help goes back to early Islamic history. During the time of the Prophet Muhammad (peace be upon him), early Muslims practiced mutual aid, pooling resources to help those in need, showing principles of mutual responsibility and solidarity (El-Gamal, 2006). Modern Takaful started in the 20th century, with the first Takaful company established in Sudan in 1963. This marked the start of structured Islamic insurance, aligning financial protection with Shariah principles (Grais & Pellegrini, 2006). By 2020, the global Takaful market was worth about USD 36 billion, and it is expected to grow to over USD 50 billion by 2025 (PwC, 2020). This growth shows the increasing adoption of Takaful in different regions and the rising demand for Shariah-compliant financial products.

Principles and structure: Takaful is based on a cooperative risk-sharing model, driven by Islamic principles of mutual help and solidarity. Participants contribute to a common pool to support each other in times of need, following the principle of "tabarru" (donation) (Hassan & Lewis, 2007). Any extra funds are either shared among participants or reinvested for the group's benefit. Conventional insurance, on the other hand, is based on risk transfer. Policyholders pay premiums for coverage against specific risks, often involving speculative elements and interest, which go against Islamic ethical standards (Khan, 2017).

Risk management and financial transactions: In Takaful, risk is shared among participants instead of being transferred to an insurer. This collective approach helps reduce moral hazard, as all participant's care about keeping the pool stable. The ban on interest and speculative activities ensures that all financial transactions follow Shariah principles (Siddiqui, 2011). Conventional insurance focuses on risk transfer and profit maximization, which can lead to conflicts of interest and moral hazard, as insurers may try to minimize claims and maximize investment returns (Grais & Pellegrini, 2006).

Governance and compliance: Takaful has a governance framework to ensure Shariah compliance through Shariah boards. These boards, made up of Islamic finance experts, oversee practices to ensure they align with Islamic law. This promotes transparency and ethical behavior, setting high standards for financial operations (El-Gamal, 2006). Conventional insurance is regulated by secular financial standards, which ensure legal and market stability but may not address the ethical considerations important to Islamic finance.

Social impact and inclusivity: Takaful is important for promoting financial inclusion and community welfare. It offers Shariah-compliant alternatives to conventional insurance, providing financial protection to those who might otherwise be excluded due to religious or ethical concerns. The growth of Takaful has increased financial accessibility and social equity, supporting underserved populations and fostering collective responsibility (Hassan & Lewis, 2007).

Takaful and conventional insurance are two different approaches to risk management and financial protection. Conventional insurance focuses on risk transfer and profit, while Takaful is based on a cooperative, ethical framework rooted in Islamic principles. The historical development and growth of Takaful show its importance as an ethical alternative in the global financial landscape.

2.3. Previous Research on Takaful Governance: Insights and Regional Perspectives

The governance of Takaful, which is a key part of Islamic finance, has been studied a lot. This research shows how important it is for Takaful to follow Shariah principles and maintain financial integrity. Different studies have looked at the development, challenges, and regional differences in Takaful governance. Early studies on Takaful governance highlight the importance of Shariah compliance and the role of Shariah boards. These boards, made up of scholars in Islamic law, oversee Takaful operations to ensure they follow Islamic principles. Grais and Pellegrini (2006) found that these boards are essential for maintaining trust and credibility in Takaful institutions. Their research shows that Shariah boards help improve transparency and accountability.

Hassan and Lewis (2007) discuss the different governance structures in various countries. They note that regulatory frameworks and Shariah governance practices vary by region. For example, Malaysia has a well-developed regulatory framework for Takaful, with detailed guidelines from Bank Negara Malaysia. This has helped Malaysia become a leading market for Islamic finance, with Takaful assets growing from RM 5 billion in 2007 to RM 16.8 billion in 2020 (Bank Negara Malaysia, 2020). There are also regional differences in Takaful governance practices. In the Gulf Cooperation Council (GCC) countries, such as Saudi Arabia and the UAE, Takaful governance is shaped by local regulations and international standards. In Saudi Arabia, the Saudi Arabian Monetary Authority has strict guidelines to ensure Takaful operators follow Shariah principles. According to the Islamic Financial Services Board (IFSB) (2019), the Saudi Takaful market has grown significantly, with total assets reaching SAR 16.4 billion by 2018, showing the effectiveness of these governance practices.

In Bahrain, the Central Bank of Bahrain has created a comprehensive regulatory framework for Takaful, promoting transparency and ethical conduct. Al-Jarhi (2011) explains that Bahrain's approach includes regular audits and

Shariah board reviews, which help maintain the stability and growth of its Islamic financial sector. However, in emerging markets like Indonesia and Pakistan, Takaful governance faces challenges such as inconsistent regulations and varying levels of Shariah board expertise. Despite these issues, both countries have seen significant growth in their Takaful sectors due to increasing demand for Shariah-compliant financial products. For instance, Indonesia's Takaful assets grew from IDR 18 trillion in 2015 to IDR 35 trillion in 2020, reflecting regulatory improvements and market expansion (OJK, 2020).

There are ongoing challenges in Takaful governance, such as the need for better standardization and the adoption of international best practices. Ahmed and Khan (2018) emphasize the need to harmonize Shariah compliance frameworks across different regions to facilitate cross-border Takaful operations and ensure consistent governance practices. Research on Takaful governance shows its crucial role in maintaining Shariah compliance and promoting financial integrity. While there has been significant progress, especially in established markets like Malaysia and the GCC countries, challenges remain in emerging markets. Continued research and regulatory advancements are needed to address these challenges and strengthen Takaful governance globally.

2.4. Sustainable Practices in Takaful: Bridging Finance and Responsibility

Sustainable practices in Takaful combine ethical finance with caring for the environment and society. Since Takaful is based on Islamic principles of fairness, honesty, and community support, it is well-suited to promote sustainability in financial services. This fit is not a coincidence but matches the core values of Islamic finance, which stress responsible use of resources and social welfare.

1. *Adding environmental and social criteria*: Recently, Takaful companies have started including environmental and social factors in their practices. Shariah principles that guide Takaful naturally support caring for the environment and society. For example, Takaful does not invest in harmful industries like gambling, alcohol, and tobacco, ensuring funds go to ethical and sustainable projects (Hassan & Lewis, 2007). Many Takaful providers are now using environmental, social, and governance (ESG) criteria to measure the impact of their investments on sustainable development goals. In Malaysia, the Takaful industry leads in adopting sustainable practices. The Malaysian Takaful Association has guidelines that encourage using ESG factors in investment decisions. This ensures Takaful investments help environmental conservation and social well-being. As a result, Malaysian Takaful companies increasingly invest in green bonds and projects supporting renewable energy and sustainable development (Bank Negara Malaysia, 2020).
2. *Promoting transparency and accountability*: Transparency and accountability are key to sustainable practices in Takaful. Governance structures, especially the role of Shariah boards, ensure ethical and transparent operations. Shariah boards oversee compliance with Islamic law and the ethical management of funds. This helps prevent investments in harmful activities and reinforces

the commitment to sustainability (Grais & Pellegrini, 2006). Research shows that Takaful companies are publishing sustainability reports to show their environmental and social impact. These reports highlight the use of ESG factors in investment decisions, promotion of socially responsible initiatives, and efforts to reduce their carbon footprint (Siddiqui, 2011). This transparency builds trust and shows a commitment to responsible finance.

3. *Case studies and global practices*: Around the world, Takaful companies have adopted various sustainable practices showing their commitment to environmental and social responsibility. In the GCC region, the Dubai Islamic Insurance and Reinsurance Company (AMAN) has a sustainability strategy that includes investments in green technologies and reducing environmental impact. Takaful companies in Saudi Arabia also use sustainability criteria in their investments, focusing on projects that support energy efficiency and environmental conservation (Al-Jarhi, 2011). In Indonesia, Takaful providers support sustainable development by offering micro-insurance programs for underserved communities. These programs enhance financial inclusion, promote social stability, and empower economically, aligning with sustainable development goals (OJK, 2020).
4. *Future practices*: The future of sustainable practices in Takaful looks promising as the industry evolves. Ongoing research and industry developments suggest that Takaful companies will increasingly focus on innovative solutions to enhance sustainability. This might include using advanced technologies for environmental monitoring and adopting stricter ESG standards. By sticking to its core principles of ethical finance and community support, Takaful is well-positioned to lead in integrating sustainability into financial services.

Sustainable practices in Takaful blend Islamic finance principles with modern environmental and social responsibility. By using ESG criteria, promoting transparency, and committing to ethical investments, Takaful companies are advancing sustainable finance while staying true to their values.

3. Takaful Models and Operations

Different models: Mudharabah, Wakalah, Waqf.

The architecture of Takaful is underpinned by various operational models, each embodying distinct principles of risk-sharing and management in alignment with Islamic finance's ethical standards. Among these models, Mudharabah, Wakalah, and Waqf stand out as fundamental frameworks that define the operational dynamics of Takaful, shaping how risk is managed and how returns are distributed.

1. Mudharabah model

   The Mudharabah model is grounded in the concept of profit-sharing. Fig 11.1 represents the flowchart of Mudharabah model, one party provides the capital (the Rab al-Mal), while the other party provides expertise and management

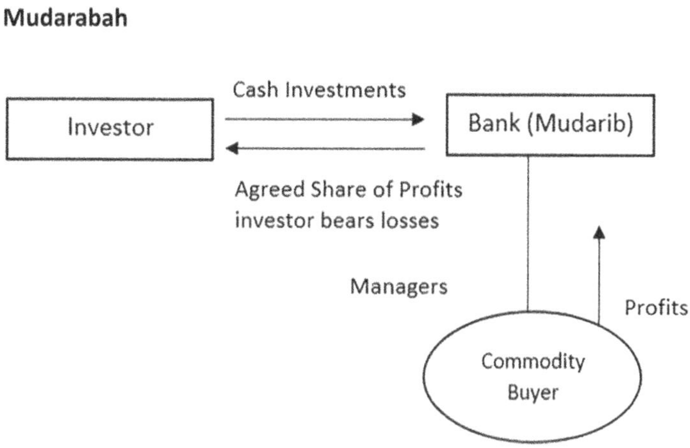

Fig. 11.1. Flowchart of Mudarabah Transactions.

(the Mudarib). The profits generated from investments are shared according to pre-agreed ratios, while losses are borne solely by the capital provider (Hassan & Lewis, 2007). Within the Takaful framework, Mudharabah can be employed to manage the investment component of the Takaful fund. Here, the Takaful operator invests the contributions of participants in Shariah-compliant ventures, and the returns are distributed based on the agreed profit-sharing ratio (Ghlamallah et al., 2021). This model promotes a participatory approach where both the operator and participants benefit from the financial success of the investments, aligning with the principle of mutual cooperation.

2. Wakalah model
   In contrast, the Wakalah model operates on an agency basis. Fig. 11.2 illustrates the flowchart of Wakalah transactions model, and the Takaful operator acts as an agent (Wakeel) who manages the Takaful fund on behalf of the participants in exchange for a fixed fee or commission. The Wakalah model emphasizes transparency and accountability, as the agent's compensation is clearly defined, and their role is limited to managing the fund and its investments (Grais & Pellegrini, 2006). The Wakalah model is prevalent in modern Takaful practices due to its straightforward nature and ease of implementation. Participants contribute to the Takaful fund, and the operator manages the investments and operations with the fee structure predetermined (Ghlamallah et al., 2021). This model ensures that the operator's compensation is separate from the investment returns, maintaining clarity and avoiding potential conflicts of interest.

3. Waqf model
   The Waqf model represents a unique approach where assets are donated for charitable purposes and managed as an endowment. In Takaful, the Waqf model involves creating a charitable endowment fund using contributions

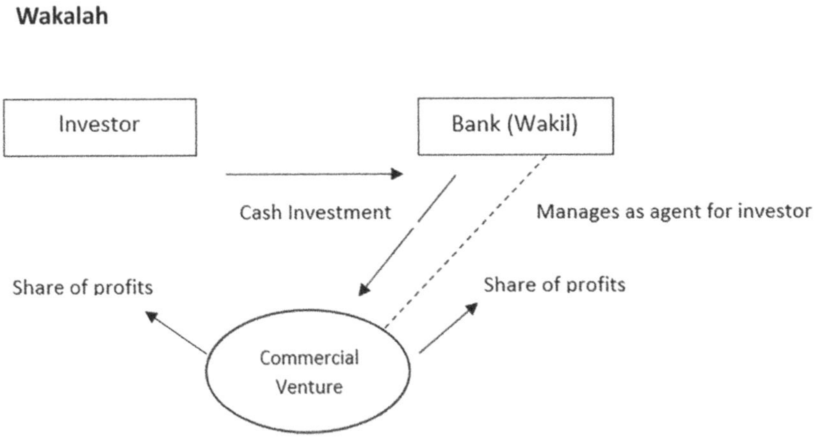

Fig. 11.2. Flowchart of Wakalah Transactions.

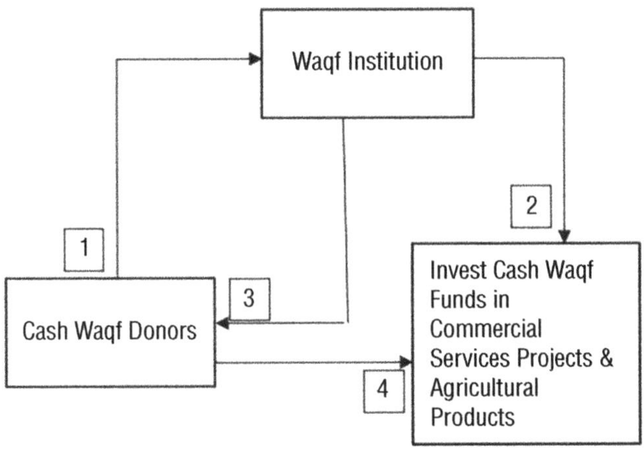

Fig. 11.3. Flowchart of Waqf Transactions.

from participants. This fund is then used to provide financial assistance to those in need or to support various community projects (Siddiqui, 2011). Fig. 11.3 shows the flowchart of Waqf transactions model aligns with the principle of social responsibility in Islamic finance, as it emphasizes the collective benefit and charitable aspect of Takaful. The Waqf fund is managed by a trustee, ensuring that the assets are utilized in accordance with Shariah principles and for the betterment of the community (Ghlamallah et al., 2021). This model not only provides financial protection but also reinforces the Takaful objective of fostering social welfare (see Fig. 11.3).

Role of participants, operators, and regulators in Takaful: A symbiotic framework

The Takaful system works because of a close relationship between participants, operators, and regulators. Each group has an important role in making sure the system runs well, stays ethical, and follows rules. This teamwork shows the spirit of cooperation and shared responsibility in Islamic finance.

1. Participants: The foundation of mutual help
   Participants are the heart of the Takaful system. Unlike regular insurance where people pay premiums, Takaful participants contribute to a common fund to help each other (tabarru). These contributions are like donations, not premiums (Grais & Pellegrini, 2006). This creates a sense of community and shared responsibility, which is central to Islamic finance. Participants have two roles: they give money to the fund and can also receive help from it if they need to make a claim. They also share in any surplus money that remains if there are fewer claims than expected. This surplus can be given back to participants or reinvested in the fund (Khan, 2017).

2. Operators: Ethical managers of the fund
   Takaful operators, or Takaful companies, manage the fund. They handle contributions, investments, and claims according to Shariah principles. Their job includes managing the money, assessing risks, and processing claims, all with complete transparency (Hassan & Lewis, 2007). In the Wakalah model, operators act as agents for the participants and earn a fee for their services. In the Mudharabah model, they share in the investment profits. No matter the model, operators must follow Islamic finance rules, which require fairness and honesty (Grais & Pellegrini, 2006).

   A key job for operators is to make sure all investments follow Shariah law. They do this through careful checks and regular audits by Shariah boards. These boards ensure that everything the operator does aligns with Islamic principles, building trust among participants (Siddiqui, 2011).

3. Regulators: Keeping the system safe and fair
   Regulators ensure the Takaful industry stays stable and trustworthy. They create and enforce rules that all Takaful operators must follow, making sure practices comply with Islamic principles and financial regulations (El-Gamal, 2006). Groups like the IFSB and national authorities set the standards for Shariah compliance and financial stability. Regulators ensure Takaful operators follow strict rules about capital, risk management, and protecting participants. They conduct regular checks to make sure rules are followed, protecting participants' interests and maintaining trust in the system (Bank Negara Malaysia, 2020). Regulators also help the Takaful industry grow by providing support like education and incentives for new ideas. For example, Malaysia has a well-developed regulatory framework that includes specific rules for Takaful. This has helped Malaysia become a leader in Takaful with strong growth (Bank Negara Malaysia, 2020). In the GCC countries, regulatory frameworks promote transparency and Shariah compliance, helping the Takaful industry grow (Al-Jarhi, 2011).

   The roles of participants, operators, and regulators in Takaful are interconnected and ensure the system's strength and ethical foundation.

Participants give to and benefit from the mutual fund, operators manage the fund ethically, and regulators enforce rules and stability. This teamwork upholds the principles of Islamic finance and shows that Takaful can be a sustainable and ethical alternative to conventional insurance.

4. Governance Frameworks

4.1. Key Principles and Standards in Takaful Governance: Upholding Integrity and Transparency

The governance of Takaful is built on principles that ensure ethical management and transparency, in line with Islamic finance values. This system protects participants' interests, maintains public trust, and promotes the growth of the Takaful industry. By following strict governance rules, Takaful institutions not only comply with Shariah law but also boost their credibility and reliability in financial markets.

Ethical integrity and Shariah compliance: At the core of Takaful governance is a strong commitment to ethical integrity and Shariah compliance. Takaful operations must avoid riba (interest), maysir (gambling), and gharar (excessive uncertainty) as per Islamic law. This ensures that all financial activities are fair, transparent, and just. The Shariah board plays a crucial role in overseeing and ensuring all operations and investments follow Islamic principles (Hassan & Lewis, 2007). The board's regular audits and reviews help maintain the ethical integrity of Takaful, building trust among participants.

Transparency and accountability: Transparency and accountability are essential in Takaful governance. Operators must keep clear and detailed records of all transactions and regularly report to participants and regulators. This transparency ensures participants know how their contributions are managed and how the Takaful fund is performing. Strong internal controls and risk management systems further ensure that the operator's actions are in the best interest of the participants (Grais & Pellegrini, 2006).

Effective risk management: Effective risk management is a key part of Takaful governance. Operators must use comprehensive risk assessment and mitigation strategies to protect the Takaful fund from potential losses. This includes diversifying investments, keeping adequate reserves, and regularly monitoring financial performance to ensure solvency and stability (El-Gamal, 2006). By managing risks wisely, Takaful operators can protect the fund's financial health and ensure it can meet its obligations to participants in times of need.

Stakeholder engagement: Engaging stakeholders is another important principle of Takaful governance. Operators must involve all stakeholders, including participants, regulators, and Shariah boards, in the governance process. This approach promotes cooperation and mutual respect, which is vital for Takaful's success (Khan, 2017). Additionally, Takaful operators are committed to treating all participants fairly and equally. This means processing claims promptly and fairly and distributing surplus funds transparently.

Regulatory oversight: Regulatory oversight is crucial for maintaining Takaful governance integrity. Regulatory bodies like the IFSB and national authorities set and enforce the standards that govern Takaful operations. These standards cover capital adequacy, investment practices, and consumer protection (Bank Negara Malaysia, 2020). By following these standards, Takaful operators ensure their practices comply with Islamic principles and international best practices.

Continuous improvement and innovation: The Takaful industry is always evolving, so continuous improvement and innovation are essential. Takaful operators are encouraged to develop new products and services that meet participants' changing needs while adhering to Shariah principles. This innovation is supported by ongoing research, collaboration with regulatory bodies, and input from industry stakeholders (Siddiqui, 2011). By fostering a culture of innovation, Takaful operators can enhance their competitiveness and contribute to the broader Islamic finance industry's growth. The key principles and standards in Takaful governance ensure ethical integrity, transparency, and accountability. By following these principles, Takaful operators can build trust with participants, meet regulatory requirements, and promote sustainable industry growth. This strong governance framework aligns with Islamic finance values and positions Takaful as a credible and reliable alternative to conventional insurance.

4.2. Regulatory Bodies and Their Roles

The regulatory framework of Takaful is designed to make sure all operations follow Islamic finance principles while maintaining high governance and financial stability standards. Regulatory bodies oversee Takaful operations, enforce Shariah compliance, and protect participants' interests. They create a strong foundation that supports the growth and integrity of the Takaful industry, making it a reliable and ethical alternative to conventional insurance.

1. *IFSB*: The IFSB is an important international organization that sets standards for the Islamic financial services industry, including Takaful. The IFSB creates global guidelines that help keep the industry stable and strong. These guidelines cover risk management, governance, capital adequacy, and disclosure requirements (IFSB, 2018). By setting these standards, the IFSB ensures that Takaful operators follow best practices and remain financially healthy, protecting participants' interests and maintaining public confidence.
2. *Accounting and auditing organization for Islamic financial institutions*: The accounting and auditing organization for islamic financial institutions (AAOIFI) also plays a key role in Takaful governance. AAOIFI develops standards for accounting, auditing, governance, ethics, and Shariah compliance for Islamic financial institutions, including Takaful operators. These standards ensure that Takaful operations are transparent, consistent, and follow Shariah principles strictly (AAOIFI, 2017). AAOIFI's governance standards provide detailed guidelines on the roles and responsibilities of Shariah boards, enhancing Takaful institutions' overall governance framework.

3. *National regulatory authorities*: Besides international bodies like the IFSB and AAOIFI, national regulatory authorities regulate and supervise Takaful operations within their countries. Authorities like Bank Negara Malaysia, the Securities and Exchange Commission of Pakistan, and the Dubai Financial Services Authority create and enforce local regulations that align with international standards and domestic needs. For example, Bank Negara Malaysia has developed a comprehensive regulatory framework for Takaful, including guidelines on governance, risk management, and consumer protection (Bank Negara Malaysia, 2020). These national bodies ensure that Takaful operators maintain financial stability, protect participants' interests, and promote industry growth in their markets.
4. *Shariah supervisory boards*: Shariah supervisory boards (SSBs) are essential to the governance of Takaful operations. These boards consist of scholars who are experts in Islamic finance and law. They provide continuous oversight to ensure that all Takaful operations comply with Shariah principles. The SSBs review and approve Takaful products, investments, and practices, making sure they avoid riba (interest), maysir (gambling), and gharar (excessive uncertainty) (Grais & Pellegrini, 2006). Their role is critical in maintaining the ethical and religious integrity of Takaful operations, building trust and confidence among participants.

Regulatory bodies also work to ensure market stability and protect consumers. They implement measures to prevent market abuses, promote fair competition, and make sure Takaful operators maintain enough capital reserves to meet their obligations. By enforcing strict disclosure requirements, regulators ensure that participants are well-informed about their Takaful policies, enhancing transparency and protecting consumer rights (Hassan & Lewis, 2007). Regulatory bodies also oversee the resolution of disputes and grievances, providing a framework for fair and equitable treatment of participants.

4.3. Shariah Compliance and Ethical Considerations in Takaful: The Core of Islamic Financial Governance

The foundation of Takaful is built on strict adherence to Shariah law and strong ethical values. These principles ensure that Takaful operates in line with Islamic teachings, promoting fairness, justice, and mutual support. This sets Takaful apart from regular insurance and highlights its important role in Islamic finance and corporate governance. The principles behind Takaful date back to early Islamic history based on the idea of mutual help and protection. In the time of Prophet Muhammad (PBUH), people practiced various forms of cooperative risk-sharing. For example, "aqila" was a practice where tribe members contributed to a fund to help those who suffered a loss due to an accident or injury (Alhabshi & Razak, 2011). This practice reflects the core values of Takaful, emphasizing solidarity and mutual guarantee central to Islamic teachings.

Ensuring all Takaful operations, from underwriting to investment, follow Islamic law is crucial. This means avoiding riba (interest), gharar (excessive uncertainty), and maysir (gambling). Takaful products and contracts are designed to avoid these forbidden elements, fostering a system based on mutual assistance and shared risk (Grais & Pellegrini, 2006). SSBs, composed of scholars with deep knowledge of Islamic law, closely oversee these operations. They review and approve all aspects of Takaful to ensure strict adherence to Shariah principles (Hassan & Lewis, 2007). A key ethical aspect of Takaful is its investment strategy. Funds collected from participants must be invested in Shariah-compliant ventures, excluding businesses involved in harmful or unethical activities like alcohol, gambling, and interest-based financial services (riba). This approach not only follows religious principles but also encourages socially responsible investing, benefiting the wider community (El-Gamal, 2006).

Transparency and fairness are vital in Takaful governance. Operators must be clear and open in all their dealings with participants, from collecting contributions to paying claims. Clear communication about the terms, conditions, and performance of the Takaful fund builds trust among participants (Khan, 2017). Additionally, treating all participants equally is essential. Claims must be processed fairly and efficiently, and any surplus from the Takaful fund should be shared among participants or reinvested for their benefit. Takaful is rooted in the principles of social responsibility and mutual cooperation. The word "Takaful" comes from the Arabic word "kafala," meaning "guaranteeing each other." This reflects the idea of mutual assistance, where participants share the burden of risk. Takaful funds are designed to support participants in times of need, fostering a strong sense of community and solidarity (Siddiqui, 2011). This model not only distinguishes Takaful from conventional insurance but also highlights its role in promoting social welfare and economic justice.

Regulatory bodies ensure Shariah compliance and ethical governance in Takaful. Organizations like the IFSB and national regulators set comprehensive standards and guidelines that Takaful operators must follow. These regulations cover governance, risk management, and consumer protection, ensuring Takaful practices align with both Islamic principles and global best practices (IFSB, 2018). Regular audits and reviews by regulatory bodies and Shariah boards ensure ongoing compliance, maintaining the integrity and credibility of Takaful operations. Takaful also aims to promote financial inclusion and empowerment. Takaful products are designed to be accessible to many people, including those excluded from conventional insurance due to religious or economic reasons. By offering affordable and Shariah-compliant financial protection, Takaful enhances financial inclusion, contributing to broader economic stability and empowerment (Bank Negara Malaysia, 2020). This inclusive approach ensures more individuals and communities can benefit from risk-sharing mechanisms, promoting overall financial resilience. Shariah compliance and ethical considerations are crucial to Takaful operations and governance. These principles ensure Takaful adheres to Islamic law while promoting fairness, transparency, and social responsibility. By upholding these values, Takaful strengthens its position as a key component of Islamic finance, offering a sustainable and ethical alternative to conventional insurance.

5. Case Studies of Takaful Operators with Robust Governance

Takaful companies are known for their strong governance, which follows Islamic finance principles and corporate responsibility. Here are some examples of Takaful companies with excellent governance, showing their commitment to Shariah compliance, transparency, and ethical management.

5.1. Malaysia: Syarikat Takaful Malaysia Berhad

Syarikat Takaful Malaysia Berhad (Takaful Malaysia) is a leading Takaful company. Founded in 1984, it is known for its strong Shariah compliance and corporate governance. The company has a dual-board structure, with a Board of Directors and a Shariah Advisory Council made up of Islamic scholars. This council ensures all products and operations follow Islamic principles (Bank Negara Malaysia, 2020). This dual structure promotes compliance, transparency, and accountability. Takaful Malaysia also follows strict ethical investment guidelines, avoiding sectors like alcohol, gambling, and conventional banking. This ensures their investments align with Shariah principles and promote socially responsible investing (IFSB, 2018). The company's commitment to transparency is shown in their detailed annual reports and regular updates to stakeholders, building trust and confidence among participants and investors.

5.2. Saudi Arabia: Salama Islamic Arab Insurance Company

Salama Islamic Arab Insurance Company, also known as Salama, is another top Takaful company. Established in 1979, Salama is one of the largest Takaful companies worldwide. A key part of Salama's governance is its SSB, which ensures all operations comply with Islamic law (El-Gamal, 2006). This board oversees product development, investment decisions, and corporate strategy. Salama is also committed to ethical and transparent management. The company provides regular financial disclosures and detailed reports on its performance, keeping participants and stakeholders informed. Salama's strong risk management and internal controls help protect participants' interests (Grais & Pellegrini, 2006).

5.3. United Arab Emirates: Noor Takaful

Noor Takaful, part of the Noor Investment Group, is a notable Takaful company in the UAE. Founded in 2009, Noor Takaful upholds high standards of Shariah compliance and corporate governance. The company is guided by a SSB that ensures all products, services, and investments follow Islamic principles (Siddiqui, 2011). Noor Takaful's governance includes a dedicated risk management committee and an internal audit function. Noor Takaful emphasizes transparency and ethical management by regularly publishing detailed financial statements and performance reports. The company also engages in community development and promotes financial inclusion through innovative Takaful products (Khan, 2017).

5.4. Indonesia: PT Asuransi Takaful Keluarga

PT Asuransi Takaful Keluarga, Indonesia's first Takaful company, was established in 1994. The company is known for strong governance and Shariah compliance. A SSB ensures that all operations align with Islamic law (Bank Indonesia, 2019). This board is crucial in product development, investment strategies, and overall corporate governance. The company values transparency and participant engagement, providing regular updates on the Takaful fund's performance. This builds trust and loyalty among participants. PT Asuransi Takaful Keluarga also focuses on social responsibility, participating in community development projects and promoting financial literacy (IFSB, 2018).

These case studies show how different Takaful companies practice strong governance. They highlight the importance of Shariah compliance, transparency, and ethical management in maintaining the integrity and success of Takaful operators. Companies like Takaful Malaysia, Salama, Noor Takaful, and PT Asuransi Takaful Keluarga follow these principles, providing ethical and sustainable financial solutions for their participants and stakeholders.

6. Sustainable Practices

Sustainability in Takaful, like in Islamic finance, involves a holistic approach. This means it looks at economic success, social fairness, and environmental care, all following Shariah principles. It goes beyond just making money, focusing also on ethical management, helping society, and protecting the environment. This matches the main ideas of Islamic finance, which stress justice, mutual benefit, and careful use of resources. To be sustainable, a Takaful company must be financially strong. This means managing risks well, running operations efficiently, and making profits ethically. Unlike regular insurance, Takaful cannot earn money from interest (riba), risky transactions (gharar), or investments in harmful sectors like alcohol, gambling, and pork products (El-Gamal, 2006). Instead, they invest in Halal ventures that support real economic growth (Grais & Pellegrini, 2006).

Social fairness is a key part of Islamic finance and Takaful. The idea of Takaful is based on mutual help and shared responsibility. Participants pool their money to protect each other against losses, reflecting community solidarity, a central Islamic value (Siddiqui, 2011). This ensures benefits are shared fairly among participants, promoting justice (adl) and social welfare. Takaful companies also engage in charitable activities (sadaqah) and fund social development projects, improving the communities they serve (Bank Negara Malaysia, 2020). Environmental care is becoming important in Takaful. Islamic teachings promote the responsible use of natural resources and protecting the environment (Khalid, 2019). Therefore, Takaful companies are starting to include environmental factors in their business. This means investing in green technologies, supporting eco-friendly projects, and promoting practices that reduce environmental harm. This aligns with the ethical goals of Islamic finance and contributes to global sustainable development (IFSB, 2018).

Strong governance is crucial for Takaful sustainability. This includes high standards of transparency, accountability, and ethical management. Takaful companies are overseen by both regular corporate governance frameworks and SSBs. These boards ensure all practices follow Islamic principles (Hassan & Lewis, 2007). This dual oversight strengthens the integrity of Takaful institutions, ensuring they are financially stable, ethical, and socially responsible. Sustainability in Takaful includes economic, social, and environmental aspects, all guided by Islamic finance principles. By following these principles, Takaful companies not only secure their own future but also contribute to social justice and environmental care. This approach makes Takaful a strong tool for promoting ethical finance and corporate responsibility in our interconnected world.

6.1. Integration of Sustainable Practices in Takaful Operations: Harmonizing Ethical Finance and Corporate Responsibility

Takaful combines economic success with social welfare and environmental care, following Shariah principles. These practices help Takaful companies build a strong ethical base, improve their market reputation, and support sustainable development.

Ethical investment strategies: Takaful companies invest in socially responsible and environmentally friendly projects. They avoid industries like alcohol, gambling, and interest-based financial services. Instead, they invest in Halal (permissible) areas, including green technologies and renewable energy projects (El-Gamal, 2006). This ensures compliance with Shariah and supports a sustainable financial system.

Transparency and accountability: Transparency and accountability are key to sustainability in Takaful. Takaful companies provide clear information about policies, fund management, and surplus distribution. Regular audits and SSBs ensure that operations follow Islamic principles (Grais & Pellegrini, 2006). This builds trust and loyalty among participants.

Social responsibility and community engagement: Takaful companies emphasize social responsibility and community engagement. They allocate part of their profits to charity (sadaqah) and community projects. These actions support social justice (adl) and improve the well-being of communities (Bank Negara Malaysia, 2020). By supporting education, healthcare, and poverty alleviation, Takaful companies promote inclusive growth.

Environmental stewardship: Environmental care is becoming important in Takaful. Islamic teachings encourage responsible use of natural resources and environmental protection (Khalid, 2019). Takaful companies adopt eco-friendly practices, reduce their carbon footprint, and support green projects. These efforts help conserve the environment and meet the values of participants who care about sustainability.

Innovative Takaful products: Innovation is key to integrating sustainable practices in Takaful. Companies create new products that meet participants' needs while promoting sustainability. For example, micro-Takaful products provide affordable coverage to low-income individuals and small businesses, enhancing financial inclusion (Khan, 2017). Takaful products that support renewable energy projects or sustainable businesses also show the industry's commitment to a green economy.

Global standards and best practices: Takaful companies follow global standards and best practices in sustainability and governance. Bodies like the IFSB provide guidelines on risk management, ethical investment, and corporate social responsibility (IFSB, 2018). By following these standards, Takaful companies improve efficiency, reduce risks, and build sustainable business models.

6.2. Impact of Sustainability on Stakeholders: Evidence from Takaful Operations

Takaful integrates sustainable practices to ensure ethical finance and corporate responsibility. By focusing on ethical investments, transparency, social responsibility, environmental care, and innovation, Takaful companies not only ensure their own sustainability but also contribute to broader sustainable development goals. These practices, rooted in Shariah principles, make Takaful a key player in creating a fair, equitable, and sustainable financial system. Sustainable practices in Takaful have significant benefits for various stakeholders, including participants, operators, regulators, and the broader community. These practices help Takaful companies fulfill their ethical duties while improving their competitiveness, resilience, and social acceptance.

i. Participants: Enhanced trust and financial security
For participants, sustainable practices in Takaful lead to greater trust and financial security. A 2019 survey by the IFSB showed that 78% of Takaful participants value ethical investment and transparency when choosing Takaful over conventional insurance (IFSB, 2019). This trust is strengthened by the fair distribution of surplus funds among participants. For example, in 2020, Syarikat Takaful Malaysia Berhad shared 20% of its surplus with participants, boosting their financial well-being (Takaful Malaysia, 2020).

ii. Operators: Competitive advantage and market growth
Sustainable practices give Takaful operators a competitive edge, leading to market growth and resilience. According to the World Bank, Takaful companies with strong sustainability strategies grow by 15% annually, compared to 10% for those that don't focus on sustainability (World Bank, 2020). This growth is driven by increasing consumer demand for ethical and responsible financial products. Noor Takaful, for instance, saw a 25% rise in new policyholders after launching eco-friendly and socially responsible Takaful products in 2019 (Khan, 2019).

iii. Regulators: Enhanced compliance and risk management
For regulators, integrating sustainability into Takaful operations improves compliance and risk management. Regulatory bodies like Bank Negara Malaysia and the Dubai Financial Services Authority have set strict guidelines

for governance, ethical investment, and social responsibility. Following these rules not only reduces operational risks but also ensures financial stability in the Islamic finance sector. The International Monetary Fund (IMF) found that Takaful companies with strong sustainability practices had 30% fewer regulatory breaches compared to conventional insurers (IMF, 2020).

iv. Broader community: Social and economic benefits
The broader community benefits greatly from the sustainable practices of Takaful companies. Programs like micro-Takaful provide affordable insurance to low-income individuals, helping with financial inclusion and poverty reduction. In Indonesia, PT Asuransi Takaful Keluarga's micro-Takaful program has covered over 500,000 low-income families, reducing financial vulnerability and promoting economic stability (Bank Indonesia, 2019). Additionally, Takaful investments in green technologies and sustainable projects help conserve the environment and support economic development, benefiting the community at large.

v. Environmental impact: Supporting sustainable development
Sustainable practices in Takaful also positively impact the environment. By investing in renewable energy projects and adopting eco-friendly operations, Takaful companies help reduce carbon emissions and promote sustainable development. A 2020 report by the Islamic Development Bank noted that Takaful investments in renewable energy in the Middle East and North Africa reduced CO_2 emissions by approximately 1.2 million metric tons annually, showing the sector's commitment to environmental care (Islamic Development Bank, 2020).

Sustainability in Takaful benefits all stakeholders, from enhancing trust and financial security for participants to providing competitive advantages and growth for operators. Regulators see improved compliance and risk management, while the broader community gains social and economic benefits. The environmental impacts further highlight the industry's role in achieving global sustainability goals. These outcomes demonstrate the vital role of sustainability in building a resilient, ethical, and inclusive Islamic finance sector.

7. Conclusion

Takaful shows how Islamic finance principles match modern ethical and sustainable business practices. One key finding is that Takaful companies follow ethical investment strategies. They avoid investing in sectors like alcohol and gambling, which are considered harmful and unethical by Shariah law. This not only ensures they follow Islamic principles but also aligns with global trends toward socially responsible investing (El-Gamal, 2006). By focusing on ethical investments, Takaful companies enhance their financial integrity, leading to long-term stability and growth. Sustainability in Takaful significantly increases trust and market growth. Participants are drawn to Takaful products because they align with ethical values and offer transparency. According to the IFSB (2019), 78% of participants prioritize ethical investment and transparency, showing a strong market preference for sustainable Takaful solutions. Takaful operators that embrace sustainability see higher growth rates. For example, Noor Takaful saw a 25% increase in new policyholders after introducing eco-friendly products (Khan, 2019). This shows that sustainability helps expand the market and build consumer loyalty.

Sustainable practices in Takaful also improve regulatory compliance and risk management. By following strict Shariah guidelines and global standards, Takaful companies effectively manage risks and reduce regulatory breaches. A study by the International Monetary Fund (2020) found that Takaful operators with strong sustainability practices had a 30% lower incidence of regulatory issues. This proves that these practices help maintain operational integrity and meet regulatory requirements. Takaful's commitment to social responsibility benefits the broader community. Programs like micro-Takaful and investments in social development projects help improve financial inclusion and socio-economic stability. For instance, PT Asuransi Takaful Keluarga's micro-Takaful program has provided coverage to over 500,000 low-income families in Indonesia, helping with poverty alleviation and economic empowerment (Bank Indonesia, 2019). These efforts show how Takaful companies positively impact society beyond their business operations.

Environmental care is a growing part of Takaful's sustainability efforts. By investing in renewable energy and adopting eco-friendly practices, Takaful companies help conserve the environment and promote sustainable development. The Islamic Development Bank (2020) reports that Takaful investments in renewable energy projects have reduced CO_2 emissions by 1.2 million metric tons annually. This shows the sector's role in supporting global environmental goals and its commitment to sustainable development. Sustainability in Takaful brings many benefits, including better ethical investment practices, increased trust from stakeholders, improved regulatory compliance, and positive social and environmental impacts. These findings show how Takaful aligns with both Islamic finance principles and modern sustainability expectations, positioning it as a sector committed to ethical and sustainable growth.

7.1. Importance of Governance and Sustainability in Takaful

Governance and sustainability are very important in Takaful. They ensure the system works well and is trusted by everyone involved. Governance is like the backbone of Takaful. It ensures that all operations follow Shariah principles, which are the Islamic laws guiding the business. This structure includes a SSB that checks all transactions and investments to make sure they comply with Islamic rules. This careful oversight helps avoid ethical and financial problems, builds trust among participants, and makes sure everything is transparent and accountable (Grais & Pellegrini, 2006).

Sustainability means taking responsibility beyond just following the rules. It involves creating long-term value and being ethical stewards of resources, aligning with Islamic principles and global sustainability standards. Sustainable practices in Takaful include making ethical investments, avoiding harmful industries, and promoting environmental conservation and social welfare. By doing this, Takaful operators contribute to larger societal goals like reducing poverty and protecting the environment, showing they are responsible corporate citizens (El-Gamal, 2006; Islamic Development Bank, 2020).

Governance and sustainability together make Takaful effective and reputable. A strong governance framework ensures that sustainability initiatives are implemented properly and align with Shariah principles. This alignment increases the credibility of Takaful and boosts market growth, as more participants look for financial products that reflect their values and ethics. Takaful operators that focus on sustainable investment strategies often see higher participant engagement and growth rates, showing the positive impact of combining governance and sustainability (Khan, 2019).

Focusing on governance and sustainability also helps reduce risks and build resilience. Good governance practices, along with a commitment to sustainability, help Takaful operators handle regulatory challenges and meet market demands more effectively. This not only strengthens the financial stability of Takaful operators but also creates a more resilient financial system overall (International Monetary Fund, 2020). The governance and sustainability are key to the success and integrity of Takaful. A well-structured governance framework ensures Shariah compliance and transparency, while sustainable practices show a commitment to ethical and long-term value creation. Together, these elements build participant trust, drive market growth, and contribute to a more responsible and resilient financial system.

8. Policy Recommendations

Improving governance in Takaful is crucial for ensuring these institutions operate with integrity, transparency, and in line with Shariah principles. Good governance is the foundation of a trustworthy Takaful operation. It upholds the ethical and religious standards of Islamic finance and protects the system from risks and inefficiencies. A key part of Takaful governance is the SSB. This board ensures that all practices, transactions, and investments follow Islamic law. The board's independence and expertise are essential for maintaining the credibility of Takaful institutions (Grais & Pellegrini, 2006). To be effective, the SSB needs clear authority, sufficient resources, and a well-defined role to oversee and advise on all aspects of the institution's operations.

Besides Shariah oversight, Takaful governance frameworks benefit from best practices in corporate governance. This includes transparent reporting, regular audits, and strong risk management processes. Transparency builds trust with participants and ensures all financial dealings are open and accountable. A study by the International Monetary Fund (2020) shows that Takaful operators with strong governance practices have fewer regulatory issues and more stable operations, highlighting the importance of these measures. Including stakeholder feedback in governance practices can greatly enhance Takaful operations. Engaging participants, regulators, and other stakeholders in discussions ensures that governance frameworks comply with Shariah and meet the needs and expectations of those they serve. This participatory approach fosters a culture of accountability and continuous improvement, essential for adapting to changing market dynamics and regulatory requirements (Khan, 2019).

Using technology-driven solutions for monitoring and compliance is also important for modernizing Takaful operations. Leveraging data analytics and digital tools can improve the efficiency of governance processes, enhance risk assessment capabilities, and ensure more accurate and timely reporting. This technological integration helps streamline operations and improve the overall effectiveness of governance frameworks (El-Gamal, 2006). Enhancing governance in Takaful involves a multi-faceted approach that includes strong Shariah oversight, transparent reporting, robust risk management, stakeholder engagement, and technological innovation. By focusing on these areas, Takaful institutions can uphold their ethical standards, build trust with participants, and ensure operational resilience in an increasingly complex financial landscape.

8.1. Promoting Sustainable Practices Within the Industry

Promoting sustainable practices in the Takaful industry is very important. It helps align financial operations with both ethical standards and environmental care. As the world increasingly values sustainability, Takaful institutions can adopt these practices in a way that reflects their principles of fairness and social responsibility. Promoting sustainability in Takaful involves green investments, social responsibility, eco-friendly operations, innovative products, community engagement, and transparency.

Green investments: Takaful operators are focusing on green investments by putting money into environmentally sustainable projects like renewable energy and sustainable infrastructure. These investments follow Islamic principles by avoiding harmful industries and help fight climate change. For example, the Islamic Development Bank reports that Takaful investments in renewable energy have significantly reduced carbon emissions (Islamic Development Bank, 2020). This approach not only benefits the environment but also attracts eco-conscious investors.

Social responsibility: Social responsibility is also very important. Takaful institutions support social development programs, like micro-Takaful schemes, which provide coverage to underserved communities. These programs promote financial inclusion and help reduce poverty, reflecting the sector's commitment to social justice. For example, PT Asuransi Takaful Keluarga in Indonesia has provided essential coverage to over 500,000 low-income families, showing the positive impact of Takaful on social welfare (Bank Indonesia, 2019). By prioritizing social responsibility, Takaful operators align their business goals with broader societal goals.

Eco-friendly operations: Takaful institutions are adopting eco-friendly operational practices. This includes using energy-efficient technologies, reducing waste, and managing resources better. Many Takaful institutions now use digital platforms to reduce paper use and streamline processes, which lowers costs and minimizes environmental impact. According to a 2020 report by the International

Monetary Fund, Takaful operators that adopt sustainable practices achieve greater efficiency and cost savings (IMF, 2020).

Sustainable product development: Takaful providers are designing products that include sustainability criteria, like coverage for green buildings, eco-friendly vehicles, and sustainable agriculture. These products meet the needs of environmentally conscious consumers and encourage sustainable practices in various sectors. By offering such products, Takaful institutions promote environmental sustainability and create new market opportunities.

Community engagement and education: Sustainability also involves engaging with the community and providing education. Takaful institutions invest in programs that raise awareness about environmental issues and promote sustainable practices. Initiatives like environmental workshops, educational campaigns, and partnerships with local NGOs foster a culture of sustainability and empower people to make informed decisions that benefit the environment and society.

Innovative sustainability reporting: Adopting innovative sustainability reporting practices enhances transparency and accountability. Takaful operators use advanced reporting frameworks to disclose their ESG performance. These reports provide stakeholders with insights into the sustainability impacts of Takaful operations and investments, reinforcing the sector's commitment to responsible business practices. According to the Global Reporting Initiative (2021), such transparency builds trust and drives continuous improvement in sustainability practices across the industry.

Promoting sustainable practices in Takaful is not just a response to contemporary financial and environmental challenges but also a reflection of the sector's adherence to its core ethical values. By integrating green investments, supporting social development, implementing eco-friendly operations, developing sustainable products, engaging with the community, and embracing innovative reporting, Takaful institutions enhance their competitive advantage and contribute to a more sustainable and fair global economy. These efforts show how Islamic finance can lead in the pursuit of sustainability, aligning financial growth with ethical and environmental responsibility.

8.2. Recommendations for Regulators and Policymakers

The recommendations for regulators and policymakers cover many strategic actions to improve the Takaful industry's governance and sustainability. These actions include strengthening governance, promoting sustainable investments, fostering innovation, engaging stakeholders, and implementing comprehensive sustainability reporting. By addressing these areas, regulators and policymakers can enhance the integrity, efficiency, and ethical alignment of Takaful institutions, ensuring they meet Shariah requirements and global standards.

i. Strengthening governance frameworks
   To improve the Takaful industry, regulators must focus on strengthening governance frameworks. This involves ensuring the SSBs are independent, skilled, and have clear authority. Regulators should require regular training for board members to keep up with changing financial practices and Shariah

interpretations (Grais & Pellegrini, 2006). Transparency in governance is also essential, requiring detailed disclosures of financial operations and Shariah compliance reports to build trust and keep stakeholders informed. Additionally, clear guidelines for managing conflicts of interest within Shariah boards can ensure impartial decisions aligned with Islamic principles.

ii. Promoting sustainability
Promoting sustainability in the Takaful sector involves several steps. Policymakers should encourage investments in green technologies and sustainable projects by offering tax benefits or subsidies. This strategy supports global environmental goals and the ethical dimensions of Islamic finance. For example, the Islamic Development Bank's work in renewable energy shows how targeted support can foster sustainable investment (Islamic Development Bank, 2020). Policymakers can also integrate sustainability criteria into regulatory frameworks for product development to encourage Takaful operators to design products that meet environmental and social sustainability standards. Guidelines for evaluating the sustainability of Takaful products and investments will help align industry practices with broader sustainability goals.

iii. Fostering innovation
Innovation within the Takaful sector is crucial. Encouraging the use of digital technologies can streamline operations, reduce costs, and improve service delivery. Policymakers should consider establishing regulatory sandboxes to allow Takaful institutions to test new technologies and business models in a controlled environment. This helps innovation while ensuring it fits with existing regulatory standards and Shariah principles (IMF, 2020). Supporting research and development in FinTech and InsurTech within the Takaful industry can drive technological advancements and improve efficiencies.

iv. Enhancing stakeholder engagement
Improving stakeholder engagement is key to developing effective regulatory frameworks. Regulators should facilitate forums and discussions that include Takaful operators, Shariah scholars, consumers, and other stakeholders. These platforms help identify challenges, share best practices, and develop collaborative solutions. Regular industry consultations can address issues related to Shariah compliance and operational transparency, leading to more effective regulations (Khan, 2019). Forming dedicated committees with diverse stakeholder representation can ensure all perspectives are considered in policy development.

v. Adopting comprehensive sustainability reporting
Comprehensive sustainability reporting standards promote transparency and accountability. Regulators should require Takaful institutions to provide detailed reports on their ESG performance. These reports should follow established frameworks, like those from the Global Reporting Initiative, to ensure consistency (Global Reporting Initiative, 2021). Transparent reporting

builds trust and provides valuable insights into the impact of Takaful operations on societal and environmental issues. Encouraging Takaful operators to publish integrated reports combining financial and non-financial performance metrics provides a complete view of their impact.

vi. Supporting capacity building and training
Supporting capacity building and training is vital for enhancing the Takaful industry's governance and sustainability. Policymakers should promote educational programs and workshops on the latest developments in Islamic finance, sustainability practices, and governance standards. These programs should be tailored for various stakeholders, including regulators, Takaful operators, and Shariah board members, ensuring they have the skills and knowledge to implement effective practices.

vii. Encouraging international collaboration
Encouraging international collaboration is key to advancing the Takaful industry's governance and sustainability. Regulators should facilitate partnerships with global financial institutions, regulatory bodies, and industry associations to share best practices and harmonize standards. This approach helps address cross-border challenges, like varying regulatory requirements and differing interpretations of Shariah compliance, fostering a cohesive global Takaful market.

viii. Enhancing regulatory technology adoption
Regulators should encourage the adoption of regulatory technology (RegTech) solutions to improve oversight and compliance. RegTech tools can automate compliance processes, monitor transactions for suspicious activities, and ensure adherence to regulatory requirements more efficiently. Using advanced technologies like blockchain and artificial intelligence can enhance regulatory reporting, fraud detection, and risk management, increasing operational efficiency and compliance.

ix. Promoting ethical investment practices
Regulators should promote ethical investment practices by setting clear guidelines on permissible investments within Takaful portfolios. Encouraging investments that support social and environmental causes, while avoiding those conflicting with Islamic ethical principles, can enhance the impact of Takaful operations. An ethical investment framework that aligns with Shariah principles and sustainability objectives will help Takaful institutions make responsible investment decisions and contribute positively to societal well-being.

x. Implementing risk-based supervision
Implementing risk-based supervision helps regulators focus on high-risk areas. This approach involves assessing the risk profile of Takaful institutions and tailoring oversight accordingly. By concentrating resources on

high-risk areas, regulators can ensure that Takaful operators manage their risks effectively and maintain financial stability in the sector.

To enhance the Takaful industry's governance and sustainability, regulators and policymakers should focus on strengthening governance frameworks, promoting sustainable investments, fostering innovation, enhancing stakeholder engagement, adopting comprehensive sustainability reporting, supporting capacity building, encouraging international collaboration, enhancing RegTech adoption, promoting ethical investment practices, and implementing risk-based supervision. These strategies will improve the integrity and efficiency of Takaful institutions, aligning them with global ethical and environmental standards.

References

Accounting and Auditing Organization for Islamic Financial Institutions (AAOIFI). (2017). *AAOIFI standards*. AAOIFI.

Ahmed, H., & Khan, M. M. (2018). *Islamic finance: The principles and practice*. Routledge.

Alhabshi, S. O., & Razak, S. H. A. (2011). *Enhancing corporate governance in Islamic financial institutions: Challenges and strategies*. International Shariah Research Academy.

Al-Jarhi, M. (2011). *Islamic finance and investment: A guide to principles and practice*. World Scientific.

Bank Indonesia. (2019). *Annual report 2019*. Bank Indonesia.

Bank Negara Malaysia. (2020). *Annual report 2020*. Bank Negara Malaysia.

El-Gamal, M. A. (2006). *Islamic finance: Law, economics, and practice*. Cambridge University Press.

Ghlamallah, E., Alexakis, C., Dowling, M., & Piepenbrink, A. (2021). The topics of Islamic economics and finance research. *International Review of Economics & Finance*, *75*, 145–160.

Global Reporting Initiative (GRI). (2021). *Sustainability reporting standards*. GRI.

Grais, W., & Pellegrini, M. (2006). *Corporate governance in institutions offering Islamic financial services*. World Bank policy research working paper no. 4050.

Hassan, M. K., & Lewis, M. K. (2007). *Handbook of Islamic banking*. Edward Elgar Publishing.

Islamic Development Bank. (2020). *Sustainable development report*. Islamic Development Bank.

International Monetary Fund (IMF). (2020). *Fintech, financial stability, and governance in Islamic finance*. IMF Publications.

Islamic Financial Services Board (IFSB). (2018). *Standards and guidelines*. IFSB.

Islamic Financial Services Board (IFSB). (2019). *Takaful participants survey 2019*. IFSB.

Khalid, A. (2019). *Fintech and Islamic finance: Synergies for growth and governance*.

Khan, M. M. (2017). *Islamic insurance: A comprehensive guide*. Routledge.

Khan, M. M. (2019). *Islamic insurance: A comprehensive guide*. Routledge.

Moualla, S. (2013). *Islamic finance: Principles and practice*. Palgrave Macmillan.

OJK. (2020). *Indonesia financial services authority annual report 2020*. Otoritas Jasa Keuangan.

PwC. (2020). *Islamic finance: A global industry at the crossroads*. PricewaterhouseCoopers.

Siddiqui, M. A. (2011). *Islamic finance and the new financial world*. Oxford University Press.

Takaful Malaysia. (2020). *Annual report 2020*. Syarikat Takaful Malaysia Berhad.

World Bank. (2020). *World Bank Takaful growth report 2020*. World Bank.

Chapter 12

Musharakah Mutanaqisah Financing for Elderly Care: Integrating Financial Literacy for Sustainable Retirement in Malaysia

Lee Chin Yee[a], *Ng Sok Choo*[b] *and Rosylin Mohd Yusof*[c]

[a]*School of Accounting and Finance, Taylor's University, Malaysia*
[b]*Universiti Malaya-Wales, Malaysia*
[c]*Universiti Utara Malaysia (UUM), Malaysia*

Abstract

The elderly face financial challenges due to reduced workforce capacity and rising healthcare costs, which strain their savings. To meet SDG 1.3, ensuring access to adequate social protection systems, a sustainable financial model is needed for post-retirement stability. Islamic finance has gained prominence, comprising 41% of Malaysia's local banking system as of 2022. Thus, Islamic finance products are vital to support the elderly during retirement. This study proposes the Musharakah Mutanaqisah Reverse Mortgage (MMRM), providing an annuity income to retirees while allowing them to stay in their homes. Promoting better financial management for retirement is essential to enhance financial preparedness, especially among middle-aged individuals. The research explores MMRM's potential in addressing elderly poverty in Malaysia, a country facing an aging population. By assessing financial literacy and proposing consumer protection guidelines, this study aims to ensure elderly financial stability without displacing them. A survey measures public financial literacy on retirement to develop suitable consumer protection frameworks. The findings will aid social protection governance

Islamic Finance and Corporate Governance: Synergies for Sustainable Growth, 203–217

doi:10.1108/978-1-83662-346-520251025

in creating an effective retirement system using this innovative financial product.

Keywords: Financial literacy; retirement planning; financial support; Musharakah Mutanaqisah Reverse Mortgage; financial sustainability

1. Introduction

People are expected to take greater responsibility for their financial security as they approach their retirement years. Nevertheless, research showed that many people lack financial management skills in terms of having enough savings for retirement (Niu et al., 2020). Although retirement planning is one of the important financial planning tools, a smaller proportion of self-employed people in Malaysia are worried about having enough savings for their retirement (Mustafa et al., 2023). Although most people understand the importance of raising their level of financial literacy, there is still a noticeable gap between their understanding and the actions that they are taking to achieve their financial freedom (Aziz & Kassim, 2020). Therefore, for most Malaysians, a comfortable retirement at the age of 60 years old may currently seem to be an unattainable goal (Zulfaka & Kassim, 2021).

Under Malaysia's retirement benefits program for the private sector, the contributions are made at a predetermined rate based on the employee's monthly wages by both the employer and the employee (Amin et al., 2021). However, as Malaysia is moving toward an aging population by 2030 and with the limitations to provide a sufficient level of income support, these trends present a threat to the viability of underfunded pension systems (Cipriani & Fioroni, 2021). The social security system, which was initially introduced to ensure retirement security, is now becoming a more political concern as the population ages and health care costs increase. The inherent effect of the aging population and rising healthcare costs also affects how people plan their careers and how firms manage their labor force (Henkens, 2022; Ramnath et al., 2021). Due to the lack of adequate social security, self-employed workers are more likely to fall into the risk of not having adequate savings for their retirement life. Thus, sustainable retirement planning is extremely important for them to maintain a stress-free retirement life (Janposri, 2021).

To achieve SDG 1.0 which is no poverty, it is crucial to achieve financial sustainability for the elderly during their retirement. Therefore, policymakers are becoming more interested in focusing on financial competency because many people find themselves in difficult financial situations, especially when the economy is weakening (Abidin & Zainuddin, 2021). With 76.9% of home ownership in Malaysia, the elderly might enhance their retirement wealth by using real estate as a financial asset. With the reverse mortgage model, borrowers (the elderly) can access their home's equity without having to move out after selling their own house. In other words, they can receive an annuity by not having to sell their own house instead they can still stay in their existing residences (Ashok & Dhingra, 2020). The reverse mortgage model can translate into a product that will benefit most of the people worldwide.

With the limited mandate of the social security system in providing a stable financially stable retirement income, it is crucial to understand the readiness of the people for retirement. Although the reverse mortgage is an innovative financial product to provide financial assistance to the elderly, the financial institutions must understand the needs of the people and the potential of the MMRM. Therefore, this study examines financial literacy among rural and urban areas and how it relates to saving for retirement in Malaysia, a nation that is going to have an aging population by 2030. The research findings could provide an insightful implication for the policymakers of Malaysia in getting the nation better preparation in handling poverty among the elderly.

2. Literature Review

In Malaysia, financing toward social protection is not limited to the fiscal policy, which individuals need to save from the income to the Employee Provident Fund (EPF). It is to ensure that the people can have sufficient savings for their retirement (Choong & Firouz, 2020; Mohd Jaafar, 2021). With the high withdrawal during the COVID-19 pandemic, EPF account holders face financial difficulties after their retirement as they have withdrawn their retirement funding for their current expenses. Since Malaysia is becoming an aging population, financial stability in retirement is a major concern for the elderly population (Awang et al., 2020). To encourage the people and get more people to be prepared for their retirement, the government is now encouraging the public to go for the private retirement savings scheme by providing tax deductions. However, most Malaysians did not create a retirement plan for themselves to achieve financial stability in their retirement due to their lack of awareness and preparation for retirement (Zulfaka & Kassim, 2021).

Around the world, people are still concerned about retirement planning as employees are relying on their savings to spend on their retirement life (Abidin & Zainuddin, 2021; Mustafa et al., 2023). According to Aziz and Kassim (2020), all Malaysians, regardless of their age or background, are having inadequate financial literacy. Other than earning from employment or business, many Malaysians were unaware of other financial products, such as insurance which can provide them with financial protection in unexpected situations. The natural tendency for retirement planning involves more financial literacy, and someone who has immediate exposure to financial knowledge can benefit from financial literacy (Hajam, 2020). Although it can be difficult to plan for retirement, not doing so can lead to some disappointment after retirement (Kumaraguru et al., 2022). Hence, with the current social security system, an innovation of financial products is crucial to assist people in getting ready for retirement.

Lacking insights into financial planning results in consumers being more likely to act on their stated intentions. People who are loaded with financial information messages are more likely to improve their retirement planning intentions

(Hoffmann & Plotkina, 2020). Concerns regarding the viability of these (mostly unfunded) social security systems and the sufficiency of households' private retirement savings have grown (Cocco & Lopes, 2020), the exposure to other financial products should be widely shared with the people so that they are equipped with more product knowledge and prepare themselves better for their retirement. A reverse mortgage is one of the financial products that can provide the elderly with a replacement income during their retirement (Yee & Chong, 2023).

With the high percentage of home ownership in Malaysia, the reverse mortgage is an equity release scheme that can increase income and reduce the liquidity risk for the elderly to achieve financial stability (Boj del Val et al., 2022; Martinez-Lacoba et al., 2021). A reverse mortgage which is also known as "house-for-pension" effectively integrates and demonstrates the combined benefits of the financial market, insurance market, and real estate markets (Wang & Han, 2021). To cater to most citizens in the world, the evolution from the reverse mortgage to MMRM will become one of the innovative products to mitigate elderly poverty. By having the property, the elderly can realize the residual value of their property by applying the reverse mortgage and using it as part of their retirement funding (Wang & Han, 2021).

Financial literacy plays an important role in taking up reverse mortgages as it changes the evaluation that consumers make of reverse mortgages (Choinière-Crèvecoeur & Michaud, 2023). The complexity of financial instruments such as reverse mortgages increases the need for individuals to have stronger financial literacy which will increase their financial well-being and resilience (Lusardi & Messy, 2023). According to Bialowolski et al. (2022), there is a relationship between financial literacy and the cost of borrowing (interest rate). One of the beneficial impacts of having high financial literacy will enable a person to decide on a more cost-effective mortgage term with a better-reduced interest rate. There are three separate approaches that financial literacy could affect one's retirement planning: (i) considering post-retirement financial needs, (ii) creating long-term financial strategies, and (iii) obtaining private pension insurance (Niu et al., 2020). To introduce an effective MMRM to the Malaysian market, it is crucial to study the level of financial literacy on retirement in Malaysia nation.

3. Methodology

This study employed a quantitative method in which a questionnaire was used as the research tool to examine the readiness of middle adulthood financial literacy for retirement and the consumer protection required to achieve financial stability during retirement. In most studies measuring financial literacy, participants' fundamental knowledge of risk diversification, inflation, and interest compounding was assessed (Amka, 2020).

To rigorously examine the readiness and financial literacy of Malaysia's middle-aged population for retirement, along with the consumer protection necessary for financial stability in later life, this study employs a quantitative research methodology. By adopting the questionnaire by Niu et al. (2020), this research assesses fundamental financial literacy concepts like risk diversification, inflation, and interest compounding among participants. The study applied a convenience sampling strategy, targeting a demographically and geographically diverse participant pool across Malaysia, reflecting the nation's concern over elderly poverty. Out of Malaysia's 33.4 million populace in 2023, with 70% falling within the 15–64 age range, the primary data of this study were gathered from 512 adults aged 18–59.

The questionnaire is structured into four sections: demographic information, basic financial literacy, advanced financial literacy, and the construction of variables for empirical analysis. This structure was designed to evaluate respondents' financial literacy, with a focus on their knowledge of interest rates, inflation, time value of money, risk and return, wealth management, and investment strategies. Furthermore, the survey also explores respondents' financial planning, retirement preparation, risk assessment capabilities, and their self-assessed financial literacy level.

Descriptive analysis of the primary data enables a detailed examination of the relationships between financial literacy and retirement readiness, delineating both the independent and dependent variables within the study. This methodological approach provides a comprehensive understanding of the current state of financial literacy and its impact on retirement planning among Malaysians, thereby informing the development of targeted financial education and product innovation strategies.

4. Results and Discussion

512 respondents had completed the Google Survey Form. Data from the questionnaires was analyzed by using the SPSS program. The results were presented in five parts: analysis of the respondents' demographics, analysis of financial literacy, retirement preparation, and other variables, and multivariate analysis of retirement preparation. Out of 512 questionnaire respondents, 292 or 57.03% were males. Most of the respondents are income earners (353 respondents), followed by entrepreneurs/businessmen (128 respondents) and unemployment/retirement (31 respondents). Table 12.1 shows the results from the demographic section.

The responses to questions about basic literacy are compiled in Table 12.2. It provides information on the percentage of respondents that answered each of the five fundamental financial literacy questions correctly, incorrectly, or "do not know." Based on the responded, it was found that other than interest rate level, Malaysian has a good financial literacy on numeracy, interest compounding, inflation, and time value of money by which the percentage of correct answers between 75% and 89%. However, there are only 32.03% of respondents were able to answer all five questions correctly. In general, the participants have a restricted comprehension of fundamental financial literacy.

A second set of financial literacy questions was used to collect more sophisticated financial information about investing and portfolio selection to test financial literacy more thoroughly. These questions, compiled in Table 12.3, specifically test the knowledge of the central bank, intricate financial products like stocks, bonds, mutual funds, and wealth management offerings from banks, financial

Table 12.1. Demographic Analysis.

Variables	**Category**	**Frequency**	**Percentage (%)**
Gender	Male	292	57.03
	Female	220	42.97
Age group	18–25	61	11.91
	26–30	57	11.13
	31–35	80	15.63
	36–40	95	18.56
	41–45	62	12.11
	46–50	40	7.81
	51–55	55	10.74
	56–59	62	12.11
Race	Bumiputera	4	0.78
	Chinese	316	61.72
	Indian	48	9.38
	Malay	144	28.12
Education level	SPM/O-Level	20	3.91
	STPM/A-Level	40	7.81
	Degree	256	50.00
	Master	140	27.34
	PhD/DBA	40	7.81
	Professional certificate	16	3.13
Individual income level	B40	154	30.08
	M40	210	41.02
	T20	148	28.90
Occupation	Unemployed	31	6.05
	Employed	353	68.95
	Self-employed/ businessman	128	25.00

concepts like risk diversification and the trade-off between risk and return, and stock market operations. The responses revealed a more concerning pattern than the questions on basic financial literacy. On average, the percentage of correct responses drops significantly. Approximately half of respondents do not know the answer to the question about banks' wealth management.

To assess the awareness of retirement preparation in Malaysia, this study employed several factors such as age, income level, financial literacy, and financial

Table 12.2. Basic Financial Literacy.

	Percentage of Total Number of Respondents				
	Interest Rate Level	**Numeracy**	**Interest Compounding**	**Inflation**	**Time Value of Money**
Correct	46.1%	80.5%	86.7%	88.3%	75.8%
Incorrect	43.7%	16.4%	10.2%	9.4%	17.2%
Do not know	10.2%	3.1%	3.1%	2.3%	7%

Table 12.3. Advanced Financial Literacy.

	Percentage of Total Number of Respondents		
	Correct	**Incorrect**	**Do Not Know**
In general, investment opportunities with high returns have high risks. True or False?	95.3%	3.1%	1.6%
Buying a company stock usually provides a safer return than a stock mutual fund. True or False?	72.7%	15.6%	11.7%
Which bank formulates and implements monetary policy?	79.7%	9.4%	10.9%
Normally, which asset is riskiest?	85.2%	11.7%	3.1%
What happens if somebody buys the stock of firm B?	62.5%	32.8%	4.7%
Which statement about mutual funds is correct?	65.6%	21.1%	13.3%
Which statement about banks' wealth management products is correct?	26.6%	50.7%	22.7%
Which statement describes the main function of the stock market?	71.9%	17.9%	10.2%

planning to associate the Malaysian general public's readiness toward retirement planning. The association between each factor and retirement planning is presented in Table 12.4.

The dependent variable, which is retirement planning, was translated to the outcome value of "Yes" or "No." Due to the binary nature of the dependent variable, logistic regression was applied to investigate the relationship between each of these factors and their impact on national retirement planning. In this model, the retirement planning variable is the dependent variable while age, income level, financial literacy, and financial planning variables are the predictors for the model. Logistic regression can estimate the probability of an observation

Table 12.4. Factors to Assess Retirement Planning.

Variable	Scale	Class
Age	18–25	1
	26–30	2
	31–35	3
	36–40	4
	41–45	5
	46–50	6
	50–55	7
	56–59	8
Income level	<RM5,250	B40
	RM5,251–RM11,819	M40
	>RM11,819	T20
Financial literacy	Completely disagree	1
	Disagree	2
	Neither agree nor disagree	3
	Agree	4
	Completely agree	5
Financial planning	Much higher than peers' average level	1
	Higher than peers' average level	2
	At peers' average level	3
	Lower than peers' average level	4
	Much lower than peer's average level	5
	Do not know	6

Table 12.5. Effect of Age on Retirement Planning.

Model	Deviance	AIC	BIC	df	X^2	p
H_0	709.783	709.783	709.783	512		
H_1	588 265	604.265	638.172	504	121.518	< 0.001

belonging to the class. Table 12.5 presents the estimation result for retirement planning based on age factor. The survey data collected show the statistical significance of the age factor on retirement planning. The data trend on the estimates plot (Fig. 12.1) depicts the change in predicted probability of retirement planning as the age changes. It can be observed from the age range 36–59 that the probability of retirement planning increases as age increases. This finding is aligned with Afthanorhan et al.'s (2020) finding that when a working person's age and income increase, they become more motivated to start planning for retirement. The odds of retirement planning are 12.75 times greater in the age group of 51–55 compared to the lower age group (18–25) as shown in Table 12.6.

Table 12.6. Coefficient for Each Age Group on Retirement Planning.

	Estimate	Standard Error	Odds Ratio	z	Wald Test		
					Wald Statistic	df	p
Age group (18–25)	0 433	0.262	1.542	1.652	2 728	1	0.099
Age group (26–30)	0.035	0.265	1.036	0.132	0.018	1	0.895
Age group (31–35)	0.847	0.244	2.333	3.473	12.061	1	< 0.001
Age group (36–40)	0.318	0.208	1.375	1.532	2.349	1	0.125
Age group (41–45)	1.056	0.290	2.875	3.639	13.239	1	< 0.001
Age group (46–50)	1.386	0.395	4.000	3.507	12.300	1	< 0.001
Age group (51–55)	2.546	0.519	12.750	4.902	24.034	1	< 0.001
Age group (56–59)	1.427	0.321	4.167	4.440	19.710	1	< 0.001

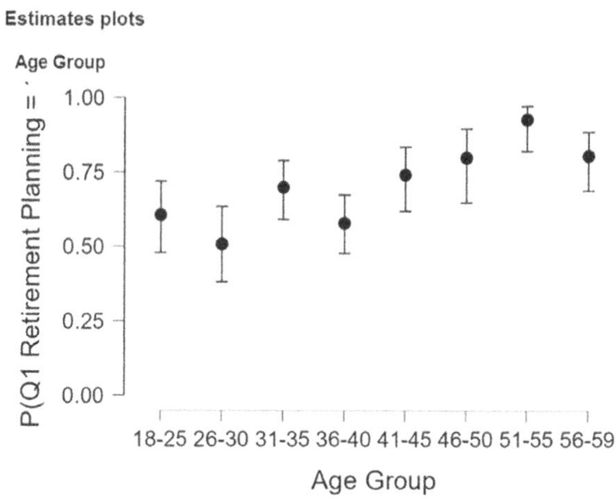

Fig. 12.1. Estimate Plot of Retirement Planning Probability Based on Different Age Groups.

Table 12.7 presents the estimation result for retirement planning based on income level. The analysis result shows the statistical significance of income level on retirement planning. The data trend on the estimates plot (Fig. 12.2) shows the changes in the predicted probability of retirement planning in different income level groups. The T20 has a higher probability for retirement planning compared to B40 and M40. The M40 demonstrates higher retirement planning probability than B40 although the growth in probability is not prominent (Table 12.8). This finding is aligned with Baker et al.'s (2021) finding that annual income and retirement planning behavior have a positive correlation.

Table 12.9 presents the estimation result for retirement planning based on financial literacy. The analysis result shows the statistical significance of financial literacy on retirement planning. The data trend on the estimates plot (Fig. 12.3) shows the changes in the predicted probability of retirement planning at different financial literacy levels. The analysis result shows that the one having higher financial literacy than his peer's average level would have a higher probability of retirement planning. The one with much higher financial literacy than the average level would have the odds of retirement planning 15.00 times greater than the group with lower financial literacy on average (Table 12.10). The probability of retirement planning is decreasing relatively as one's financial literacy value is lower. It should be noted that group 6 in the estimates plot (Fig. 12.3) are the respondents who do not know about their financial literacy. This finding is aligned with Janposri (2021), whereby the financial literacy analysis shows that the rise in the probability of retirement planning may be explained by financial knowledge, financial behavior, and financial attitude, all of which are positively significant.

Table 12.7. Effect of Income Level on Retirement Planning.

Model	Deviance	AIC	BIC	df	X^2	p
H_0	709.783	709.783	709.783	512		
H_1	585.364	591.364	604.079	509	124.419	< 0.001

Table 12.8. Coefficient for Each Income Level on Retirement Planning.

	Estimate	Standard Error	Odds Ratio	z	Wald Test		
					Wald Statistic	df	p
Income level (B40)	0.341	0.164	1.406	2.085	4.347	1	0.037
Income level (M40)	0.567	0.144	1.763	3.949	15.597	1	< 0.001
Income level (T20)	2.110	0.265	8.250	7.972	63.550	1	< 0.001

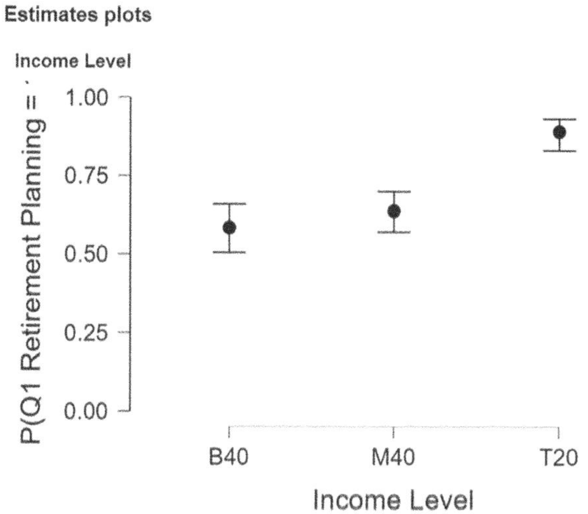

Fig. 12.2. Estimate Plot of Retirement Planning Probability Based on Different Income Levels.

Table 12.9. Effect of Financial Literacy on Retirement Planning.

Model	Deviance	AIC	BIC	df	X^2	p
H_0	709.783	709.783	709.783	512		
H_1	558.140	570.140	595.570	506	151.643	< 0.001

Table 12.10. Coefficient for Each Financial Literacy Level on Retirement Planning.

	Estimate	Standard Error	Odds Ratio	z	Wald Test		
					Wald Statistic	df	p
Income level (B40)	0.341	0.164	1.406	2.085	4.347	1	0.037
Income level (M40)	0.567	0.144	1.763	3.949	15.597	1	< 0.001
Income level (T20)	2.110	0.265	8.250	7.972	63.550	1	< 0.001

Table 12.11 presents the estimation result for retirement planning based on financial planning. The analysis result shows the statistical significance of financial planning on retirement planning. The data trend on the estimates plot (Fig. 12.4) shows the changes in the predicted probability of retirement planning at different financial planning levels. The analysis result shows that one having

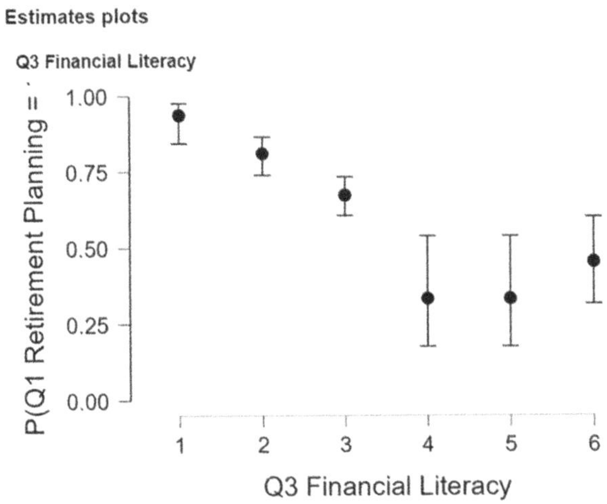

Fig. 12.3. Estimate Plot of Retirement Planning Probability Based on Different Financial Literacy Level.

Table 12.11. Effect of Financial Planning on Retirement Planning.

Model	Deviance	AIC	BIC	df	X^2	p
H_0	709.783	709.783	709.783	512		
H_1	536.219	546.219	567.411	507	173.564	< 0.001

Table 12.12. Coefficient for Each Financial Planning Level on Retirement Planning.

	Estimate	Standard Error	Odds Ratio	z	Wald Test		
					Wald Statistic	df	p
Q2 Financial planning (1)	1.386	0.559	4.000	2.480	6.150	1	0.013
Q2 Financial planning (2)	−0.336	0.293	0.714	−1.149	1.321	1	0.250
Q2 Financial planning (3)	−0.000	0.162	1.000	-2.220×10^{-16}	4.930×10^{-32}	1	1.000
Q2 Financial planning (4)	1.213	0.172	3.364	7.064	49.906	1	< 0.001
Q2 Financial planning (5)	3.178	0.510	24.000	6.229	38.805	1	< 0.001

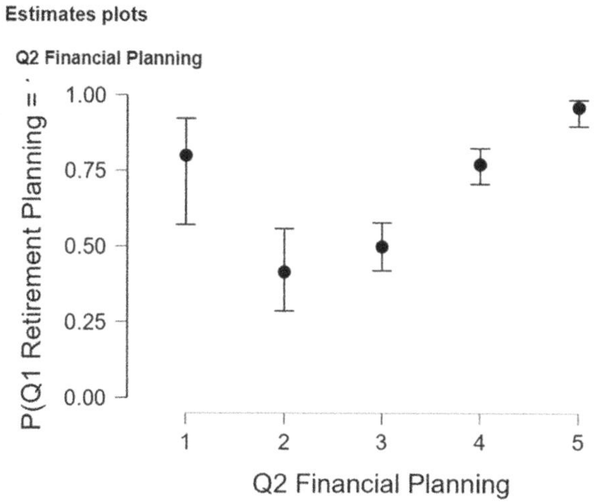

Fig. 12.4. Estimate Plot of Retirement Planning Probability Based on Different Financial Planning Level.

long-term financial planning would have a higher probability of retirement planning. The probability of retirement planning is increasing relative to one's financial planning level except for the group 1 observation who responded "completely disagree" when they were asked if they have long-term financial planning (Table 12.12).

5. Conclusion

Based on the above result, it found that most of the respondents have a basic level of financial literacy; however, when it comes to implementation, the practical knowledge might not be as high as their financial knowledge as the financial decision is vary depends on their financial status and profile. As financial literacy reflects financial knowledge, financial behavior, and financial attitude, therefore, it is crucial to enhance the financial literacy of the individual while promoting new innovative financial products to cater to the individual needs. In the middle stage of the cycle, it might be challenging for the individual to prepare for their retirement; therefore, it will be good to improve financial literacy to increase awareness of retirement planning needs before launching a new financial product. For the retirement plan, an innovative financial product, MMRM, is part of the Private Retirement Plan. MMRM is an innovative product that needs more financial knowledge on the financial decision to opt for the annuity term; therefore, it encourages the policymaker to put more effort into building financial literacy as it will get the individual to make a wise choice before enrolling to the financial product.

For future research, it will recommend working on the education and awareness of the MMRM before launching the product. Sufficient education is required to ensure the potential borrower is aware of the consequences of the product and their actual post-retirement needs to achieve financial stability. At the same time, the financial institutions may consider conducting an introduction or briefing before accepting the application from the prospect to ensure they are the person who needs this annuity, and the usage of the annuity is for the post-retirement needs so that the financial support from MMRM can achieve the product objective.

References

Abidin, Z. Z., & Zainuddin, A. (2021, August). *Financial literacy on retirement planning among working single women in private sector, Selangor*. International conference on innovations in social sciences education and engineering (ICOISSEE) (Vol. 1, No. 1).

Afthanorhan, A., Mamun, A. A., Zainol, N. R., Foziah, H., & Awang, Z. (2020). Framing the retirement planning behavior model towards sustainable wellbeing among youth: The moderating effect of public profiles. *Sustainability*, *12*(21), 8879.

Amin, N. S. B. M., Mohamed, A. A. A., & Torla, A. (2021). Retirement benefit in Malaysia: Understanding the legal framework and its challenges to the migrant workers. *IIUMLJ*, *29*, 199.

Amka, A. (2020). *A structural equation modelling study of the determinants of retirement preparedness*. A structural equation modelling study of the determinants of retirement preparedness.

Ashok, S., & Dhingra, D. (2020). Reverse mortgage: A financial planning tool for the retirees – Case study approach in India. *South Asian Journal of Business and Management Cases*, *9*(3), 375–386.

Awang, H., Rashid, N. F. A., Peng, T. N., & Mansor, N. (2020). Factors associated with savings and withdrawals among employees provident fund members. *UPM PERTANIKA Journals*, *28*(3), 2239–2263.

Aziz, N. I. M., & Kassim, S. (2020). Does financial literacy really matter for Malaysians? A review. *International Journal of Banking, Accounting, and Finance*, *2*(2), 13–20.

Baker, H. K., Tomar, S., Kumar, S., & Verma, D. (2021). Are Indian professional women financially literate and prepared for retirement?. *Journal of Consumer Affairs*, *55*(4), 1416–1441.

Bialowolski, P., Cwynar, A., Xiao, J. J., & Weziak-Bialowolska, D. (2022). Consumer financial literacy and the efficiency of mortgage-related decisions: New evidence from the panel study of income dynamics. *International Journal of Consumer Studies*, *46*(1), 88–101.

Boj del Val, E., Claramunt Bielsa, M. M., & Varea, J. (2022). Reverse mortgage and financial sustainability. *Technological and Economic Development of Economy*, *28*(4), 872–892.

Choinière-Crèvecoeur, I., & Michaud, P. C. (2023). Reverse mortgages and financial literacy. *Journal of Financial Literacy and Wellbeing*, *1*(1), 79–102.

Choong, C., & Firouz, A. (2020). Social protection and fiscal policy in Malaysia. *Khazanah Research Institute Discussion Paper*, *9*, 20.

Cipriani, G. P., & Fioroni, T. (2021). Endogenous demographic change, retirement, and social security. *Macroeconomic Dynamics*, *25*(3), 609–631.

Cocco, J. F., & Lopes, P. (2020). Aging in place, housing maintenance, and reverse mortgages. *The Review of Economic Studies*, *87*(4), 1799–1836.

Hajam, M. A. (2020). The effect of future orientation and financial literacy on family retirement planning mediated by saving attitude. *Jurnal Sosial Humaniora (JSH)*, *13*(2), 176–189.

Henkens, K. (2022). Forge healthy pathways to retirement with employer practices: A multilevel perspective. *Work, Aging and Retirement*, *8*(1), 6.

Hoffmann, A. O., & Plotkina, D. (2020). Why and when does financial information affect retirement planning intentions and which consumers are more likely to act on them?. *Journal of Business Research*, *117*, 411–431.

Janposri, P. (2021). The role of financial literacy in retirement planning and wealth accumulation among self-employed Thai workers. *Journal of Population & Social Studies*, *29*(1), 177–194.

Kumaraguru, L., Geetha, C., & Mohidin, R. (2022). The factors influencing retirement preparation among Gen Y in Malaysia. *Advanced International Journal of Banking, Accounting, and Finance*, *4*(10), 01–12.

Lusardi, A., & Messy, F. A. (2023). The importance of financial literacy and its impact on financial wellbeing. *Journal of Financial Literacy and Wellbeing*, *1*(1), 1–11.

Martinez-Lacoba, R., Pardo-Garcia, I., & Escribano-Sotos, F. (2021). The reverse mortgage: A tool for funding long-term care and increasing public housing supply in Spain. *Journal of Housing and the Built Environment*, *36*, 367–391.

Mohd Jaafar, N. I., Awang, H., Mansor, N., Jani, R., & Abd Rahman, N. H. (2021). Examining withdrawal in Employee Provident Fund and its impact on savings. *Ageing International*, *46*, 70–82.

Mustafa, W. M. W., Islam, M. A., Asyraf, M., Hassan, M. S., Royhan, P., & Rahman, S. (2023). The effects of financial attitudes, financial literacy and health literacy on sustainable financial retirement planning: The moderating role of the financial advisor. *Sustainability*, *15*(3), 2677.

Niu, G., Zhou, Y., & Gan, H. (2020). Financial literacy and retirement preparation in China. *Pacific-Basin Finance Journal*, *59*, 101262.

Ramnath, S., Shoven, J. B., & Slavov, S. N. (2021). Pathways to retirement through self-employment. *Journal of Pension Economics & Finance*, *20*(2), 232–251.

Wang, P., & Han, W. (2021). Decision analysis of the elderly participating in the housing reverse mortgage: Based on bequest motivation constraint. *Journal of Intelligent & Fuzzy Systems*, *40*(4), 8569–8586.

Yee, L. C., & Chong, C. C. (2023). *Willingness to accept reverse mortgage*. European proceedings of social and behavioural sciences.

Zulfaka, A., & Kassim, S. (2021). Retirement awareness among the working population below 40 in Malaysia. *Journal of Islamic Finance*, *10*, 101–110.

Chapter 13

Strategic Zakat Management to Amplify Social Impact in Corporate Social Responsibility

Nor Shaipah Abdul Wahab and Muhammad Ali

School of Accounting & Finance, Taylor's University, Malaysia

Abstract

This chapter explains the concepts of zakat and corporate social responsibility (CSR) to enhance the understanding of the two concepts in society. In Islam, the zakat is considered a religious obligation, which is further connected with CSR and societal well-being. It offers various benefits to society such as economic empowerment, poverty reduction under the faith-based mechanism, and sustainable development. This chapter also highlights that hoe zakat and CSR can provide dual benefits for organizations, namely, addressing societal issues and religious commitments. It also she light on the ethical business practices, transparency, and corporate legitimacy while overcoming potential misalignments between profit-seeking and social responsibility motives. This chapter further discusses the role of effective top management in the zakat-CSR governance mechanism to increase positive societal outcomes.

Keywords: Zakat; corporate social responsibility; social impact; strategic management; sustainability; Islamic finance

Islamic Finance and Corporate Governance: Synergies for Sustainable Growth, 219–227

doi:10.1108/978-1-83662-346-520251028

1. Introduction

Zakat, an obligatory duty following Islamic principles, serves to ease the burdens of communities (Mawardi et al., 2023). In contrast to CSR provisions, in which the contribution is voluntary, zakat payment is compulsory with well-defined beneficiaries, and governed by the Islamic authority, for example, Zakat Board in Malaysia and Ministry of Religious Affairs in Brunei (Borneo Bulletin, 2023; MyGovernment Malaysia, 2024). Despite the differences, zakat and CSR share a similar focus on improving social well-being. Significant efforts by governments in integrating zakat with CSR activities are at the increasing phase. For example, the United Nations Development Programme (UNDP) in Indonesia collaborates with Amil Zakat National Agency, the national zakat collection agency in Indonesia, to support SDG-related initiatives (UNDP & Badan Amil Zakat Nasional, 2018). In Malaysia, Lembaga Tabung Haji, the Islamic statutory body that provides and manages the welfare of Malaysian hajj pilgrims and deposits, distributes zakat through its CSR programs to assist underprivileged, for example, through CSR program Ehsan, Iqra', Mobility, Ikhtiar' and A'fiat that, respectively, targets at providing supports for Eid preparation, education support for tertiary level, assistance in providing vehicles for the funeral, financial support for business, and medical equipment for medical centers and hospitals (Lembaga Tabung Haji, 2024).

Despite the shared values of zakat and CSR, legitimacy issues may arise when integrating both almsgiving and contribution methods. Given the Islamic principles and ethical norms, integrating zakat principles into CSR activities may raise misalignments between the activities and the social responsibility motives. By principle, zakat distribution is strictly for eligible Muslims and the distribution for eligible non-Muslims is restricted from the provisions for converts and poverty (Al-Bawwab, 2023; Razak, 2020). The definition of beneficiaries of CSR contributions is, however, more relaxed as the boundary of the beneficiaries can span any communities or stakeholders (Filipeanu et al., 2024; Razak, 2020). Thus, integrating zakat in CSR activities requires careful consideration of the alignment between the activities and the principles set forth within the zakat framework to ensure impactful zakat contribution.

Integrating zakat in CSR also requires the top management team's (TMT) commitment to ensure strategic alignment between zakat and CSR efforts with the firms' strategic focus (Amer, 2023). Conflicting aims between profit-seeking and social responsibility motives may reduce the impact of zakat and CSR on the firm's mission and vision. Similarly, transparency and accountability in zakat and CSR can be questioned if the reporting of the collection and distributions is weak and, hence, raises questions on the accountability, including on allocated resources for zakat and CSR initiatives, which the distribution should be made based on the initiative's impacts, alignment with the firm's values, and stakeholders' expectations. Therefore, this chapter aims to explore impactful zakat within CSR practices, policy implications, and recommendations for zakat-CSR integration.

2. Integrating Zakat and CSRs

Previous studies justify firms' zakat contribution to fund CSR activities as a religious commitment termed *Fard Kifayah* (Brahim & Arab, 2020; Razzak et al., 2024). CSR, on the other hand, is termed as activities carried out to ensure the legitimacy of the firms (Bitektine & Song, 2023; Velte, 2022). This implies that zakat can be a corporate strategic tool to ensure the existence of the firms legitimate in the eyes of the stakeholders. In integrating Islamic contributions, including zakat, and CSR, Raimi et al. (2013) introduce a faith-based model as the underpinning framework to align the contributions toward the economic and social improvements of Muslim majority nations, which the improvements are expressed as comprises poverty reduction, enterprise development, and economic empowerment.

Legitimacy theory (Dowling & Pfeffer, 1975), focuses on social responsibility activities as the initiative to ensure the legitimate existence of firms with a larger spectrum of contributions or funds, that is, beyond Islamic contributions. The theory argues the intention of firms when engaging in CSR activities as the acts to seek alignment with social expectations, norms, and values, which, in turn, increases the firms' legitimacy. Previous studies, however, find CSR activities affect firm value in mixed directions (Fahad & Busru, 2021; Roy et al., 2022; Tasnia et al., 2021). Positively, CSR activities are viewed by shareholders as firms' commitment to community well-being and, hence, increase the firm value (Qiu et al., 2021; Roy et al., 2022). In contrast, firm value can be affected negatively by CSR when the activities are perceived as a waste of resources, especially when firms' financial performance is weak (Fahad & Busru, 2021; Lopez et al., 2022).

Thus, in the context of zakat and CSR, the integration of a faith-based model and legitimacy theory can induce zakat-CSR synergy, in which the integration can balance the negative connotation of legitimacy as the value of the CSR activities is underpinned by the Islamic awareness or principles, in which "honesty" and "truthfulness" of an intention are key of good conduct (Ab. Wahab & Masron, 2020). This also broadens the role of zakat in amplifying social impact beyond religious preaching initiatives. The dynamics of both theories also highlight the need for effective governance and management to ensure the firm value is preserved while pursuing the corporate strategic mission and vision through CSR activities.

Drawing upon the faith-based model and legitimacy theory, the synergy between zakat and CSR is in terms of shared objectives, intended impact, and strategic integration with sustainability development. Through shared objectives, integrating zakat and CSR promotes ethical business practices in addressing social and community development (Razzak et al., 2024). This can then improve the social impact of zakat by complementing the CSR initiatives through funding and resources. At the top management level, the synergy between zakat and CSR can improve sustainability development by integrating social responsibility practices with Islamic principles, fostering ethical business conduct, and enhancing positive impact on both society and the environment (Hoque et al., 2023).

Therefore, this chapter aims to explore impactful zakat within CSR practices and its policy implication. Understanding both facets of zakat-CSR synergy allows for informed recommendations that help firms strategically plan for zakat-CSR integration. This can then shed light on the potential benefits of integrating zakat and CSR, not only from an ethical standpoint but also in terms of a long-term sustainability perspective. In addition, by understanding the synergies between these two frameworks, organizations can develop robust strategies that contribute positively to both their financial performance and societal well-being.

3. TMT in Zakat-driven CSR Initiatives

The TMT is elementary in driving zakat-driven CSR initiatives as the team sets the tone at the top. Hence, impactful zakat-CSR synergy requires TMT's commitment and effective leadership in ensuring strategic alignment and efficient resource allocation (Huang et al., 2022; Zhao et al., 2023). TMT's commitment to stakeholder management, transparency, and reporting is also crucial to strategically govern the zakat-driven CSR initiatives. As the TMT has more access to the firm's resources compared to the stakeholders, the rent-seeking motive may underrate the impact of zakat and CSR synergies. Agency theory terms this as a conflict of interest (Meckling & Jensen, 1976), which includes contradicting expectations and motives between the TMT and the fund contributors.

While TMT pursues the legitimacy objective, stakeholders are targeting to increase the social well-being of communities (Dowling & Pfeffer, 1975; Islam et al., 2021). Balancing the expectations and motives is important for strategic zakat management in amplifying the social impact within the CSR initiatives. TMT members are argued by upper echelon theory as influenced by their behaviors, beliefs, cognitions, social interactions, values, and perceptions (Carpenter et al., 2004; Hambrick & Mason, 1984). Thus, the decisions, choices, and actions of the TMT can be associated with their psychological- and social attributes (Carpenter et al., 2004), which, through their powerful roles, can affect the social impact of zakat-CSR initiatives. This is because TMT's functional areas can directly influence the decision on the extent that the zakat within the CSR context can be strategically framed as firms' strategic decisions.

TMT, via endorsement and advocacy, may demonstrate a significant commitment to integrating zakat and CSR, through which active endorsement of the integration can be exhibited. The advocacy of the TMT during the communication and approval process can be simplified to reduce the red tape for the zakat-CSR integration to be materialized at a smooth pace. This includes communication in both internal and external contexts. Within this commitment perspective, TMT's leadership role is key in shaping the firms' approach to forming zakat as a fund for CSR initiatives. Potential issues may arise surrounding unawareness of TMT on zakat principles and cultural sensitivity. As zakat is an Islamic almsgiving, its impact on society depends on the execution of the approach that aims to alleviate the social problem while adhering to Islamic principles (Razak, 2020). Neglecting this can further undermine the impact of zakat and can induce cultural sensitivity. The latter is more apparent within multinational firms due to background and cultural diversity (Luu et al., 2023). The TMT is, therefore, important to be equipped with the knowledge and understanding of cultural sensitivity in integrating zakat and CSR.

Impactful integration of zakat and CSR also requires TMT's strategic alignment between zakat-driven CSR and the firm's strategic plan. TMT's effective zakat-CSR governance ensures the initiatives align with the sustainability strategies of the firm. Decoupling both short-term and long-term objectives of zakat-CSR initiatives leads to immature and disconnected societal impact in the long run, through which the form of the societal impact will outperform its substance and this, in turn, will lead to a reduction in trust by the stakeholders in the long run. Thus, TMT's commitment to ensuring a robust measure of societal impacts is necessary to serve both legitimacy and social well-being objectives simultaneously in the firm's long-run strategic initiatives. Careful planning on the sustainability of the zakat-CSR initiatives is closely related to resource allocation endorsed by the TMT. This includes manpower and monetary provisions (Huang et al., 2022, 2023), which can place the TMT in the contradicting objectives, that is, increase shareholder value through profit-seeking versus enhancing social impact of the zakat-CSR initiatives.

Within the resource allocation context and in a similar vein to upper echelon theory, TMT members decide with their value, cognition, and perception as a fundamental driving force during the decision-making process (Hambrick & Mason, 1984). From the budget allocation counterpart, TMT endorses and decides the allocation of zakat along with the CSR budget. With high social- and psychological-inspired motivation, TMT members with strong value, cognition, and perception of impactful contribution to communities weigh the budget allocation against the societal impact (Carpenter et al., 2004). After the cost–benefit analysis and should the latter outweigh the former, the strategies of zakat allocation within the CSR budget are to be revisited to ensure the cost-effectiveness of the CSR activities. Similarly, as human resource allocation forms a substantial cost in a firm's budget (Kieling et al., 2021), TMT is to play a significant role in setting the policy on personnel and manpower allocation for the CSR activities and zakat funds allocation. Assigning the roles and responsibilities to run the zakat-CSR initiative also requires TMT's prudence as conflict of interest may arise because there can be a grey line to separate firm's objective and personal's intentions, especially within the information asymmetry setting between the managers and the stakeholders (Meckling & Jensen, 1976).

TMT's roles are, therefore, important to strengthen the firm's stakeholder engagement as effective communication can be useful to diagnose any discrepancies during zakat-CSR integration. While TMT communicates with employees to engage internal stakeholders in the zakat-CSR initiatives, engagement with external stakeholders can be in the form of communication with customers, communities, and other external parties. This can serve both motives of legitimacy and social impact. Involvements of internal and external stakeholders in the zakat-driven CSR may also increase stakeholder engagement and, hence, enhance the rapport between the stakeholders and the firm. Consequently, from the governance perspective, the negative impacts of information asymmetry between the management and the shareholders can be reduced (Aben et al., 2021).

Initiatives to reduce the information asymmetry span increased transparency and reporting (Hamrouni et al., 2022). TMT's accountability is the key to ensuring that transparency is in practice by the management. In the zakat and CSR reporting, the integrated zakat-CSR reporting is essential to ensure transparent zakat distribution, including through CSR activities (Azrai et al., 2024). Report on the impacts of zakat utilization and its links with CSR initiatives is important to showcase the firm's strategic zakat management in amplifying the social impact through CSR initiatives. Several reporting mechanisms can be employed, including annual reports, interactive media delivery and events. To sum up, TMT's commitment and roles in impactful zakat-driven CSR are important to ensure ethical conducts in integrating zakat and CSR that warrants positive impacts of zakat-CSR initiatives.

4. Impactful Zakat Within CSR Practices

Zakat is believed as one of the essential pillars of Islam. It has been considered a tool for social justice and wealth distribution among the Muslim society. The integration of the zakat mechanism with CSR practices can be a unique way to generate a real impact on society for wealth distribution management. Zakat provides an avenue for organizations to meet social responsibilities and religious obligations. It can provide socioeconomic development and enhance the well-being of marginalized communities. Furthermore, CSR practices and zakat concepts transcend the idea of traditional charity, addressing the pressing needs of social challenges. The organizations that adopt zakat and CSR practices together help societies in multiple ways such as poverty alleviation, economic empowerment, fair distribution of wealth, healthcare, and educational advancements. This helps companies to secure sustainable values for the people they serve in society.

The key challenge for companies to attain the maximum benefit of zakat and CSR practices is the prioritization and identification of the beneficiaries. According to the Islamic concept, zakat is the right of those who meet its criteria such as people in debt, striving in the cause of Allah, and the poor. In a corporate setting, managers translate zakat benefits to the vulnerable population and improve wealth inequalities in society. In this context, various organizations shared zakat funds to initiate various programs such as financial assistance for small businesses, provide funds for skilled-based programs, and allocate finance for health and related services for underserved communities. Additionally, the inclusion of zakat benefits in CSR practices can be a useful way to improve corporate reputation among the stakeholders. It is a common phenomenon that investors and consumers give high value to the social and ethical behavior of companies. Similarly, the two concepts also comply with Islamic ideology by demonstrating a strong commitment to improving social justice. However, businesses and organizations need to maximize the actual benefits of zakat within the CSR framework. This objective can be obtained through strategic zakat management which includes transparency in zakat-funded projects, careful allocation of funds, and continuous monitoring.

5. Policy Implication and Recommendation

The combination of zakat and CSR practices has important implications in the field of Islamic finance and corporate governance. To increase the benefits of zakat in social justice, regulators, managers, and policymakers should create opportunities for companies where zakat management becomes an integral part of corporate governance under CSR initiatives. This process demands impactful policy guidelines, reforms in existing frameworks, promotion of zakat benefits, and improved CSR activities that follow Islamic ideology. Furthermore, the establishment of zakat management standards in terms of collection, calculation, and later its distribution to the eligible communities. At present, there is a lack of consensus among Muslim scholars on the uniform standards of zakat distribution which also creates inconsistencies and underutilization of zakat funds. In this context, comprehensive and standard guidelines should be adopted by the organizations for zakat management, thereby increasing the best CSR practices and the greater impact on society.

Another key policy recommendation is tax flexibility and leverage for the organization that integrates the zakat system into its CSR activities. The support from authorities by offering tax credits may increase the active participation of companies. This policy has dual benefits which include social development through zakat funds and the increased engagement of corporations in socially responsible activities. Additionally, companies may include zakat contributions under CSR expenditure which can be reported in financial statements as a part of their commitment toward sustainability disclosures.

Likewise, there is a pressing need for collaboration between public and private partnerships to promote zakat and CSR initiatives. Both stakeholders can create a pool of resources under zakat management for impactful interventions in society. In this regard, companies and nongovernment organizations can collaborate with authorities to develop zakat-funded projects. This working partnership can improve healthcare and education systems and decrease poverty in society. Similarly, there is a strong need for capacity-building programs for zakat management and CSR initiatives. This required training, seminars, and workshops to equip managers for the effectiveness of zakat and CSR activities. For this purpose, universities, colleges, and Islamic institutions can play a significant role in delivering a robust capacity-building curriculum for zakat and CSR management.

Lastly, zakat funds and CSR initiatives are finance-based activities where policymakers should maintain accountability and transparency in the system. The adoption of an effective evaluation and continuous monitoring system can be a useful tool for zakat and CSR funds' credibility. The policymakers can include independent audits, feedback surveys, and robust impact assessment software to create trust in zakat management. Therefore, it can be concluded that the integration of CSR and zakat concepts can be a powerful medium to enhance social impact under Islamic principles. To attain maximum benefits of zakat and CSR activities, the above discussion in this chapter is essential for advancing regulatory framework, capacity building, fostering stakeholder partnerships, and promoting incentives for the benefit of sustainable socioeconomic development.

References

Ab. Wahab, M., & Masron, T. A. (2020). Towards a core Islamic work value: Evidence from Islamic legal texts and the muftīs' verification. *Journal of Islamic Accounting and Business Research*, *11*(1), 179–200.

Aben, T. A., van der Valk, W., Roehrich, J. K., & Selviaridis, K. (2021). Managing information asymmetry in public–private relationships undergoing a digital transformation: The role of contractual and relational governance. *International Journal of Operations and Production Management*, *41*(7), 1145–1191.

Al-Bawwab, R. A. J. I. E. S. (2023). Zakat: Changing the framework of giving. *Islamic Economic Studies*, *30*(2), 86–103.

Amer, M. (2023). Systematic review of religiosity and social responsibility. *Journal of Business Socio-Economic Development*, *4*(3), 254–271.

Azrai, A., Harahap, M. G., Haidir, H., & Saragih, A. (2024). Distribution of zakat towards poverty alleviation. *Innovative: Journal of Social Science Research*, *4*(2), 635–644.

Bitektine, A., & Song, F. (2023). On the role of institutional logics in legitimacy evaluations: The effects of pricing and CSR signals on organizational legitimacy. *Journal of Management*, *49*(3), 1070–1105.

Borneo Bulletin. (2023). *MoRA launches new department*. Retrieved August 12, 2024, from https://borneobulletin.com.bn/mora-launches-new-department/

Brahim, N. B., & Arab, M. B. (2020). Social disclosure: Compliance of Islamic banks to governance standards No. 7 of AAOIFI (2010). *Journal of Islamic Accounting Business Research*, *11*(7), 1427–1452.

Carpenter, M. A., Geletkanycz, M. A., & Sanders, W. G. (2004). Upper echelons research revisited: Antecedents, elements, and consequences of top management team composition. *Journal of Management*, *30*(6), 749–778.

Dowling, J., & Pfeffer, J. (1975). Organizational legitimacy: Social values and organizational behavior. *Pacific Sociological Review*, *18*(1), 122–136.

Fahad, P., & Busru, S. A. (2021). CSR disclosure and firm performance: Evidence from an emerging market. *Corporate Governance: The International Journal of Business in Society*, *21*(4), 553–568.

Filipeanu, D., Hertug, I., Maha, L. G., Tiganas, C. G., & Viorica, E. D. (2024). The aftermath of communicating CSR campaigns' results: A perception study. *Corporate Social Responsibility Environmental Management*, *31*(6), 6150–6166.

Hambrick, D. C., & Mason, P. A. (1984). Upper echelons: The organization as a reflection of its top managers. *Academy of Management Review*, *9*, 193–206.

Hamrouni, A., Bouattour, M., Ben Farhat Toumi, N., & Boussaada, R. (2022). Corporate social responsibility disclosure and information asymmetry: Does boardroom attributes matter? *Journal of Applied Accounting Research*, *23*(5), 897–920.

Hoque, N., Uddin, M., Islam, M. T., Mamun, A., Nazim Uddin, M., Ahmad, A., & Thowhidul Islam, M. (2023). Pursuing sustainable development goals through integrating the aspirations of zakah and CSR: Evidence from the perspective of an emerging economy. *International Journal of Social Economics*, *50*(9), 1232–1247.

Huang, H., Hao, S., & Chen, Y. (2023). The more the better? Service transition for shaping sustainable development in manufacturing firms and the role of top management team attributes. *Corporate Social Responsibility and Environmental Management*, *30*(6), 3255–3270.

Huang, J., Duan, Z., Hu, M., & Li, Y. (2022). More stable, more sustainable: Does TMT stability affect sustainable corporate social responsibility? *Emerging Markets Finance and Trade*, *58*(4), 921–938.

Islam, M. T., Kokubu, K., & Nishitani, K. (2021). Corporate social reporting in the banking industry of Bangladesh: A test of legitimacy theory. *Social Responsibility Journal*, *17*(2), 198–225.

Kieling, E. J., Rodrigues, F. C., Filippetto, A., & Barbosa, J. L. V. (2021). Human resource allocation in projects: A systematic mapping study. *International Journal of Business Information Systems*, *37*(4), 505–521.

Lembaga Tabung Haji. (2024, August 12). *CSR Zakat programmes*. https://www.tabung-haji.gov.my/en/corporate/corporate-sosial-responsibility/csr-zakat-programmes

Lopez, B., Rangel, C., & Fernandez, M. (2022). The impact of corporate social responsibility strategy on the management and governance axis for sustainable growth. *Journal of Business Research*, *150*, 690–698.

Luu, T. D., Mai, K. H. N., Huynh, C. C., Phan, N. H. T., Le, N. T., & Le, T. N. D. (2023). Performance of franchisee: The role of reciprocal resources, relationship quality and cultural sensitivity. *International Journal of Emerging Markets*. Vol. ahead-of-print No. ahead-of-print. https://doi.org/10.1108/IJOEM-04-2022-0581

Mawardi, I., Widiastuti, T., Al Mustofa, M. U., & Hakimi, F. (2023). Analyzing the impact of productive zakat on the welfare of zakat recipients. *Journal of Islamic Accounting Business Research*, *14*(1), 118–140.

Meckling, W. H., & Jensen, M. C. (1976). Theory of the firm: Managerial behavior, agency costs and ownership structure. *Journal of Finanacial Economics*, *3*, 305–360.

MyGovernment Malaysia. (2024, August 12). *Managing Zakat*. https://www.malaysia.gov.my/portal/content/27674

Qiu, S. C., Jiang, J., Liu, X., Chen, M.-H., & Yuan, X. (2021). Can corporate social responsibility protect firm value during the COVID-19 pandemic? *International Journal of Hospitality Management*, *93*, 1–12.

Raimi, L., Patel, A., Adelopo, I., & Ajewole, T. (2013). Tackling poverty crisis in the Muslim majority nations (MMNs): The faith-based model (FBM) as an alternative policy option. *Advanced Journal of Business Management and Entrepreneurship*, *1*(1), 1–12.

Razak, S. H. A. (2020). Zakat and waqf as instrument of Islamic wealth in poverty alleviation and redistribution: Case of Malaysia. *International Journal of Sociology and Social Policy*, *40*(3/4), 249–266.

Razzak, A., Ahmad, M. A., Awad, G., & Mohammad, N. (2024). The effect of digital zakat and accounting on corporate sustainability through financial transparency. *Asian Economic Financial Review*, *14*(3), 228–249.

Roy, P. P., Rao, S., & Zhu, M. (2022). Mandatory CSR expenditure and stock market liquidity. *Journal of Corporate Finance*, 721–729.

Tasnia, M., Syed Jaafar AlHabshi, S. M., & Rosman, R. (2021). The impact of corporate social responsibility on stock price volatility of the US banks: A moderating role of tax. *Journal of Financial Reporting and Accounting*, *19*(1), 77–91.

UNDP & Badan Amil Zakat Nasional. (2018). *Unlocking the potential of zakat and other forms of Islamic finance to achieve the SDGs in indonesia* (pp. 1–19). e Intellectual Seminar Series at Islamic Economics Institute of King Abdul Aziz University, Kingdom of Saudi.

Velte, P. (2022). Meta-analyses on corporate social responsibility (CSR): A literature review. *Management Review Quarterly*, *72*(3), 627–675.

Zhao, L., Yang, M. M., Wang, Z., & Michelson, G. (2023). Trends in the dynamic evolution of corporate social responsibility and leadership: A literature review and bibliometric analysis. *Journal of Business Ethics*, *182*(1), 135–157.

Printed and bound by CPI Group (UK) Ltd, Croydon, CR0 4YY
15/09/2026
14962485-0004